Soccer Dad

ALSO BY THE SAME AUTHOR

Souvenirs (1981)

Vermont River (1984)

The Man Who Loved Levittown (1985)

Hyannis Boat and Other Stories (1989)

Chekhov's Sister (1990)

Upland Stream (1991)

The Wisest Man in America (1995)

The Smithsonian Guide to Northern New England (1995)

Wherever That Great Heart May Be (1996)

North of Now (1998)

One River More (1998)

Small Mountains (2000)

Morning (2001)

This American River (2002)

A Century of November (2004)

On Admiration (2010)

The Writing on the Wall (2012)

Soccer Dad

A Father, a Son, and a Magic Season

W. D. Wetherell

Skyhorse Publishing

Skyhorse Publishing books may be purchased in bulk at special discounts for sales promotion, corporate gifts, fund-raising, or educational purposes. Special editions can also be created to specifications. For details, contact the Special Sales Department, Skyhorse Publishing, 307 West 36th Street, 11th Floor, New York, NY 10018 or info@skyhorsepublishing.com.

Skyhorse° and Skyhorse Publishing° are registered trademarks of Skyhorse Publishing, Inc.°, a Delaware corporation.

Visit our website at www.skyhorsepublishing.com.

10 9 8 7 6 5 4 3 2 1

Paperback ISBN: 978-1-62087-716-6

Library of Congress Cataloging-in-Publication Data

Wetherell, W. D., 1948-

Soccer dad : a father, a son, and a magic season / W.D. Wetherell.

p. cm.

ISBN 978-1-60239-329-5 (alk. paper)

1. Soccer players--Family relationships--United States. 2. Fathers and sons--United States. 3. Wetherell, W. D., 1948- I. Title.

GV944.U5W47 2008

796.334092--dc22

2008017118

Printed in the United States of America

Contents

1

THE FIELDS OF WINTER

In the life of a young man, in the life of his father, there are many goals.

One is downstairs in our basement. A finished basement—small bedrooms for each kid, a windowless closet for the computer, a drafty half bath. In the course of a normal day, I might go down there three of four times total, but so far—on the kind of bitterly cold February morning these New Hampshire hills still know how to dish out—I've already been down a dozen times, making up errands to disguise a heavy case of nostalgia. Daughter Erin is away at college, which I've grudgingly gotten used to, but son Matthew is finishing off his junior year in high school with a semester in the Bahamas—and yesterday was his flight down. A long story—it's a nontraditional school emphasizing "real-world" learning, environmental stewardship, interaction with the local community—but the bottom line for me, on a morning like this one, is that I have an awful lot of alone time in a house that suddenly seems very empty.

The empty-nest syndrome: my older readers are probably nodding their heads in sympathy, having been through it themselves. Not the real thing yet, not with another year of high school to go through with Matt, but enough of a foretaste to let me know it's every bit as hard as they say it is.

(How hard? Celeste called from work while I was downstairs, and the first thing I asked her was, "Want to have another kid?")

I feel closer to Matt when I'm in the basement. On the left of the stairs hangs a poster showing the famous Manchester United midfielder Paul Scholes with his tongue plugged determinedly against his cheek, his cleats stepping over a soccer ball in a trademark shift of balance—a poster advertising his team's U.S. tour in 2003, when we saw them play at Giants Stadium. Just beyond is a poster fashioned by Matt himself—caricatures of his favorite players made by cutting out photos of their heads from soccer magazines and superimposing them atop crazy body parts cut out at random from other magazines.

The posters form a portal to the trophies in his room, over there in the corner on a wedge-shaped shelf. There's a first-place trophy from the Southington Invitational tournament of 2005: a square little pedestal atop which stands the gold-plated, leg-swinging soccer player with the resolutely blank expression who must adorn 98 percent of the world's the world's soccer trophies. He's also on the first-place trophy from the RYSA Columbus Day tournament of 2001, and, being no snob, adorns the third-place trophy from the Londonderry United Labor Day tournament of 2003. Ribbons and medals from the low-budget tourneys hang on nearby nails. The two smallest of these are Matt's most precious: winner's medals from the New Hampshire state high school championships, one from his sophomore year, one from his junior.

On the walls above Matt's bed is tacked a line of twenty-two five-by-seven photos—pictures of all the Bayern Munich teams of 2002, with players named Zvjezdan Misimović and Bixente Lizarazu, as well as more famous ones, like the great goalie Oliver Kahn. Below it is a shelf with his soccer books, his collected issues of *FourFourTwo* (the glossy British soccer magazine), his soccer videos. On the table beside his bed are bobble heads of David Beckham and Rio Ferdinand, along with a Manchester United clock, which keeps the most accurate time in the house. *FIFA 07*, the frighteningly realistic computer game, is also down here somewhere, but I'm so used to seeing it on his screen, I just imagine its e-players live there in a kind of electronic locker room, changing under the keyboard, showering in the hard drive, trotting onto the screen ever ready for another game.

This is the paraphernalia of any soccer-crazy kid, albeit one who is lucky enough to play on the best high school team in his state. But in his closet is a treasure, an album, that is uniquely Matthew's. When he was ten, wanting to surprise sister Erin for her birthday, he wrote letters to all the members of the U.S. women's soccer team, asking for their autographs. After a delay long enough to make us think they wouldn't answer, in came a flood—personal letters and signed pictures from almost everyone on the team, including stars like Kristine Lilly and Brandi Chastain.

Success with the women prompted Matt to try the men. Getting addresses of various teams is easy enough with the Internet, but what took him longer was writing carefully worded letters to each player, explaining that he was an American boy who loved soccer, admired his playing, and would love an autograph. The results were amazing— far beyond what he would have gotten from baseball or basketball stars. Player after player sent Matt his signature, including immortals like Franz Beckenbauer (aka "the Kaiser") and contemporary stars like David Beckham and our poster boy Paul Scholes. Even better, many included personalized notes. For Matthew, Beckenbauer took the time to print. The French star Emmanuel Petit wrote, "*To Matthew: I wish you all the best for the new year, take care!*" A signature on Howarth Timber stationery came from the legendary English goalie Gordon Banks.

The real prize has some poignancy attached. Many consider George Best to have been the most talented soccer player who ever laced up boots, but with a liking for birds and booze that cut his career short. ("If I had been born ugly," he once famously quipped, "no one would ever have heard of Pelé.") Matt read about him in his books, listened to my memories of him (playing out of shape in the old NSL), suffered my brief lecture about how talent can be both a blessing and a curse, then went out and found a black-and-white picture showing Best following through after a vicious shot on a foggy English field back in the sixties. He cut it out, stuck it in an envelope, figured out the return postage so George wouldn't have to be bothered, and then, only a month or two before Best died, back came the picture, not only signed, but with a note on the bottom in surprisingly elegant script.

Dear Matthew. Thank you very much for your lovely letter. Hope you are well. I have signed the photograph for you. All the best, George.

I carefully returned the autographs to their hiding place, but I wasn't quite finished with the nostalgia. A few paragraphs back I mentioned something about goals. Basement goals are what I was talking about, though only Matt and I know they're there. Once, when he was five or six, we both happened to be in the hall outside his bedroom at the same time. What's more, there turned out to be a ball at our feet, one of the innumerable plastic balls or NERF balls or beach balls that just appear from nowhere when you have kids that age. I looked down at it, had a sudden inspiration, stuck my foot out, and shot it toward the door at the hall's far end, the door that led to the furnace room. It hit the door square in the middle. "Goal!" I yelled, throwing up my arms. Matt, instantly understanding, ran to the ball, turned, kicked it past me toward the door at my end of the hall, the door that led to the computer room. "Goal!" he yelled, in his croaky little kid voice. "One to one!"

That started it, our little indoor soccer game, the innumerable matches that decorated our winter nights for a good six or seven years, until the day when, with his fakes and fancy footwork, he would inevitably beat me eleven to zip. Great hours these, and what I realized, as I looked unsuccessfully around for a ball to shoot (tactical genius—shoot while he was in the Bahamas!), was that it was the physical contact of these games I missed most—the roughhouse kind of affection we shared as we tried forcing our way past the other in midhall, shoulder to shoulder, leg against leg . . . the kind of contact that presses love in deep, without you ever thinking about it much, not at the time, not when you're laughing and grunting and yelling all at once.

I popped my head into Matt's room to check the time on his Man U clock: 8:15—which meant fourteen hours of this beginner's empty nesting yet to go before Celeste would come home and help me cope.

Luckily, I had scheduled myself an errand. At 9:00, I was meeting a man in Vermont to talk about buying his vintage wood and canvas canoe. I went upstairs and cleaned up the breakfast dishes, grabbed my coat and boots, and ventured a little warily outside. It had been a windy night, and branches had blown down off the oldest of our trees—many had landed vertically in the snow, so our meadow looked impaled by javelins. While the car warmed up, I went around collecting these, adding them to the pile of brush we burn in the spring. This led me, inevitably, toward the second of our goals. Friends down in Hanover bought it for their son when it looked like he would be the high school's starting goalie, and because they're the kind who always buy the best, it's professional quality, with metal uprights I half suspect are genuine silver. Unfortunately, their son didn't get to play much, and, knowing Matthew loved the game, they took apart the goal, stacked it in their truck, drove to Lyme, and reassembled it on the house side of the birch-covered knoll we call Sunset Hill.

I walked over to it now, on snow that was hardened by the six inches of sleet that had fallen over the weekend. The sky was a dirty slate, there were already a few snowflakes wafting down, but that didn't stop the goalposts from shining as brilliantly as ever. I wasn't the only recent visitor here; behind the goal were the prints of a deer, and I wondered if, famished, he had been nuzzling the net. Last autumn's yellow grass was caught up in the twine, forming what looked like a collection of miniature beards hung out to dry. The twine had taken a beating over the years. There were cannonball-sized gaps top left and top right, and much of the twine had been repaired with plastic twist ties, duct tape, and sutures of old fly line.

The goal, with the snowy base, seemed smaller than it did in summer, and standing in the middle I had no difficulty touching the upper bar. We had long ago passed the point when I could parry any of Matt's shots, but I felt that if he were there now, I might have a chance, with a reduced target area. A chickadee flew down to perch on the side post, but either I frightened it or the metal was too cold, because it immediately flew off again.

Bradford, Vermont, is over on the other side of the Connecticut River, a twenty-minute drive past what remain of our local farms. When I got to the canoe man's garage, there was no sign of him, or rather, there was a sign, scrawled hastily over cardboard and propped against the bay door: EMERGENCY BACK LATER.

Bradford sits on two plains: the Upper Plain, supporting the shabby-genteel downtown, and the Lower Plain, with a cow-pasture golf course, a water treatment plant, and the historic old train station. It's a floodplain, this lower one, and now in midwinter it looked sunk so far below the rest of the town that it seemed to rest in a different century. At a loss, needing to kill some time until my man appeared, I walked down a winding road that soon turned to dirt, sent around a last curve, and came out into an open area of about ten acres: the site—the lonely, all-but-forgotten site—of the town's fairgrounds.

This was vintage, out-of-season Vermont, all right. Vintage, out-of-season America. Behind me was a long open shed, with an undulating roof sheltering hay that still exuded a warm calf smell, even in winter. Out in front were piled concrete blocks for ox-pulling contests, twenty-four of them in a fortresslike pile. A baseball backstop was in the old style: chicken wire nailed between telephone posts, backing an infield of flint and gravel. COKE IS IT! read a faded red sign from an ad campaign that must have been new in 1949. On the flattest, driest patch of land sat a dilapidated bandstand, and I climbed the steps for the view. Look west, and you could see the town sitting on its twenty-foot-high bluff—the church spires, the turrets of the town hall, were as sharp as dunce's caps, framed against a high wooded esker. Look east, and you could see a blue-white sliver of the Connecticut's choppy ice, cheese on a messy grater, and then rising clear of it the clean brown ridges of New Hampshire. The fairgrounds, the town, even New Hampshire: in the wintry gray of that lonely morning, they teetered on the tremulous edge that separates benign neglect from out-and-out abandonment.

So palpable was the *temps perdu* texture that it took me longer than it should have to remember Matthew had once played soccer here. This would have been third or fourth grade, playing for his elementary school team—nine years ago, nearly a decade. It probably represented the farthest north soccer had ever taken him—as the years went on, as his skills developed, the current of his game swept south. Curious, I took a little walk, following a snow fence's bulging pickets. FIRST AID read a sign over a frozen mud puddle. Just beyond it, I found the soccer goals, two of them, dragged to the very edge of the woods. Dumped there—that's the effect it gave—and I wondered why whoever went through the effort of dragging them hadn't finished the job by tipping them over into the swamp. They were the normal, basic, no-frills rec-ball kind of goals, but even so, they seemed extraordinarily foreign and exotic—modern transplants that were the only thing visible belonging indisputably to the twenty-first century.

I ran my hand along the netting, plucking out some of the swamp grass caught up in the twine. A Natural Ice beer can lay on the ground in the center of the goal, and snowflakes were sticking to its metal before they were anything else. I wondered how many goals Matt had scored against this twine, where exactly he had made it bulge. "Watch out for the kid in goggles!" the Bradford players would call to each other—Matt, nearsighted, was already wearing sports goggles in third grade.

So. Soccer even here, in this frozen, forgotten slice of 1949. I pulled the collar of my coat up against the wind blowing in from the river, walked up the dirt road back to town. There was bad news and good news at the garage. Still no canoe man, but the emergency sign was gone.

I looked at my watch. 9:30. A long day yet to fill—I had absolutely no desire to return to an empty house. But standing by those forgotten fairgrounds goals, the germ of an idea had begun to form. Matt, when I stopped and thought about it, had in the course of twelve years played soccer across a good stretch of Vermont and nearly all of New Hampshire, games that I had mostly driven him to and almost all of which I had watched. Would it be possible, in the course of one short February day, to retrace my way to all of these fields or at least some of the most significant? To sneak up on the entire soccer experience while its passion was hibernating? To thaw out, at least a little, its fields of memory?

Ever the novelist, I thought immediately of John Cheever's famous short story, "The Swimmer," wherein suburbanite Neddy Merrill, drinking gin one night at a party, suddenly realizes he can swim from one backyard pool to another and make it all the way home entirely by water. "He seemed to see, with a cartographer's eye, that string of swimming pools, that quasi-subterranean stream that curved across the country." Well, I could see with a cartographer's eye myself: a soccer cartographer, with many years of experience.

It's a long way from rural Vermont in the north to suburban New Hampshire in the south, hard by the Massachusetts border. Could I cover that distance before it got dark? It was snowing lightly, I was late getting started (well, not so late—counting the basement, our backyard goal, and Bradford's, I already had three fields under my belt), and I wasn't totally sure I could find my way around without the e-mailed maps, sent by parent "coordinators," that I had always navigated with before.

As it turned out, the next few fields were easy to find, but disappointing. Three towns form a line down the Vermont side of the Connecticut, from stubbornly working-class Fairlee to picture-postcard Thetford to affluent Norwich, the richest town in the state. Matt had played elementary school soccer against all three, but this was in the great-galloping-herd stage of soccer—twenty-two kids chasing a defenseless ball—and it was hard to separate any specific memories, particularly in light of feeling (as one does now when visiting elementary schools anywhere) that you are a suspect to be monitored and tracked. And there were no goals hibernating in the snow that I could find.

Norwich's main street ducks under I-91, then crosses the Ledyard Bridge to Hanover in New Hampshire. I drove uphill through the Dartmouth campus past students who looked stunned by the cold, took a left on busy Lebanon Street, and parked behind the co-op food store, which abuts one of the college's largest, lushest athletic fields. Wildest, too. The Appalachian Trail, on its long winding way from Georgia to Maine, cuts past the field's edge, and I followed its blazes toward what a sign said were velvet rocks. Another sign, this one to my left, announced ATHLETIC FIELDS ARE FOR DARTMOUTH COLLEGE ACTIVITIES ONLY, but that wasn't quite threatening enough to stop me, especially since, ten steps in from the parking lot, the landscape was as bleak and empty as tundra. A bulldozer was stuck in the frozen sleet; a new soccer stadium was going up for the college team, though winter seemed to have halted progress. Closer, abutting a flimsy-looking radio tower, was what I was looking for: goals, the college soccer goals, sixteen of them grouped in what looked like two separate villages or clusters. I walked over to them, following the tracks of someone's snowshoes. The goals were classy, of course, this being Dartmouth—the kind with squared-off tops and nets made of plush black twine. They had been handled pretty roughly for all that—if this was a village of soccer goals, it was a dilapidated one, with goals lying sideways against other goals, the uprights half canted toward the ground.

Matt had played on these fields many times as part of the Lightning Soccer program run by Dartmouth's soccer coaches. And the field nearest the parking lot, the one where the snowshoe prints were thickest, had been the site of a key moment in my own soccer life. In April 1986, as a young man trying to help his wife during her first pregnancy, I had driven down to the co-op to do our food shopping. It was bitterly cold and damp, but when I got out of the car, I noticed a group of young boys and girls sitting in a semicircle near a soccer goal on the Dartmouth field. They were listening attentively to a tall, ruggedly handsome man who stood in their center, lightly tossing a soccer ball from hand to hand—hands so big and sure that they reduced the soccer ball to something the size of a lemon.

"You need to brrrring the ball with you as you make your run," he said, in a loud and distinct Scots accent. "Understand that, lads? Understand that, lassies?"

I didn't know this at the time, but the man dispensing so much energy, passion, and humor to a shivering set of kids on that muddy field on an atrocious April day was none other than Bobby Clark, already a legend in Scotland, soon to be a legend in the States. He had been the goalie for Aberdeen when it had been one of the best pro teams in Europe, coached by the young Alex (not-yet-Sir-Alex) Ferguson. After a stint playing goal for Scotland's national team, he had emigrated to America and taken the vacant Dartmouth head coach job. He was to prove spectacularly successful at this, bringing Dartmouth into the college soccer big time before moving on to even greater things with Stanford and Notre Dame.

I learned this about Clark later, as well as the fact that here in Hanover he had started something called Lightning Soccer for local kids, including three of his own. What hit me with immediate impact is a bit harder to explain. Although I had played soccer in high school and enjoyed it thoroughly, I had given the game hardly a thought in the twenty years since. I was busy establishing a career, I had no kids, and after the demise of the New York Cosmos, there was no soccer in America compelling enough to catch my attention . . . until now. The boys and girls were up on their feet, juggling balls from foot to foot, but it was as if one of them had blasted a shot into my groin, so dramatic was the effect. When I had played soccer, when I had last even thought about it, it was strictly an autumn sport; even our best players—boys who went on to become all-Americans in college—put their cleats away in November and didn't pick them up again until the following August.

That soccer was now a year-around sport was news to me; that there was something called "travel-team" soccer was a complete surprise; that kids started seriously playing so young now, I had no idea.

And it wasn't just a cultural wake-up call, either. It occurred to me, watching these kids go through their paces, listening to Bobby Clark's happy, generous exhortations, that it might be nice, once we had kids of our own, to introduce them to soccer ourselves, buy them a little ball, play with them in the yard. Nothing more than that; visions of glory, of stardom, of eventual scholarships did not flash before my eyes. Kicking a soft ball over soft grass with a laughing little girl or boy—that's what came to me, even in that April miasma. How nice that would be!

So. This is the spot where it all began, the place Matthew's soccer life was conceived—and mine reborn. It was worth a moment's reflection—in that cold, a moment's reflection was all that it got— and then I walked back to the parking lot, reached in my car for my ski hat and scarf, and continued on across the street to Hanover High School.

Hanover High was built in the 1920s, the proud red-brick era of American public schools, so it looks like the kind of high school Mickey Rooney would have attended with Judy Garland. Unfortunately, it looked like that on the inside, too, with halls and classrooms that had steadily darkened with the passage of years. The good news is that renovations, after many battles and votes, were at long last under way. Construction trucks were everywhere now, and students, to get from class to class, had to detour outside, hugging themselves in the cold, skipping around the slushy puddles. I walked to the back where a new floodlit, artificial turf field was going in. It was almost finished now, raw in a newborn kind of way, and its final neatening would have to wait until spring.

The soccer field—natural grass—remained where it had always been: to the north of the high school, directly across the street from Dartmouth's ivy-covered football stadium. Not much had changed here, though I noticed the swamp along the sidelines had been patched with fresh sod. There was no sign of any goals, and the field looked a little pointless without them. Where was the goal that Jeff Levin had found with a spinning shot with five seconds left in regulation against Fall Mountain to send us through to the semifinals last fall? Where, for that matter, was the goal that had been nearly lifted off its base from the force of Lucas Dahlstrom's shot when we beat archrival Lebanon in a quarterfinal shootout Matt's sophomore year, a game that will go down in local history as the most melodramatic, epic sporting event ever played in the Upper Valley? (A thousand spectators forming a semicircle around the goal; the sun setting through the autumn twilight; the yearning, the hope, the fear, so palpable it formed a twilight all its own; the parents, the students, the teams, spontaneously holding hands—yes, epic, the stuff of legends.)

I walked around to where the old football field had been, past a sign that read HANOVER HIGH SCHOOL HOME TO THE MARAUDERS above a weary-looking pirate with a patch over his eye and a dirk between his teeth. No goal there, either, at least no soccer goals. I had to skip aside from the beep of a construction truck backing up, but at least this nudged me in the right direction, and I finally found the two netless goals leaning up against an old brown shed, their overlap forming a steel butterfly pattern. The snowplows had left a drift here, and I climbed to the top to reach over and touch the closest goal—touching goals seemed an important part of my little journey.

I looked back toward the high school, wondering whether anyone sitting bored in math class was watching me. I half expected Matt to appear, felt disappointed that he didn't. Okay, he's in the Bahamas—get used to it, Dad. I hoped maybe one of his teammates would come out, Casey Maue, say, the gentlemanly giant, or Eric Barthold, shy and thoughtful. It would be good to reminisce with them about last season's miraculous championship, when a team that had lost nearly all its stars to graduation won the states on teamwork and sheer intelligence. For that matter, I was surprised that Rob Grabill didn't appear, Hanover High's charismatic head coach. There wasn't a soccer field in a fifty-mile radius that Rob didn't haunt, and it wasn't like him to take the winter off.

A great spot to linger, if it wasn't for the cold—and then I had many soccer miles to go before I slept.

Hanover, with its Ivy League credentials, likes to think of itself as the center of the universe, but when it comes to soccer geography, it lies well off the mainstream. To find suitable competition, travel teams have to head southeasterly to the suburbs, which means a good ninety minutes of I-89 through the range of rugged hills that have always isolated western New Hampshire from the rest of the state. (As affluent and sophisticated as Hanover is, the teams we play in the suburbs think of us as hicks.)

Driving the same road in winter, I could relax and indulge myself in some memories. Driving alone with Matthew, we would talk about the upcoming game, what to expect, but not too seriously, and we were just as apt to talk about British Premier League games or even the Italian Serie A. Sometimes a teammate would be in back, and quite often this was Sam Peterson, whose trademark way of listening to you, grave and amused at the same time, always lifted my spirit. He and Matt would start talking about computers, but their adrenaline kept careful track of the mileage; by Concord, they were putting on their cleats and shin guards; by Manchester, they'd be asking me to find some pump-up music on the radio, which had to be played as loud as my ears could stand.

February days are short, and my goal was to make it as far south as Derry before turning around—Derry, drab suburban Derry, which was once rural enough to give Robert Frost his poems. I would pass a town, take the exit, drive until I found the field Matt had once played on—Bow's at an elementary school; Concord's at the New Hampshire Technical Institute; Manchester's at Rock Rimmon Park;

Hudson's at the Budweiser plant (a field so lush we parents joked it had been watered with suds)—park my car, walk across the snowy field, search for the soccer goals, give them a totemic pat, remember a bit, get back in the car, drive on. It was snowing hard enough now to make me wonder if my impromptu expedition wasn't getting a little too compulsive. Neddy Merrill, as he swims across the suburbs, wonders similarly. "Why, believing as he did that all human obduracy was susceptible to common sense, was he unable to turn back? Why was he determined to complete his journey even if it meant putting his life in danger? At what point did this prank, this joke, this piece of horseplay become serious?"

With daylight fading, I decided not to fool around with any of the satellite fields that ring the city of Nashua, but to go right to Stellos, which is the Old Trafford of New Hampshire soccer, our Maracanã, our Wembley. It's a stadium, modest enough by the standards of larger states, but big-time for us, and the site of the high school championships each November. Set next to the Nashua River, its highest stands face west, and so there is always a sunset behind the players when they're introduced, enlarging their shadows, lending a bittersweet quality to it all, making it seem as if the game, even before it's started, is slipping nostalgically into the past.

CLOSED FOR THE SEASON POLICE TAKE NOTICE, read the sign on the stadium's fence, but I had come too far to pay attention to warnings like that. I walked over toward the second, inner fence, gave the black padlock an exploratory tug, then contented myself with staring through the wire mesh to what I could see of the field.

The snow, covering the artificial turf, looked artificial itself, it was so smooth and unblemished. The wind made a tinny sound against the metal risers, then found the halyards of the twin flagpoles, making them rattle and snap like the rigging on a barque. The soccer goals were in the far corner, and their shadows stretched to meet me halfway—but again, there was no way of bucking that fence.

All the other fields I visited cast a lonely, forgotten feel that was easy on the spirit; Stellos, even in the depth of winter, reeked of tension, nerves, and high anxiety. Partly, this came from soccer's very nature; with goals so hard to come by, almost any game is liable to be close, and with the top teams in New Hampshire being very evenly matched, this means the state title is usually decided by a single goal, often in overtime, when the suspense and drama have been wound to their maximum tightness. Memories here, even good memories, come coated in anguish.

I remembered Matt's sophomore season, the title game against Bow, our players galloping forward in a rainy mist so thick it seemed to form a barrier across the Bow goal—how else to explain why shot after shot somehow missed? And then finally, deep in overtime, when it seemed we would have to come back in two nights for a replay, our star Ben McKinnon turned from outside the box and struck the ball goalward with all his left-footed strength, a speculative effort that probably would have sailed wide, too, except for Andrew Hathaway, our snowboarding right midfielder (not to be confused with Kevin Pearce, our snowboarding left back, who was already a celebrity on the world professional snowboarding circuit and had only returned to high school for the soccer season)—"Drew" Hathaway, that is—who suddenly bent over like a praying mullah, jerked his head down in an abrupt, perfunctory bow, met the ball, and sent it obliquely past the sprawling Bow keeper, to set off a wild celebration from players, parents, and fans.

And then the following year, with Matt as a starter now, in the final against Lebanon. A mix-up by our goal, the comic Keystone Kops kind of moment that comes when a team collectively stops paying attention. Matt sensing this, like an alert drummer in a jazz big band when the overall rhythm begins to sag . . . running over not just to clear the ball from the box, but dribbling it out, shouting, waking his teammates up again, turning the play the other way. Memorable, at least for his dad. And then there was Mike Grant with his flip throws, his acrobatic somersaults as he threw the ball deep toward the Lebanon goal, flip throws that require long run-ups, so he would force his way through the burning bushes that lined the far edge of the field, disappear into the darkness, then suddenly appear again in the lights with a tremendous flourish, bursting through the hedges and releasing the ball on a fast, flat trajectory that almost scored us a winner just before halftime . . . a winner that came, finally came, deep in overtime, when Angus Kennedy somehow got a foot to the ball in the box and with agonizing (for Lebanon), triumphant (for us) slowness—we all had time to rise to our feet, suck in our breaths, stare, wish, yearn—the ball rolled behind the keeper and won us our second state championship in a row.

Suspense of this kind doesn't melt quickly. Then, of course, I couldn't come to Stellos without worrying whether the lads would be good enough to win their way here next season, in Matt's senior year. Hanover had always fielded one of the best teams in the state, but never had they won the state championship three years running.

Time to head back north to the hills. But if I thought I was in charge of this journey, I was now learning that, like Neddy Merrill, the journey was in charge of me.

Rush-hour traffic in southern New Hampshire can be heavy, so I decided to try a shortcut to avoid I-91. On my left, not far from Stellos, I passed an elementary school, and past this, a kind of satellite field, part school playground, part civic park. But it was something about the parking lot that caught my attention, got the bells ringing. It had an odd way of opening, a choke collar leading to a staggered set of terraces. Matt had played here, I sensed that instantly, and the only thing it took me a bit longer to remember was when.

A Columbus Day soccer tournament the year he was thirteen—the Nashua Invitational tournament for elite New England teams, one that our Lightning team, the hicks from the sticks, felt flattered even to attend. I pulled over, squinted through the windshield to make sure, but I already knew, from what I was feeling, that I had the right spot. It wasn't nostalgia this time, a burnished, pleasant memory, but something with a harder bite, something I wanted to duck away from: a recovered memory, the kind a psychiatrist might pry out of you after long hours of therapy.

I got out and walked over to where I remembered the goals having been, though there was no sign of them now. The snow was scrappier here than it was on the other fields, and there was enough grass exposed that I had no difficult finding a long, yellowed scar that was perfectly goal sized, with a matching scar ninety yards away near the woods. I would say our game here instantly came back, but it had already come back the moment I pulled into the parking lot, and walking across the field only sharpened what was already far too clear.

Columbus Day 2003. We have done well in the first round games. Now even a tie will send us through to the quarterfinals. Our opponents are the U-13 team from West Hartford, Connecticut. Dressed in black, they go through their warm-ups with cocky nonchalance. They look twice as big as our lads (that's the thing about travel-team soccer: the other team always looks bigger, even if they're smaller). Two of them—I'm not making this up—wear mustaches and goatees. Their dads look very much alike: endomorphs; middle height or even shorter; still in shape, but barely; tomato-red complexions; a few years either side of forty; gold necklaces on some, Rolex watches on others. I notice one thing with surprise and even alarm. There are no soccer moms watching West Hartford. No civilizing influence. The women-folk have all been left at home.

The game goes all their way at first, but the West Hartford dads are still not happy. One man, built like a fireplug, keeps angrily yelling, "Kick the ball, guys! Why in hell don't you kick the ball!" which pretty much exhausts his supply of tactical suggestions. Another father, this one wearing a red warm-up suit, keeps yelling out, "Lob him, Omar! Lob him!" A third, my favorite, shouts triple-digit numbers to his son, which must be a private code; this same father also keeps a notebook and scribbles something down every time his boy's foot touches the ball.

Cal Felicetti, our shifty midfielder, makes a run down the left, and their tall striker, the one with the mustache, rushes in to cut down the angle.

"Stop him!" a shrill voice yells to my right. "Break his ankles!"

On our end of the line, the Lightning end, thirty synchronized heads swivel eyes right toward the West Hartford end. Have we heard right? The yellow-shirted referee, who is huskier and beefier and angrier-looking than any West Hartford tough, runs across the grass, stops at the sidelines, juts his chin out, stares into the suddenly blank faces.

"Who yelled that!" he demands.

None of the West Hartford dads says a word or even flinches. Luckily, one of our parents, arriving late, happens to be standing right next to the perpetrator. Kevin Peterson, who at six-foot-four takes no shit from anyone, jabs his thumb down at the dad who said it.

"He did, sir."

The referee goes right over to the guilty dad, nearly butts him with his chest. "Those are kids out there!" he yells. "One more word out of you, and you're outta here!"

Four minutes left to go. West Hartford attacks yet again, trying to spread our defense thin—and then suddenly their winger turns the corner and crosses it toward the goalmouth. Ben Harwick, our keeper, rushes out to intercept, but the ball scoots under him. Matthew races up to help—with Ben sprawled on the ground, our goal is totally unprotected—and he is just about to kick it to safety over the touch-line for a corner when a West Hartford player barges into him from behind, forcing Matt's foot forward just far enough to deflect the ball in the back of the net.

1-0 West Hartford. An own goal. A goal scored by Matthew for the wrong team, the hateful team, the ones who are now celebrating like they've won the World Cup, ditto their fathers, ditto the man who screamed. An own goal by Matthew. A fatal mistake by my son.

He plays furiously for the next three minutes, trying to atone, but time runs out. He and the other lads have to shake hands with the West Hartford team (West Hartford, to rub things in, take the souvenir patches the teams exchange before the game and throw the ones we gave them into the mud). Matthew grabs his Adidas duffel bag and starts walking toward the parking lot by himself on an angle designed to keep it that way as long as possible.

"You okay?" I ask, when our converging paths finally meet at the car.

He nods, gets in, slumps sideways against the door.

"Hungry? Thirsty?"

He doesn't answer, stares silently out the window—it's like a hole has opened in his foot, draining out all his animation. Somehow we make it to I-91, then I-89, where the country begins. With the sun shining through the cruller-shaped clouds, the foliage on the surrounding hillsides is at its peak—brilliant reds and gorgeous oranges and even some deep, luxurious purples. Breathtaking—and yet it can't do anything against our numbness, and when I tap my finger on the windshield, Matt hardly bothers glancing up.

I know what you're feeling, I want to say. It's been a long time since I was thirteen, but not that long, and anyway the capacity for major fuckup failure is far from being just a feature from my past. To fight so valiantly against those who would humiliate you, then have the bastards laugh in your face when you, YOU, are the one who gives them their chance. Sure, it's only a game, just a sport, boys kicking around a dimpled ball, but to you on this golden afternoon it's everything, and why pretend otherwise? If life has to teach you this lesson, it can use soccer as well as it can use any of its other tools, and there isn't much you can do about it now except take the defeat deep inside where it can get its hurting over with, kick and punch you all it wants, and only then, just when you think you can't stand anymore, can you start the necessary business of climbing back toward the top.

I'm sorry these are all clichés, Matthew—I wish I could say it better. Hell, I wish I had the gumption to say the words out loud at all. I can drive you to your games, Matt, and I can cheer for you, and I can be silent if you need me to be silent, but what I can't do, what I can't ever do, is guarantee the world will always go your way.

For two hours of the drive, we didn't exchange a single word, but then exiting the interstate, starting on the last lap toward home, Matthew suddenly straightened in his seat and stretched.

"I wonder how Man U did today."

"Yeah, I was just wondering about that," I said. "Newcastle's a strong side. Check BBC's Web site when we get home?"

"Sure."

Okay, a baby step in the right direction—but there was one step more, and when we were unpacking the car, in the last moment we had together before we had to go in and explain what had happened to the rest of the family, I took the chance.

"Hey, your first goal of the season, right? I was pretty proud of you. No one else on your team bloody well scored."

Risky, playing the jocular card early—had I blown it? Matt looked downcast, seemed about to yell, but then—and this happened in one very long second—he brought his head up and smiled.

"My left foot, too," he said. "Notice that?"

Victory. Hope. Tragedy. Suffering. Defeat. Silence. Endurance. Courage. Rebound. Recovery.

And lasagna waiting from his mom.

For me, on my winter journey, there was one stop more. I'd been driving in the dark since Manchester, but at least the snow had stopped, and along the interstate the stars were bright enough that I mistook them for taillights ahead of me on the otherwise deserted road. I drove back through Hanover past the high school and college, came out into the country again at Lyme. Just before our house is a large trout pond, and to the north of the pond, sitting in a wetland that often gets flooded, is the town's brave attempt at a soccer field. The plows clear a spot off the road for the ice fishermen, and this is where I parked. Then it was only a matter of crossing a low cable fence to the closest goal, the one that shone brightest in the moonlight.

Someone had dragged it out from the woods. Maybe it was Matthew, back in our extraordinarily mild December when he had wanted to get in a little postseason practice on his own. I didn't just touch the goal this time, but actually stepped in under the net; it was made of a higher-class twine than the days when Matt played his little-kid soccer here. Through it I could see Orion rising above the ridge east of town and the fierce glow of Sirius following it up the sky. A spotlight shone down on a cleared patch of pond ice, but it was far too cold for any skaters; a flagpole had its own small light, and the flag was still at half-mast for Gerald Ford, who had died two weeks earlier.

This is where Matt played his first games, or at least his just-for-fun soccer "activities," when he was in first grade. I remember standing to the side watching, enjoying the frantic, happy way the kids swarmed around the little balls; I remember taking a great deal of smug satisfaction in picturing how I would never become a typical American sports parent—that it was entirely a matter of indifference to me whether my son eventually played sports or not.

They played a little scrimmage at the end, if you can call it that—seven a side, but the kids soon forgot which team they were on, and the point of the game seemed merely to get your toe on the ball and giggle. Fine—but then somewhere in all this, the ball went airborne for a second, perhaps off some little girl's bony knee. Matthew was standing there, six-year-old Matthew, who had never seen a soccer game before, not a live one, not on TV. With the ball in the air above him, the cones marking the goal to his right, he jumped in the air as spontaneously as a salmon, cocked his head and shoulders back, snapped his head forward, and sent the ball rocketing through the cones. It happened so fast, I don't think the coaches noticed. But, standing twenty yards away, I noticed all right, and I remember how distinctly and with what surprise the thought formed: that's aptitude I'm seeing there, can't-be-taught soccer aptitude, and what are the implications of that?

I like to joke to my friends that after following my daughter's games and now my son's, I've come to know the whereabouts of every single soccer field in Vermont and New Hampshire. I don't, of course. Today, in a hard day's traveling, I had managed to visit perhaps twenty. Here, close to home, our starlit pitch by the frozen pond seemed much larger than it did normally, vast even, merging at the ends with the other fields I had visited, and not just these, but the invisible fields that extended north, south, east, and west of where I was standing: fields slapped down on old cow meadows, fields built atop landfills, fields sunk in wetlands, fields high on hillsides with commanding views of the White Mountains, fields tucked behind breweries, fields that were part of elaborate soccer complexes run by elite youth teams with artificial turf and sophisticated drainage systems and banks of bright blue lights. Yes, a clever, soccer-mad giant could hopscotch from one side of New England to the other and keep at least one foot in a soccer field at all times. The game is an integral part of the region's texture.

And not just the region, but the whole continent now. Fields down in New York pressed up against the high-rises, fields down in Kentucky on lush blue grass, fields out in Montana where the kids who are too small or too smart for football play framed by that end-less big sky, fields in California where some clever Latino kid dribbles circles around the Anglos or maybe vice versa, fields in Oregon, Washington, and Texas—fields (and I've seen them) even in Labrador and Alaska. And even these are only a tiny corner of the real field of the world. Add in Ghana's and Serbia's and China's and Brazil's, and you could start to get an idea of how vast a playing area I was contem-plating, a soccer dad home from his eccentric road trip, very conscious, in a world of tragic and unnecessary divisions, of how this beautiful game linked so much.

I began this journey in search of goals. Returning home now, I think of them again. My immediate goal is to help my son Matthew as he goes through his senior year in high school: that vital, busy time that may or may not be the first year of adulthood, but is certainly the last year of being a kid. In particular, it's to root him through what will perhaps be his final season of playing competitive soccer. He's a smart player who reads the game wonderfully, an on-field general, a passionate competitor who's enjoyed much success, but he may not quite be a top college prospect, at least not at the school he's interested in attending. We've talked this over and feel good about it, because it frees us both from the frenzy of those who will do anything to keep playing. We've come a long way with soccer. Almost accidentally, our mutual love for the game became the passion that bound us most closely together, and if this is his last year of playing before completely different goals come to dominate his life, then we need to make sure our closeness doesn't take a hit.

My goal, in many respects, remains the same as it has always been, ever since that day when a six-year-old Matthew rose over the other kids to make his perfect header: to handle this soccer-dad business, something that can go wrong very fast, as competently and gracefully as I can. Along the way, this will probably tempt me into offering advice or pronouncing platitudes, and, as when I'm standing on the sidelines, I'll have to ruthlessly check myself, bite my tongue. But how much of fatherhood involves keeping faith with platitudes!

And books have goals, too. This one will follow what has become a recognizable genre: following a sports team through the ups and downs of one season as they strive to win another championship. It's a team made up of talented, likable young men I've known and followed since they were little kids, young men who now form the core of the best high school soccer team in New Hampshire, this cranky, eccentric state that is just far enough removed from the American mainstream to make it interesting.

Only partly will it be an insider's view. I'm a parent. I belong on the spectators' side of the pitch, worrying, fretting, cheering, hoping. There is drama here. There are stories, lessons, heroes, villains, personalities of all sorts. Writing now in the depth of winter, it's hard to anticipate exactly where these will lead me. But this will be an unorthodox sports book, written as it is by someone who is skeptical about the over-the-top importance this culture attaches to sport, but someone who, almost despite himself, has become fascinated by soccer's beauty. It's an autumn kind of beauty, at least when your son is likely playing his last season, and so, in trying to describe it, I will have to remind myself not to root so hard I can't keep my eye on the larger picture.

Most writing about soccer in the United States takes either a defensive, prickly stance or a condescending, dismissive one, but this book will eschew both approaches and take it as a given that anyone reading it already understands and values soccer, doesn't need his or her hand held when it comes to things like explaining offsides, prefers to avoid long explanations of why pro soccer has never really caught on here, detests long sociological treatises about soccer moms and their political influence. American soccer needs, badly needs, a book of pure celebration. The world's real football, flying often under the radar, has become a venerable part of American culture, and the only ones oblivious to this are the big-time sportswriters, who, in their snobby smugness, have missed the biggest grassroots sports story of their day.

But, again, I can only speak personally here. My son, for one part of his life, became obsessed with soccer, and that's enough to make a soccer-obsessed America for me.

2

SEEKERS

Rob Grabill was put on earth to teach young men soccer, but it's interesting, watching the passion and intelligence he invests in this, to speculate what other vocations might have harnessed his special blend of talents. Given his genius at remembering names, his communication skills, his infectious grin, how about a big-city politician, a beloved mayor on the order of Fiorello LaGuardia? With his ability to multitask, his calmness under pressure, his rapid-fire show-biz wit, maybe the ringmaster at the old style of Barnum & Bailey three-ring circus? A social director at a Catskill resort? Or, playing around now with time, keeping in mind the steel that underlies his geniality, how about a Civil War general, the kind who didn't just exhort his men from headquarters but took sword in hand and led from the front?

He'd be good at all these things, a natural, but there is one occupation that would suit him even better. Picture a boy's camp in the New

Hampshire hills, so cliché perfect it's hard to believe it really exists. An idyllic lake for swimming and canoeing, mountains to climb, the weathered log buildings nestled in a gentle bowl between water and hills, the whole sheltered under the blue shade of pine. Picture a hundred boys of all ages, backgrounds, and races running around with purposeful energy, as counselors with clipboards and whistles shout out names sorting them out. Picture a boy blowing reveille on a golden coronet. Weathered log cabins that date back to 1908. A mess hall with long trestle tables piled with platters of cold cuts and homemade bread, everyone singing a corny camp song before digging in.

Picture this, then think of the organizational skills needed to run it successfully, including being able to remember names instantly, cope with emergencies big and small, exude energy exceeding anything pumped out by the boys, be sympathetic and understanding on demand, and sing louder and tell jokes better than anyone else in camp. Then and only then will you have found a job that suits—perfectly suits—Rob Grabill.

And this isn't pretend. For the last thirty-eight years, when he hasn't been coaching soccer, Rob has been the director of Camp Pemigewasset, "Camp Pemi," which, in the summer I'm writing in, is proudly celebrating its one hundredth year. Begun in 1908 by a group of Oberlin College professors when these hills were as lost and forgotten a corner of New England as you could find, it's flourished over the years as a classic boys summer camp with a reputation for doing things the good-old-fashioned way, and doing this so successfully that the waiting list to get a place for your son rivals Princeton's.

This is what Rob calls his "day job"—a demanding year-around vocation that, thanks to some adroit juggling, just gives him enough time to coach high school soccer in the fall. And so, on an outrageously beautiful June day, one of his player's parents, happening to pass by the camp on his return from a fishing trip, decides to stop in and say hello.

"Is Rob around?" I ask the first counselor I meet—a young woman, as it happens. She points toward the lake, shrugs, points toward the soccer field, shrugs again, points toward the office cabin, frowns . . . and I get her point. Rob is ubiquitous, he's liable to be anywhere, but then a boy to our right emits a mighty blast on his trumpet, and she points, much more decisively, to the mess hall.

I'm waiting by the entrance, doing my best not to get trampled by a hundred hungry boys, when Rob steps out from the mob and waves; he's as loyal to his soccer parents as he is to his players, and he's surprised and delighted to see me. He's dressed in an official U.S. National Soccer team uniform—glossy blue- and vertically white-striped shirt over glossy blue- and vertically white-striped shorts—not an outfit many fifty-six-year-olds could wear with distinction, at least off a soccer pitch, but on strong, barrel-chested Rob it looks perfect and has the utilitarian benefit of making him, the point man on so many decisions, easy to find.

He's deeply tanned, handsome as always, though the beard is new. Its closely trimmed silver-white matches the silver-white of his hair and makes him resemble photographs of Robert E. Lee, if you can imagine a happy-go-lucky Robert E. Lee. Aging athletes are often described as walking slightly pigeon-toed, with an easy roll to their gait, and Rob certainly demonstrates this, though heavy usage has made the roll veer toward a limp, the kind an old pirate might develop after spending too much time on tossing decks.

"Have time for lunch?" he asks, shaking my hand. The next thing I know, I'm sitting down at a long table passing plates, dishing out slices of boiled ham and turkey, pouring juice . . . and trying not to let flashbacks of Camp Wauwepex circa 1962 drown out Rob's happy explanations of who's who and what's going on.

We're interrupted often, but that's okay—Rob clearly enjoys making order out of chaos. Again, I thought of my Civil War general analogy, Rob presiding at a council of war, making decisions, issuing instructions, leading by example with his 100 percent genuine upbeat tone. "We scrape the iPods off them," he says, when I ask how campers have changed in his thirty-eight years here. "A lot of them suffer from nature deficit disorder, and we try very hard to find a cure."

It's this aspect of Rob—his relentless good humor—that threw me when I first met him some eight or nine years ago. Rob, after a roving soccer life, had settled down as the director of the Lightning Soccer travel program, which both my kids were then involved with. Matt's coach was missing, so Rob took over practice, and I'll admit my first impressions were negative. How could anyone pour so much passion and enthusiasm into coaching a bunch of eleven-year-olds on the hard, bare floor of an iceless hockey rink when he didn't even know their names? (Eleven minutes into practice, of course, he knew them all.) And that smile on his face—no middle-aged man I knew ever looked so happy so consistently. "Stop!" he would scream, when someone

made a timid pass. His face became tomato red; his barrel chest trembled like a keg of dynamite. Okay, here it comes, I decided—the mean, over-the-top coaching fascist reveals his true colors. But I was wrong on that. In an instant, Rob was back to laughing and cheering, and, when I got to observe him further, I decided that what threw me was absolutely his best and rarest quality: this is a man who absolutely loves what he's doing and is not afraid to show that love with every word, every expression, every gesture.

Lunch over, Rob goes over to the center of the mess hall and orchestrates a furious round of announcements. Over in the corner, the patriarch of the camp, Tom Reed (age ninety-two), the son of the founder, tells a joke, and it's a good one that makes the boys laugh. Then it's time for a camp song, "The Clam Shell Song," according to a songbook someone sticks in my hand.

I cut my foot on a damn clam shell

And the blood came a trickling down

Blood! Blood! Blood! Blood!

And the blood came trickling down!

It's a classic, a song fit for pirates, and Rob sings louder than any-one. Afterward, there are still more announcements. One of Rob's great gifts is that he has a loud/soft voice—loud in timbre and cutting power; soft in tone, in rhythm. It's a wonderful tool, enabling him to project his sensitivity at a distance, or, when he takes the softness out, enabling him to be listened to very quickly.

After lunch comes rest period, and it's amazing how swiftly so much activity subsides into so much peace. Rob and I find a bench under one of the pines; though we command a wide view of the lake and playing fields, there is absolutely no one else in sight.

"So," Rob says. "How did Matt make out in the Bahamas? I hear he's running half marathons."

"He liked it so much he's going out for cross-country in the fall, the hell with soccer."

Rob laughs. "I'll make him run twice as much as anyone else at preseason. Tell him Rob says to be scared. To be extremely scared."

Since we're on the subject, Rob explains he has big plans for Matt that might involve a change of position. Because our brilliant mid-fielder Jeff Levin has graduated, he wants to press Angus Kennedy forward to play at offensive center mid and move Matt up from central defense to act as his partner.

Rob beams at the perfect rightness of this. "Angus will set the table and Matt will clean the dishes."

This throws me considerably. "Well, Matt's smart enough, but I wonder about his speed."

"No problem. We'll use him like the U.S. national team uses Claudio Reyna."

I'm trying hard to picture exactly how the U.S. national team uses Claudio Reyna, but Rob is already on to the next subject.

This is the coming season, what the prospects are for Hanover, what goals might be within reach. "There is one challenge I'm really excited about," he says, putting, if anything, even more twinkle in his eyes than lies there ordinarily. "One accomplishment that is tough, but we might just pull off. I want the boys to win"— here he hesitates, milks the pregnant pause, continues in a rush of words— "their second New Hampshire good sportsmanship trophy in a row."

From any other coach you might suspect this was a whopper platitude, paying lip service to good sportsmanship before going on to talk about his real priority: winning the state soccer championship again, no matter how that goal is achieved. Surely some cynicism is in order here, but you'd be making a bad mistake about the man if you read Rob as hypocritical. The state sportsmanship trophy is hard to win—the coaches who vote for it usually treat it as a consolation prize—and for a school to win both the soccer title and the sportsmanship award is rare and a tribute to the kind of tone Rob sets. If he says that sportsmanship comes first for him, winning second, you can well believe him.

And Hanover hasn't always earned high marks in this department. Several years back, the girls on the soccer team showed up for a game against archrival Lebanon wearing white trash bags over their heads—making the not-so-subtle point that Hanover has more doctors, lawyers, and trust funders per capita than Lebanon does. Hanover fans also often showed up at away games wearing orange hunting hats, though the symbolism here is a bit more ambiguous; does it show that we're the hicks from the sticks, or do we think the other team are hicks?

Rob has no patience with this kind of behavior. Before last year's playoff, he sent out an e-mail to everyone in school saying he would take it as a personal insult if anyone came to support his team wearing an orange ski hat and that "appropriate and immediate" action would result if they did.

The upshot? No one wore anything even remotely offensive. Having stamped out a bad tradition, having continued the good ones (for instance, providing bagels and juices for the visiting teams before their long bus drives home), having come down hard on any hint of misbehavior on the playing field or from parents watching, Rob was deservedly proud of the team's sportsmanship award, and he would brag about this to all and sundry while saying nary a thing about the winner's trophy that flanks it on the high school's shelf.

Given this, he's a bit reluctant to indulge in any preseason chitchat about the prospects or team chemistry or who might emerge as his stars, though this is the kind of thing the soccer-mad dad sitting next to him on the bench is hungry for. Oh, he's quietly confident they'll have another strong season. Yes, he's still not sure who his strikers will be. As always, it's going to be hard making cuts; there were a few seniors who had served their time in the trenches of JV and deserved a shot, but then again, he had a good crop of freshmen, and surely at least one would force his way onto the varsity. (Rob had already in the spring made what he called "house calls" on parents of all the incoming freshmen—not recruiting them, but letting them know how the Hanover High soccer program operated.)

Our competition this year? Souhegan in the south of the state, Bow over near Concord, Oyster River in Durham (home of the University of New Hampshire), and Con-Val down near the Massachusetts border. In other words, the usual suspects.

"What about Lebanon?" I ask.

Rob smiles, winks. "Well, if you were from the *Valley News*," he says, mentioning the local newspaper, "I would have to say Lebanon is part of the mix. But they graduated the heart of their team, so I don't think we'll have to worry about them very much."

"But pretend I am a sportswriter. Any predictions?"

"We have to take luck out of the equation. How many games did we win in overtime last year? Five? Five pig-pile games, everyone jumping on the goal scorer. My heart couldn't take another season like that. We have to be so much better than the other teams that accidents can't happen. But these seniors, the ones who are going to be leading the show this year: I've never had smarter players or ones who loved the game more. Their idea of fun is going home from practice and watching Premier League highlights, then playing FIFA on their computers half the night. That's rare. Most soccer players I've had, even the good ones, go home and watch the NFL."

The talk veers from the coming season to soccer in general. Rob goes back a long way with the game. He played for Lincoln-Sudbury High School outside Boston back in the late sixties and early seventies; like me, he remembers a primitive time when high school rules forbid throw-ins and the ball was always kicked in after going out of bounds. He played four years at Oberlin, then—when he wasn't working at Camp Pemi—began coaching and refereeing, so by the time he became Hanover High's coach, he'd been around the soccer block five or six times, in many different capacities.

He'd been the head coach of Southern New Hampshire University from 1979 to 1987, making them a nationally ranked Division II team and laying the foundation of the team that won the NCAA Division

II national title in 1989. After that came spells as a college and high school referee, a couple of years as assistant coach at Dartmouth, and the directorship of the Upper Valley Lightning travel-team program. Then, starting in 2002, he worked as an unpaid volunteer assistant under Chris Cheney in Hanover. I always assumed this second-banana role must have been hard for him; he's such a take-charge kind of guy. But no, he'd enjoyed it thoroughly. Respecting Chris as he did, he found it tremendously relaxing—after the summer at Camp Pemi—to let someone else steer the ship.

Chris had left Hanover before the 2006 season to coach down the road at Kimball Union Academy, a tony boarding school. Rob took over, and there were doubts expressed by some of the more competitive parents just because Chris had been so successful. Within a few weeks, those doubts were gone. Grabill is a coach to die for, both from the player's point of view and the parent's; it's tempting to say that there is nothing wrong with high school sports in this country that cloning several thousand Grabills couldn't cure. Excellent communication skills, real sensitivity, a perspective much wider than is usually found in sports, unquenchable energy, a talent for one-liners and teasing repartee—Rob has it all. And as much as his players respect him, they're just a bit afraid of him, too. His wit is so fast, his comebacks so quick that even the most sarcastic tread warily when Rob is about. If there were any doubts about his underlying toughness, they were dispelled at the team's first scrimmage last year. Five seniors, among them the team's freest spirits, arrived three minutes late and were immediately sent home. No one was ever late again.

Last year, after Matt had worked hard to win a starting spot, he came down with pneumonia, a serious case, and came back from the hospital to find waiting for him an e-mail from Rob, assuring him that his starting spot would be there waiting for him when he recovered. That kind of gesture wins loyalty for life. Beating Lebanon for the state championship, a team that included many boys he had worked with in the Lightning program, Rob didn't throw up his arms in triumph or yell or even smile, so bad did he feel for the opposing team. While our boys celebrated, he went around the bench obsessively picking up stray water bottles, discarded warm-ups, litter—trying, I suspect, not to cry.

Quiet time is ending now as campers begin to emerge from their cabins, blinking in the bright sunlight. I won't have Rob to myself much longer, but there's something I want to ask him: whether any sport would have been enough to capture him, or whether there is something unique to soccer that made him fall in love with it so hard.

"Soccer is the true democracy sport," he said. "With the ball at your feet, you're the quarterback, you're the point guard or pitcher, you make the decision where it goes."

Yes, great, I see what he means—but is there something about the beauty of the game that really grabbed him?

"It's not a coaching-centered sport. That's why you don't see me yelling from the touchline. I do it all in practice."

No doubt about that—Rob is remarkably mellow on the sidelines and spends most of his time talking to the subs, cracking jokes, accompanying his running play-by-play with his own colorful commentary. "We have a lot of fun on the bench," is often the way he breaks it to someone that they won't be starting.

I try again to get him talking about soccer's beauty, but he's uncomfortable with mouthing off about aesthetics. Fine. He's a sensitive guy, but touchy-feely he is not. And anyway, I have something else I want to ask.

"I've always been impressed by how soccer coaches, you in particular, can rewind every game, remember every single touch, can tell, if asked, who kicked the ball to whom starting with the first whistle."

Rob laughs. "It's like remembering names. I just can."

Off by the lake a whistle blows, and Rob twists sideways on the bench gathering himself to pounce on the afternoon. I've been saving my one and only soccer parent concern: Celeste, seeing a preliminary schedule, was concerned that the St. Thomas game was scheduled on the same morning as the October SATs. But Rob knows all about that—the game had already been moved to late afternoon.

Counselors converge on us from all sides, but Rob has one more thing he's itching to tell me. This is the boyish side of him—he beams like a little kid letting me in on a secret—and it suddenly occurs to me that in all my wondering about where his talent comes from, his extraordinary rapport with boys and young men, I've missed the most obvious ingredient. He himself is a grown-up boy, possesses in unique concentration that perpetual boyish quality that was supposedly one of the secrets to Teddy Roosevelt's charismatic appeal (and Rob, shave the bear and give him rimless specs, would look a lot like TR). Boyish—and a lot more excited about the coming season than he at first lets on.

"They're doing this with each other," he said. "All the seniors." He looks over his shoulder to make sure no one can see, brings his hand down, sticks out three fingers, folds them tight across his chest.

"A secret sign, just like the Masons."

I look at his hand, but still don't get it.

"Three championships in a row. A three-peat. We're not going to talk about it, but we're not going to forget about it, not for a second."

I'm in on the secret—I now feel like an initiated camper myself. Rob shakes my hand, jumps to his feet, glances down at his watch, starts sprinting toward one of the cabins, off to teach the afternoon class in yet another of his specialties: native butterflies and moths.

It's the summer of David Beckham, as once again the corporate world tries to jump-start American soccer from the top down, this time with a gorgeous celebrity with million-dollar legs—two such, actually, counting Beck's posh wife. Meanwhile, down here in the American grass roots, soccer decorates our summer with surprising varieties of flavors and intensities.

As it turns out, English missionary zeal, which a century ago took the game to every quarter of the world, is not quite dead. An organization called Play Soccer is running three mornings of clinics for our Lyme boys and girls on the field by the pond. Yesterday, on my way for a swim, I stopped to talk with its two instructors, who cheerily introduced themselves as Paul and Silas. They were in their early twenties, obviously chosen for their personalities as much as their soccer skills; like other instructors I talked with when Matt played there, they had made it to the lower rungs of English pro soccer, realized they would advance no further, and saw a summer teaching soccer in the States as a fun thing to do before settling into a real job.

We had a nice chat about the Premier League, who they fancied. I noticed they seemed preoccupied, though, as well as a bit stunned— perhaps at finding themselves exiled so far out in the U.S. boonies?

"Uh, Tottenham's coming up," Paul mumbled, meanwhile looking intently past my shoulder toward the beach.

Silas—who when demonstrating soccer skills yelled so exuberantly it made Rob Grabill seem shy—laughed and pointed.

"He means—what's her name? The blonde lifeguard over there. What's her name and does she fancy Brits like us?"

Across the Connecticut in Norwich, on the Huntley Meadow field where the high school team will practice come fall, it's over-thirty-five soccer, with shin-guardless men and shin-guardless women wearing a collection of left-leaning T-shirts and playing without goalies on a reduced-sized field. The skills vary—obviously, a few have played in college, and even more obviously, some have hardly played at all—but what unites them is an unfailing politeness that is borderline excessive. "Nice ball!" they shout, on even the clunkers. "Oh, nice ball, Roger!" "NICE ball, Ellen!" A few players are from the med school or college, and they're yelling something in Croatian or Bantu, but it's obvious the translation can only be "Nice ball!"

A little farther west in Quechee, my friend Art Trottier organizes Tuesday night games for all-comers, no matter what the age. High school and college players show up, and there are some rough-tough soccer moms whose kids play on the nearby swings, a number of British and Irish ex-pats, even a Greek Orthodox priest who travels from northern Vermont to play. Art likes talking about all the different styles the players bring to the mix, how everyone learns from each other. "You can't coach creativity," he says. "The game teaches you creativity by itself."

This is nondiscriminatory soccer, soccer at its most democratic and Grabillian. For a more intense mix, you can go down to Hanover, where the Jeff Cook Elite Soccer Academy brings more than two hundred high school–age boys to a weeklong camp on the Dartmouth campus. Partly this functions as a skills camp helping young players learn, but the more serious part focuses on the seventeen-year-olds who want to play in college and use this camp and others like it as a way of auditioning before college coaches on the staff, including Dartmouth's smart and affable Jeff Cook. A "meat market" some call it, and there is certainly a brutal winnowing process going on. The goal is to make the camp all-star team and play in the final exhibition games, or, failing that, to at least have one of the college coaches notice you, take down your name, your SAT scores, your GPA.

Finishing an errand in Hanover, I walked over to the camp to watch. This was on the same field I had visited in the winter, the one with the neglected goals, and what had then looked like a peasant village on the frozen Russian steppe now looked like a lavish condo development on a golf course down in the Carolinas. Soccer goals and soccer players were everywhere—coaches nearly as numerous—and the atmosphere, the concentrated energy mixed with naked ambition, gave you the feeling that this must be the world's only purpose: to create soccer players, to churn them out through mass production.

I recognized five HHS players, including Eric Barthold from here in Lyme. When he saw me and trotted over, I learned that this was his third camp in row.

"Uh, let's see," he said. "There was Notre Dame, then Brown, now Dartmouth. That's my three. A lot of these players are doing six or seven."

"How's it going? You like it?"

He hesitated before answering. "I haven't played that well. A coach from Kenyon came over and talked to me at Notre Dame."

Eric, who plays with a speedy impetuosity that belies his modest personality, has always been hard on himself. He looked like he could use some cheering up.

"Kenyon's in Ohio, Eric. Take my word for it. You're a skier. You couldn't survive where there aren't any mountains."

This is the first summer in three that Matt's not attending Jeff Cook's camp with Eric; it had helped develop him as a player, but the meat-market aspect, the auditioning, is not for him. Instead, he's been playing in the New Hampshire summer league for high school players. Always before, after playing spring travel soccer, he's needed a sabbatical from the game in summer; this year, having been gone for three months in the Bahamas, he's felt the need to get some playing time in before his senior season. And it's turned out to be fun. Some coaches take summer league very seriously, demand any player who wants to make varsity take part, but on the Hanover team, Touchline, the ethic is much more relaxed: if you can make a game, fine, if you can't, no sweat.

I've enjoyed it, too, since it's recreated our quality time in the car together, driving down to away games. Matt has his license, but he's a bit too polite and deferential yet to be comfortable on the interstate, so Dad rides shotgun. This has been a summer of violent thunderstorms and blinding downpours, and he also needs some backup to deal with that.

We've had some good talks, driving together. Matt's had a hard time readjusting to life at home after his extraordinary stay in the Bahamas. There was between us the natural shyness that comes when two people haven't seen each other in a while, and all this needed to be smoothed out.

Tonight's game was at Sunapee, an old New Hampshire resort town that backs the big lake of the same name. It's an hour's drive, and, as we used to with travel soccer, we talked about almost everything on the way down.

For starters, there was a cheating scandal at Hanover High that had just become public knowledge, though Matt had heard rumors the first day he was home. Four or five students had broken into the school, found the keys to two teachers' file cabinets, taken out the final exams, gone to a local store, copied them, returned them, then distributed copies to their pals. Too many people were in on the heist to keep it quiet—and now the town's police force was investigating, lawyers had been hired by the parents of the unnamed perpetuators, and the school had canceled the final test results for a good portion of the junior class.

"You know any of them?" I asked.

"I know who some are."

"Any soccer players?"

"Football players."

"Why am I not surprised?"

Cynical of me, but that's sometimes my role. "How's the job going?" I asked, switching gears.

"Painting the picket fence? Or Dartmouth Day Care?"

"Fence."

"It's harder than I thought. All those edges."

"Everyone should paint a picket fence once in their life. Nobody does it twice."

That's the kind of fatherly wisdom I like to dispense: witty aphorisms.

"Then bikers come by and yell things like 'Hey Tom Sawyer!' or 'You missed a spot!' Dartmouth Day Care is fun. I get the seven-year-olds mostly, the Woolly Bears. They seem to like me. One boy, Jason, cried when I said I had to leave early for tonight's game."

"We need to start that college essay soon. Need to visit some more colleges, too."

"The essay's scary."

"It's simple. Dear College Admissions Director, you say. My name is Matthew Wetherell, and you're lucky I'm applying to your college. I was breast-fed as an infant, never attended day care, grew up without a TV in the house, my parents aren't divorced, I don't drink or use drugs or play violent video games. What's not to like?"

"That's all in negatives."

"My mind often works that way. Do you miss not going to the Dartmouth camp?"

"Do you mean, do I want to play soccer in college? Sort of. Sort of wish I could play."

"We've talked about that, Matt. About how even at a Division III school, soccer would be your entire life, the coach would be your dictator, your friends would entirely be soccer players, and do we actually want that?"

"I have a game. Can we talk about it later?"

The ominous black clouds, scudding in from the west, seemed to drive Matt's foot down harder on the gas pedal, and I had to remind him that racing thunderstorms is a losing proposition. I'd been studying him pretty carefully since he got home from the Bahamas. What I was looking for, of course, were ways he had changed. He had more physical confidence in himself; it was there in his very posture. He had reached the six-foot status he had long coveted, and the new maturity in his body made him stand out with more individuality than he had as a cute but otherwise ordinary-sized little kid. On a solo kayak trip, camped on a beach totally alone for the first time in his life, he had been woken after midnight by waves crashing over his sleeping bag—a storm surge, totally unexpected, a mini-tsunami. He hadn't panicked, had done the sensible thing (which was to gather his gear and retreat toward higher ground), then went to help other students who, camped farther down the flooded beach, were having a tougher time. A challenge met, and it showed in the way he carried himself.

This physical confidence and maturity are changes I naturally approve of, though not without the sentimental pang you have when the little child you brought up slips even further into the past. Other changes I'm still getting used to. Matt flourished in the small, collegial setting of the Island School, discovered (and he'd gone with lingering doubts about this) that people are drawn to him, look to him for leadership, plain old-fashioned like him. Great—but some of his new pals turned out to be not only remarkably bright and energetic, but off-the-scale rich. The first weekend he was home he got invited down to Boston to attend a party hosted by one of his fellow student's parents—a house party to raise money for Barack Obama's presidential campaign. Matt got to be the one to greet the senator when he came through the door—a heady moment for a seventeen-year-old interested in politics, but, as with driving too fast on the interstate, Dad felt it required a few words of caution.

"Matthew, that's super, having an opportunity like that. But—how shall I say it? People with this kind of money are often charming, especially the Democrats, but they can be ruthless too, or how did they make all those bucks in the first place? What I'm saying is . . . just be a little careful with them, okay?"

Matt gave me the kind of blank stare that can be read fourteen different ways. "This our exit up here?"

"Lake Sunapee. My parents brought us up here from Long Island on a family vacation in what must have been 1957. I remember, because I saw kids throwing a Frisbee around on the beach, and I thought it was the coolest thing I ever saw, and I just read that Frisbee celebrates its fiftieth anniversary this year. What was I, eight or nine? Would have been pretty strange if someone had come up to me then and told me I'd have a son someday and he'd be playing soccer right down the road."

Sunapee is one of those trophy lakes where people buy $500,000 homes on the water, tear them down, and build $3 million houses in their place. Back in the little town, a quieter, sleepier mood remains in place, and though I hadn't been here in fifty years, I immediately experience a flash of recognition. The game was at the tiny high school, on the lower of two terraced fields. On the upper one, teenage girls had a game, but it was ending now, and some of them, in little flocks like sleek and satiny birds, were coming down to cheer on the boys.

I seemed to be the only visiting-team parent. I settled down on my beach towel near where the baseball infield bulged into the soccer grass. The clouds had slid eastward, but already a new set was building, and off in the distance I could hear the first leaden bubbles of thunder.

Summer soccer can be rough-tough stuff, a lot of players making up in aggressiveness what they lack in skill, but the referees are surprisingly competent, and by and large they kept things in hand. Even at the highest level, there is a free-for-all quality to soccer that is one of its unsung appeals. Watching players fight for a fifty-fifty ball is like watching the scramble for a fumble in football or a rugby scrum—there's always the suspense of who will get it—and while soccer is all about establishing order out of chaos, it's sometimes fun to watch the chaos have its way.

I kept my eyes on Matt, of course; I was looking for evidence of how his game had changed, with his not having played since the previous fall. He's always played focused and smart, with an intellectual kind of energy that confuses the opposing players more than anything he does with his feet. The energy comes from his mother probably—the genes all but flash in neon across his chest—but there is a searching, seeking quality that is definitely Matthew's own. When he plays soccer, he seems—at every moment, under every circumstance—to be looking for something: another player, another opportunity, a weakness in the other team's alignment; what's more, looking for something that lies far beyond the confines of the field. He's a seeker, whatever else there is in him. A soccer seeker.

A somewhat slow seeker, at least in the past. At eleven or twelve, having always won the sprints in practice, he began to come in third, and then suddenly next-to-last. He had all the soccer gifts but speed, and while he learned to compensate for this with his smarts and his energy, it made it likely that he wasn't a top college prospect. This was a partial relief to us all; with the time and effort the family was putting into soccer, at least we acknowledged a limit and didn't get involved in ODP (Olympic Development Program) or the elite regional travel teams that dominated the lives of some of his more ambitious friends.

But something funny had happened. In the Bahamas, he had run—and run and run. Four miles of roadwork every morning when the students woke up, long swims after that, bike rides, kayaking, all leading to a half marathon where Matt had finished second with a very respectable time. His first day home he had run six miles to the covered bridge and back; the second day he had entered a road race and finished up there with the leaders; and now he was running all the time, and it showed on the field. Sprinting to the opposing penalty area to get in a header, running right back to defend, flying this way, then that—this was a new Matt I was seeing. Matt on wheels.

Some of the other players caught my eye. Deaf, Ethiopia-born Yosef Osheyack (nicknamed Yo-Yo) had been on varsity last year as a sophomore; he had speed galore and a quick, opportunistic foot when he was near the goalmouth. He was slim, got bundled off too many balls, but he was improving with every game. Ben Rimmer, another junior-to-be, played every summer league game as if it were the FA Cup final (he had developed a wicked powerful throw-in; one of them found Matt's forehead and went in). He was, if anything, a bit too intense; he complained often to the ref, and his petulance was something Coach Grabill would have to deal with if he wanted to win that sportsmanship award again. But at least Ben was a sharp dresser—the team wore trashy orange T-shirts, and he was the only one to have gone out and bought orange socks to match.

Our boys put the game away early, and, already relaxed enough, it being just summer ball, I relaxed even more, tried focusing on the game at large, soccer in the abstract. I realized in a way I never had before that one of the core delights of soccer is how the ball remains the center of interest, the magnet for all eyes, the pointer showing you where to look. It's soothing in the mindless way TV watching is soothing; just let the ball make all the decisions. Follow the bouncing ball, as they used to say in movie sing-alongs—being a soccer fan is often as easy as that. The ball is just the right size to see easily, muscled in seams and indented in dimples, colored a basic black and white. What's more, you can never count on its doing what you expect or what you want; the physics can be strange, so there are constant surprises that operate even in a one-sided game like this one.

With only a few quiet, well-behaved spectators watching, with none of the big-match tension that can clog up your ears (this should be studied; it's very real), I found myself trying something I've not seen attempted before: to pin down the peculiar sound of soccer or at least the characteristic blend of sounds that makes for some great aural entertainment.

And with the grass so scrappy in some places, so lush in others, the sound that struck me first was the one that twenty-two pairs of cleats, forty-four case-hardened soles, and several hundred molded conical studs made on the playing surface. This is the thundering herd effect, buffalo or longhorns stampeding—that kind of sound, with an uneven, constantly varying syncopation that comes to you mostly through the ground itself. When the play turned into taller grass, the stampede sound became muffled, more sibilant—it made me think of old men shuffling along in slippers.

Cleats on grass form the bass line that supplies the game's rhythm—always there, hardly noticed, absolutely core. The soloist, the instrument that performs the variations and riffs, is, of course, the ball itself. When it's kicked square and hard and accurately, it gives off one of the most satisfactory sounds in all sport: the solid-quality thunk you hear when a punching bag is struck hard or a football is solidly punted. It's leathery and percussive and comes to you through your chest. It can be a bass note, on a goal kick, say, and it can be a baritone on a solid pass down the flanks, and it can even be tenor—a lot of penalty kicks soar up the register, all but scream. In essence, it's a manly sound, very voicelike, and there's no mistaking when it speaks well.

Those are the good kicks. The bad kicks, the scuffed balls, the ones that are sliced, all give off very different sounds, tinny, scrappier ones, with a dissonance that, if you appreciate beautiful soccer, makes you want to cover your ears. Even in a well-played game, ugly bad-ball sounds will outnumber lovely good-ball sounds; that's something your hearing just has to accept. But there are all kinds of pleasing ancillary sounds, too, ones that, once launched, are created by the ball's flight and eventual landing. A serpentine hiss as a grass cutter picks up speed; a howitzer whoosh as a punt soars to its apogee and falls. The angry slap of a ball hitting skin; the thump of a ball well chested and trapped. Balls pinging off crossbars after a vicious high shot; a ball breaking apart the shrubbery as it's blasted out of bounds. A bad pass going off a thigh with a wet slobbery sound; the bonking sounds, eighteen varieties of bonking, as the ball finds someone's head; a threebeat muted sound as the goalie takes his three dribbles. And there are secret soft sounds, too, like the nestling, comfy whisper the ball makes as it drives into the back of the netting, entwines itself, sighs away its inertia, drops.

These are soccer's nonhuman sounds—the sounds, if you will, of soccer nature. Interesting, a real aural treat, but nature is all but drowned out by human sounds: the voices, grunts, yells, curses, laughs, pants, sobs, sighs that come from the players. What a language! What a lingo! The inarticulate sounds alone speak volumes. The exuberant slap of hands when a goal is scored or the softer slap when a sub passes the player he's replacing. The goalie's growl when he yells out something too urgent to be words. The grunt of effort, so like a tennis player's, when someone tries to put all his might into a kick. The long extended sigh that comes after a mistake—a sigh that might start deep, but, the agony building, breaks apart into a prepubescent squeak, reminding you that these seventeen-year-olds, for all their bravado and bluster, are not quite men.

Baseball chatter is famous, a venerable part of the game, but most of it comes from the dugout or coaching boxes, and the exchanges between players are usually quite limited. In basketball, things happen too fast to talk very much; lacrosse and hockey players are rendered deaf and dumb by their helmets; in football, most everything is said in the huddle. It's soccer where the conversations are the most important and influential—real information needs to be exchanged, by players who are often very far apart. If a team is too quiet, it's almost always a bad sign, and "Keep talking boys!" is one of the most frequent admonitions players will hear from their coach.

I decided to try and make a record of just some of this; I ran to the car, grabbed a piece of scrap paper, came back, started writing as fast as I could. What follows is what I heard, which probably represents a hundredth of what was actually said in the course of the game's second half.

Leave it! Come on, Yo-Yo! We're good, boys! I'm in! Let it roll! Stay tough, boys! Oh, bad luck, Trevor! Man on! Hey hey! Let's get some buildup! Keep swinging it! Ball! One more! Keeper! Down the sides! Mark him, Rimmer! Drop! Good job, Ben! That's you! One wide, Eric! Good stuff! Everybody's up white! Shit! Step up, boys, step up! Sir? Sir? Lock them in! You take it, Cal. Got me, Mattie! Let it run! Frigging hell! Who's covering 38! Win

*those, Henry! Right shoulder, right shoulder! Is that my shin guard over
there? Away away! Your throw, Aussie! Fuck! Who in hell is watching 22?
Make a run!*

Almost all of this comes with exclamation points attached, often
two or three, as the voices soar from urgent to more urgent to most
urgent. But a surprising amount is said conversationally too. "Matt, I'm
going in for this one, you stay back and cover," is typical. Exhortations,
words of encouragement, warnings, angry shouts—like a train racing
toward you, then away from you, they come at varying pitches, tend
to slur and stream. And much is missed by spectators, even on a quiet
night like this one. Matt will come over after a game complaining
about all the trash talk and swearing, and often I will never have heard
even a syllable. "You suck," one player will say to another as they fight
for the ball, and yet there's a kind of whispered intimacy about it that
never makes it past the touchline.

Other sounds? The referee adds his own authoritarian shouts—
"Hands off him, 13! Play on! We're coming out with it!"—to say
nothing of what he does with his whistle. Even if you disagree with
the call, the shrillness can be aurally satisfying, the fresh piccolo sound
above all that relentless baritone. Every ref seems to have a particular
musical style, with your tweeters, your double-dippers, your flutists—
and, my favorites, ones who like to signal full time with three regret-
fully long and wistful notes.

This is not the definitive guide to soccer sounds, only a local approximation—the kind of thing that comes to the ears on a summer evening in the New Hampshire hills. For the true soccer soundtrack, you would have to cue in the noise of the fans watching, which can form a smothering bell jar over the sounds mentioned above. Parents cheering at a travel-team game; friends and girlfriends shouting at a high school match; "You'll Never Walk Alone" sung at Anfield as Liverpool wins; the ugly ululations at a derby match in Milan; smoke bombs exploding in the terraces as rival mobs scream themselves hoarse; the crescendos of a Brazilian crowd at the Maracanã, one hundred thousand human souls singing and shouting in a happy choir.

None of that here in Sunapee, but there is another sound that quickly underlines all the others, then quickly drowns them out: thunder, as the black clouds that have been flying solo all evening now find each other and coalesce into sonic booms that stop play even before the first lightning bolts crash down. A whistle screaming, boys yelling and laughing, more thunder, the drum of rain on minivan roofs, umbrellas snapping open, squishy running sounds—game over, 6-0 Touchline, T-shirts bleeding orange in the rain.

3

ON THE BUBBLE

Huntley Meadows, on a sunny August morning, looks like a place meant for lazy effort. It's set in a bowl, with Blood Brook (less bloody than its name) purling along one side and Union Turnpike (less pike-ish than its name) winding along the others. In between are perhaps twenty-five acres of pristine grass, damp with leftover shreds of fog that the sun—still low enough in the sky that its rays slant—is in the process of burning off. Looking down on this from the dirt parking lot that widens back from a modest cliff, you expect to see a woman in sandals walking a golden retriever across it all, or a jogger going slow, or even a retired old gent, up early with a visiting grandchild, bringing her to the playground for a special treat. "High summer calm" would be the caption if this were a photo. Goldfinches tumble across the uncut grass on the edges, their wings dispersing the sunlight, giving it motion, vibrancy, and life. Chipmunks sit on their hind legs and happily peer about; red squirrels do similar. So perfect is the scene, you expect them to link arms and start humming zip-a-dee-doo-dah, zipa-dee-ay.

But this valley, beautiful as it is, is not and never has been a place for lazy effort. The locals, the few that are left now, believe in starting work at 7:00 a.m., descended as they are from ancestors to whom the phrase Puritan work ethic was not just an empty abstraction. These are the contractors and carpenters, the drywall specialists and plumbers; if you're having work done on your house, they're liable to show up on Thanksgiving or Easter ready to go, unless you specifically tell them not to. The newcomers, the flatlanders who have migrated to these hills, often work just as hard, but what sets them apart is that for them it's a Puritan play ethic that's operational; this is a land of marathoners, triathletes, mountain runners, and if you're asked by a new friend to go biking, be assured that by biking they mean a quick one hundred miles.

Down in the lower parking lot, the one closer to the field, a car door slams, then another, then a third. Young men get out, managing to look sleepy and apprehensive at the same time. Soccer bags are taken from the trunks, there is a brief swarming together near a split-rail fence as shin guards and cleats are donned, then one by one, with equine prancing motions, the boys venture out onto the grass. These are the freshmen and sophomores, fourteen- and fifteen-year olds, and the farther out on the grass they go, the more nervous their body language becomes. Somehow, from a magic soccer chute in the sky, soccer balls appear, which is a great comfort to these early arrivals. They pick out a ball, kick it, and it's like they've all found pets to play with, little terriers that race ahead of them on the grass, then wait for them to catch up—and with this, the mood of anxiety perceptibly lifts.

It's the first morning of tryouts for the Hanover High soccer team, the New Hampshire state champs—and that these are being held in Vermont is an anomaly that needs explaining. Hanover is the New Hampshire half of what was the first interstate school district ever established in the country, the Dresden school district, with Norwich being the Vermont half. Hanover, as wealthy a town as it is, has always had a beggarly field situation, relying on various satellite fields (some loaned them by Dartmouth) spread across both towns; Huntley Meadows, which usually serves as a town park for Norwich, becomes the place for summer tryouts, autumn practices, and JV games. Because a third of the players are usually from Norwich, because the meadows themselves are lovely in a secret, pastoral sort of way, no one grumbles too much about the logistical inconvenience.

The seniors, the veterans, arrive fashionably late, at least compared with the underclassmen. They remember that the official practice uniform consists of gray T-shirts over black shorts, something the newcomers don't know yet, and so right away, at least in sartorial terms, there's an "in" crowd and an "out" crowd. Many of these seniors have played soccer with each other since the age of seven, many haven't seen each other since June, and so there are a lot of those grave, formal handshakes seventeen-year-olds like to exchange with each other. But even among the returning seniors, there is apprehension. Each time a new car arrives in the parking lot, they simultaneously glance up, as if expecting someone who never quite appears. Who they're looking for is Ben McKinnon or Jimmy Alexander or Jeff Levin, stars from the teams they played on their first two years . . . and over the first forty-five minutes of practice, there is a slow dawning process, as the senior veterans painfully realize that they are the senior veterans, the leaders, the stars, and that now for the first time in their varsity careers, there is no one to look up to.

Three men, after a quick parking-lot huddle, descend to the field, and the one leading them blows his whistle. Rob Grabill (a newly clean-shaven Rob Grabill) has already shaken everyone's hand, waved to parents dropping boys off, consulted his list of players still needing forms, tossed off a half dozen of his trademark one-liners, and plunged into the season with the considerable force of his personality—or temporarily plunged. His Camp Pemi is celebrating its one hundredth anniversary with a reunion this week, so he has five hundred alumni campers to watch over, and he must quickly head back north. With him are the paladins who will be running tryouts. Assistant Coach Alex Kahan, fitter than any of his players and a very smart soccer man, carries a bundle of red flags and a clipboard; white-haired Mike Callanan, a legend among Vermont coaches (he runs our JV in semi-semiretirement), wears his usual black track suit, sips a diet soda, and smiles benignly at boys he knows, comfortable with the old familiar ritual of it all, something he's been part of for the last forty years.

The players, as they cluster around Rob, have the posture and expressions of troops listening to their colonel before setting off on a dangerous mission. Some stare straight at him, hang on every word; others, while listening just as intently, look off toward the middle distance, swat at bugs, fold their arms across their chests, and pensively frown. No one laughs, not even at Rob's joke. Only thirty have shown up for varsity tryouts, an unusually low number; triple that number will be on the field the following week when JV and reserve team tryouts are held, a figure that represents one quarter of the HHS male student population. Obviously, there's a self-selection process that's already gone on, with many potential aspirants knowing varsity soccer at the state-champ level is something they're not ready for. Among those here are five seniors who were on JV last year, having tried and failed to make varsity for three years running. This is their fourth and final attempt—and if they listen to Rob even more attentively than the others, it's with good reason.

Rob keeps his spiel short ("We peaked on November 1 last year, and this year we're going to peak on August 30," he says, rather elliptically), and once he leaves, Coach Kahan splits everyone up into four lines for twenty minutes of warm-ups.

This is the newly fashionable "dynamic stretching," which is definitely not the calisthenics that coaches favored in an earlier generation: the sit-ups, push-ups, and toe touches they ordered players to do with drill-sergeant glee. In dynamic stretching, each line follows the leader through a different set of stylized, Kabuki-like motions designed to gently loosen things up. The first set involves slow straight-leg swings to the left and then the right, the boys doing a passable imitation of arthritic Rockettes. The second involves lifting the knee to the chest, clutching it, letting it drop, while all the while moving forward toward the front of the line—picture someone saying "Oh my right leg hurts! Oh my left leg hurts!" and you can get a sense of the rhythm. After that, they step, kneel, and twist, this time with their upper torso, which makes them resemble Roman gladiators performing some ancient form of tribute or obeisance. The fourth drill has them put both hands on the grass and lean forward like they're going to do a somersault, but only a mulish one with their legs. The fifth has them make some running skips, then lower an arm and make a scooping motion over the grass—it makes you think of field hands sowing wheat or candlepin bowlers. But apparently this all works, and teams that employ dynamic stretching have far fewer injuries than teams that do not.

After this comes warm-ups with the ball. Players pair off and take turns tossing the ball to each other, trapping it with each foot, controlling it off their chests, then exchanging headers. Of all thirty players, two stand out with special distinction: the very Irish, very cocky looking Angus Kennedy ("cocky Irish" is a cliché I never thought I would use, but in Angus, it's there) and the handsome, charismatic, truly gigantic Casey Maue. Today is their first day as team cocaptains, and they seem to the manner born. Casey is the one who demonstrates the drills, and Angus, when it comes time to pair off, goes immediately over to the sole, frightened-looking freshman who's turned up and starts kicking the ball back and forth to help him feel welcome.

Much is expected of Angus and Casey this year, and in the latter's case, it has a lot to do with his size. He's six feet, five inches tall and a star of the basketball team that won the state title in a Cinderella story last winter. But it's football you think of when you look at Casey—how he escaped being drafted into being a linebacker or tight end is something of a miracle. His parents, as many do now, saw soccer as a much safer, more interesting alternative to football, and once started as a little kid, he's stayed with soccer ever since. (Add that to the Upper Valley's peculiarities: it's one of the few places in the United States where interest in soccer is higher than interest in football.) Casey carries his size well, is among the fastest runners on the team, and is certainly one of the hardest workers. His black hair comes over his forehead in a retro, semi–Prince Valiant style, and his expression is surprisingly sleepy, given his energy and the depth of his intelligence.

He's vocal and funny, and the leadership role will be no problem for him; what might be a problem, as is usual with Casey, is what he does with his feet.

As wonderful an athlete as Casey is, you get the feeling, watching him play, that soccer is not quite the perfect sport for him, striker not quite his proper position. He'll hustle to hell and back to win a ball, he intimidates defenders with his relentless drive as much as he does with his size, and he has the ability to rise to the occasion, as his brilliant overtime winner in last year's semifinal proved. It's his touch that's the problem, his feet that have never quite been up to doing the ballerina moves, the little soft touches and impish flicks that to born strikers come naturally. He's improved a lot in this respect, finishes much better, but, watching him, you get the feeling you often get watching high school soccer—of someone who would be much happier if he were allowed to use his hands. ("Casey," Rob once quipped, "is the only player who can kick the ball with one foot and trip over it with the other.")

Angus Kennedy is cut from a far different pattern. Watching him in warm-ups, he seems ordinary enough in size and physique, and it's only the real soccer buff who understands that this wiry, nondescript sort of package almost always hides the most exceptional soccer gifts. Angus is the central midfielder, by instinct a defensive central midfielder, content to clean up problems in the back and send the attack on its way rather than joining in the attack himself. This year he's going to be asked to step up to a more offensive role, and this will mean a change in his temperament, not just his tactics. He has marvelous technique, great soccer intelligence, decent speed, a fighting spirit that never quits—and the challenge is to drive all this talent goalward. The coaches know he's capable of this. Dartmouth, Notre Dame, and Williams have all talked of recruiting him, and he's the one Hanover player who's had his eye on playing in college since he was ten.

His captaincy will be another challenge. Angus is funny, he knows how to get kids to laugh, but his wit can be bitingly sharp; this is something he's going to have to soften if he wants to be the leader that his soccer skills naturally make him.

And so. The drills continue through the rest of the morning. The boys split up for two-on-two competitions, leading to three-on-three, then six on six. Seen from the distance, they look heterogeneous enough and ragged enough and enthusiastic enough to form a promising raw material: soccer dough that only needs kneading and rolling to result in something smooth.

An objective observer, looking at life beyond sports, might say that for these thirty young men, there is no need for tryouts—they've already been born into the first team. Hanover and the Upper Valley that surrounds it is one of those blessed American places that seem to have it all: beauty of setting, general affluence, culture, widespread civic engagement, a proud history, educational opportunities far above the norm. Brains are respected here, art is tolerated more than in most places, capitalism is less glorified. Winter used to be the fly in the ointment. "You have to be able to cope with our winters," newcomers would be warned; but, with climate change already a reality, winters aren't what they used to be, and the obvious attractions of living in the country near a famous college are even beginning to draw large numbers of retirees.

And it's not just the hills, rivers, and lakes that make it special. Many of the people you meet in the course of the day are actively involved in helping the world get better: doctors researching vaccines that might prevent cancer; regional planners hard at work trying to improve not just our local traffic bottlenecks, but the infrastructure of Zambia; retired seniors recruiting "localvores" to patronize our remaining farms; conservationists working night and day to save the Bicknell's thrush. Everyone has a cause, a good cause, and it creates a certain mood in the valley, a sunny haze of compassion that nestles comfortably between the hills.

It's not as rural a place as it once was—creeping surburbanization is picking up speed, particularly outward from Lebanon, where the ever-expanding Dartmouth-Hitchcock Medical Center employs more than six thousand people. "Doctors are our blue-collar workers," the local joke goes, and it's not much of an exaggeration; we must have more doctors per capita than any comparable place in America.

More and more, it's the medical center that dominates life here, not Dartmouth College.

Hanover has another good quality: it's an easy place to poke fun at. "Never trust a town that doesn't have a used car lot," the essayist Sam Pickering once said of it, after teaching for a spell at the college. There's a prissy, self-congratulatory tone that can get tiresome pretty fast; the rakish, the scruffy, the unkempt are not to be found in Hanover, and the town is considerably poorer for their absence. Then, too, almost everyone you meet is a Democrat, a rich Democrat, a Not in My Backyard Democrat, and there is as much hypocrisy, maybe even more hypocrisy, than you would find in a town that was solidly Republican.

It's a place where people are comfortable, perhaps too comfortable, with competition. Most have done very well with it, so they seem to crave even more, the way addicts crave ever-larger dosages of drugs. To give them credit, the competition is not always for the usual trophies of American prestige—the obscenely large cars, the disgustingly large houses—but for endowed professorships, chief surgeon positions, "genius" awards, Guggenheims. Competition in sport is if anything even bigger; this is a region with an unusually high number of champions in "master sports" competitions—events for those older than forty, fifty, even sixty-five—many of whom were Olympic wannabes when they were younger or achieved great glory in college sports. Of these, a high percentage engage in endurance sports like rowing, cross-country skiing, and running, and you have to drive carefully, on a foggy summer morning, not to run over the sixty-year-olds out for their morning five-mile sprint.

Anyone weighing the pros and cons of raising a child here has to be concerned about this highly competitive regional testosterone and whether it might prove toxic. When everyone is an overachiever, ordinary achievement can be viewed as outright failure, and parents, when it comes to bringing up their children, get their expectations all wrong.

One way to avoid this competition is to remove yourself from it physically. We live in Lyme, which is twelve miles north of Hanover, just enough distance to insulate us from its most irritating aspects. Lyme is locally famous for its high rate of civic participation in volunteer activities and the townwide dedication to conservation; it's perhaps the one valley town where newcomers and old-timers (many tracing their roots back to the town's founding families in the 1700s) get along best. We're far too small to have our own high school, and so students, once they complete eighth grade here, are farmed out to high schools in the neighboring towns, with Lyme picking up the tab for tuition. This is "school choice" in action, and it's not necessarily a good thing, because all the effort and care we put into getting our kids through their first eight grades (Lyme School is the centerpiece of town, our pride and our joy) is largely dissipated once our children reach the verge of adulthood, when we scatter them and all their energy across the countryside and scarcely see them again after that.

The choice can be complex. Many Lyme families truly agonize about it because it can mean splitting apart friends, but there seems to be a pattern governing their decisions. The most adventurous head up to St. Johnsbury Academy in northern Vermont, but this means an hour on the interstate each way and rules out most after-school activities (Lyme provides no high school bus service—you have to get to school on your own). The wariest old-timers, the "'twas good enough for me, by geezus!" crowd, send their kids to Rivendell Academy in Orford, one town north. The prudent, the ones who want their kids to be safe and sound in high school and fear the competition farther south, send their kids directly across the river to Thetford Academy. Those whose kids show great promise in academics and/or sports—or are expected to show great promise in academics and/or sports—choose Hanover High School and all the pressure that goes with it.

Does Hanover High deserve its exalted reputation? Matt's entering his senior year, and yet for us the jury is still out—the quality of a high school, for a parent, can be a difficult thing to judge, with less teacher-parent interaction than you get in grade school and offspring who would be mortified if they even so much as glimpsed you inside the halls. Still, we have a rough-and-ready sense of the place now. About a third of the teachers are excellent, a third are average, a third are poor—a typical enough scorecard, I would say, though my friends in other parts of the country tell me this is actually a superior percentage. The unique thing about Hanover is the overachieving student body. The typical Hanover student has his or her own film company by the time he or she is fifteen (and has had a film screening at Sundance), is right on the bubble for making the Olympics in snowboarding, has already had his or her debut cello recitals at Symphony Hall in Boston, has perfect scores on the SATs, and, withal, is a perfectly charming young man or woman, able to tell adults exactly what they want to hear. No one can achieve so much at an early age without an aggressive support system, and these superheroes are usually fueled by helicopter parents who hover, micromanaging their kids' lives. Hanover High teachers, the highest paid in the state, earn their salaries several times over dealing with much higher levels than normal of parental angst.

The administration, to give them credit, tries to find ways to reduce the competition and stress. Class rank is not kept, there is no National Honor Society chapter (so many students would deserve inclusion, the five left out would feel rotten), and, although there are honors courses, there is no advanced placement. The athletic department tries hard to include everyone; in soccer, there is not only the varsity team, but the JV team, a reserve team, a freshman team—four soccer teams a season, and if there are still boys needing a team, a fifth.

It became clear in mid-August, just as tryouts were getting under way, that the subject of competition and its possible corrosive effects on Hanover High School students would be a huge issue in the coming year. On August 18, the headline of the *Valley News* read NINE CHARGED IN HANOVER TEST THEFT, as the rumor Matt had heard in June about widespread and systematic cheating on finals had turned out to be true. Nine students have been charged with misdemeanors, accused of breaking into the school and stealing final math and chemistry exams from locked cabinets in teachers' rooms—some plotting the break-in and theft, others acting as lookouts. They're all seventeen-year-olds, so their names can be printed in the local newspaper, and the article detailed how they pulled it off. This wasn't a case of a student copying his neighbor's answer or writing answers down on her wrist; this was a complicated and carefully thought-out heist.

Judging by the chatter at tryouts, people are incensed; there are no soccer players involved, at least so far, but seniors' parents feel this might besmirch the school's reputation and lower their own child's chances with college admission, or, at the very least, cast a pall over the seniors' last year. (Fears exacerbated when the *Boston Globe*, *New York Times*, and National Public Radio all came to Hanover and did stories on the scandal.) And, in the way of such things, people express their astonishment and shock, not so much at the kids involved, but at who their parents are: one is CEO of a major hospital, once is a well-respected doctor, another is a locally famous newspaper columnist.

The last is the only parent quoted in the local article. He takes the high ground, accuses Hanover High's "high pressured academic culture" of forcing his son to cheat, demands "the entire community must be willing to take a hard look at how it might have unwittingly contributed to his problem," and defends his son—and in the same breath condemns him—by remarking that on the finals said to be stolen he got a C minus and a D.

It will be interesting to see how this all plays out, but I suspect the specifics of the scandal—and perhaps even some soul-searching as regards the school's competitive drive—will be in for some serious soccer-mom and -dad discussions along the sidelines this year. But there will be many in this valley who won't mind seeing Hanover brought down an inglorious notch. CHEATERS! I can picture the signs in the stands now.

Matt's response to attending such a high-powered place has been interesting. He's done well, his grades are right up there with the elite's, he gets along well with his teachers, and soccer has won him many good friends. And yet, he's somehow managed to keep the whole high school experience at a certain distance—high school will definitely not represent the best four years of his life—and much of this comes from going back each night to a different, much quieter rural town. "Limeys," they call the kids from here, "Lyme slyme," or "hicks," but having a refuge here is probably worth all the teasing.

Matt's not become involved in the soap-opera aspects of high school life, the endless popularity primping, hallway schmoozing, and giggly do-you-like-so-and-so. In his four years, he's never once been to a party—and this a kid who, if he went to one, would find himself the center of attention. He knows if he goes there will be booze there, there may be drugs, and he simply doesn't want to get involved with any of this—not so much the temptation, but the boring, nerdy business of just saying no. (My daughter, who attended Thetford Academy in as pretty a rural Vermont town as you can imagine, also stayed away from parties, for the same reason.) His pals are mostly from the soccer team, boys he's known since he was little, very smart, personable homebody atypical jocks who like to play poker on Friday nights, then watch a Manchester United game on delayed tape. Not many of them have girlfriends yet—they're all a little wary of plunging into high school life too deeply, seem to be waiting for college before taking any social risks. There must be other such kids in the country, but they're a subgroup (smart, personable homebody jocks) that never causes anyone trouble, and so you don't hear much about them.

Almost everyone at Hanover High goes on to college, and so senior year is when competition becomes not just the hidden undertone but something that is explicitly addressed. We're incredibly competitive here, the ethos seems to go, but for three years we're going to pretend we're not, and then the fourth year we're going to let it rip—may the best man or woman win! Knowing an elite liberal arts college is only likely to accept one or two students from the same high school each year, you become secretive when other parents ask you, oh so casually, what schools your son is considering.

How nice it would be to step aside from the complicated and competitive ordeal the college search has become. "College schmollege," you could say, when the SAT registration material arrives. "Go out into the world, and good luck to you, fella!" If your son was interested in starting his own business and knew pretty much what it was about, you could write him a check for the $200,000 that four years at a private college now costs, which would be pretty good start-up money. If he wanted to be a writer, you could rent him a garret in Paris for a year; if he wanted to be a filmmaker, you could ship him out to Los Angeles and help him find a menial job at a studio, where he could start out at the bottom.

If you were tough and brave and bold, you could do these things. For most of us, we moan and groan and end up playing the game, which means, in the senior summer, you visit colleges, most of which are a considerable distance away. We would be more than happy to send Matt to our state university, even though its tuition for in-state students is the highest in the country. But then we do the research you're supposed to do and find it's high on several national rankings, as in "best party schools" (number five), "places where professors are invisible" (number six), and "least racial diversity" (number eight). No, you decide, I don't think so. A state school in another state would actually be cheaper, but a kid who went to school with a class of twenty through eighth grade and now attends a relatively small high school would probably not feel comfortable in a university of fifty thousand students.

Matthew has sent away for information, and he's been deluged with brochures, each one slicker, more lavishly produced than the next; his father, trying to keep a lid on his cynicism, stifles comments about how the cost of college tuition must have something to do with the enormous amount of money spent on marketing. ("In my day," the stifled comment goes, "all they sent you was the catalog of courses, end of story.") All this is largely wasted, because a college's reputation comes down to the little ten-second sound bytes that parents exchange while watching a soccer game or standing in line at Starbucks. Rick is looking at Dartmouth? "Dartmouth's a big fraternity school, you have to be that type." Heather is looking at Williams? "Williams is for s.o.b's." Colin is looking at Colby? "It's out in the boonies." Hillary is looking at Middlebury? "It's a college full of preppies." Cornell? "It's cold and it's gloomy and my brother went there and there weren't any pretty girls." MIT? "Not unless you're Asian."

But, sucking in our breaths, smothering our cynicism, we've been making the obligatory college visits. It's one of life's significant rites of passage, not so much for the student, but for the parents: the first step in the final step of handing your child over to the outside world. And much of the ritual is familiar to us from when Erin was looking for a school four years ago. Following the directions to campus, looking for a place to park amid all the lavish new construction (one friend, dropping his daughter off at the University of Virginia while he searched for a parking place, hurried back to the admissions office to find she had tripped on the stairs and was lying there with a broken leg). The campus tour, with personable student guides chosen, it seems, for their ability to talk while walking backward; the little hurried, apologetic glimpses they allow you inside the dorms; the amused, superior incrowd looks you get from the students who are lucky enough to have made it in; the questions people on the tour ask, which always include "Do the dorm rooms get cable?" (from at least one "prospective" student) and "What percentage of your graduates get accepted to med school?" (from at least one "prospective" dad).

Before a tour, or sometimes after, you sit through information sessions led by someone from the admissions office. I've always found these to be a somewhat abstract exercise. The presentation is always well done, touching all the bases, explaining about things like double majors, housing options, and junior year abroad. Some parents take notes or politely raise their hands with questions, but I've never been tempted to do either. To me, the experience is like visiting an exclusive, very expensive club anyone would die to become a member of, politely asking questions about all the amenities and rules, but feeling all the while that there is a very large subject no one is addressing: will they actually let me into this club? Not knowing this—knowing, in fact, that anyone's chances of being accepted are miniscule—makes it hard to take seriously all the information you're meant to digest.

Our last visits this summer were to Cornell and Colgate in upstate New York—a long drive from here, but doable. Cornell, we ended up deciding, would require some guts and toughness; Colgate, at least to me, seemed like a gorgeous prep school, but for a boy brought up in the country, too rural to bring him much growth. Something amusing/revealing happened at the Colgate information session, as students and parents shyly found seats. One father, dressed in a white linen sports coat and a tie short enough to pass as a cravat, strolled in late with his daughter, looked around at the comely, intelligent-looking students busily burying their heads in their brochures, turned to his daughter, and, in a voice loud enough that everyone could hear, said, "Well, here's your competition!"

"Ass!" we all decided, though this is exactly the thought (Here's your competition!) that had already crossed our collective minds, especially after the admissions officer finished telling us they had 8,000 applicants for 650 spots. I decided, in the end, that the father deserved credit for making this competition explicit. Maybe that's exactly what contemporary American life needs: to have our vicious, all-against-all competition brought out into the open, made even more explicit and cutthroat than it already is, the hell with mealymouthed euphemisms or arrogant, nonverbal posturing. At soccer games, let the conversation between parents begin with the words "My son is ten times the player your son is." At parties, tell me exactly how many times bigger your house is than mine or what Ivy League school your kid got into, and don't bother hiding the contemptuous sneer, either. At swimming pools or country clubs or ski slopes, go ahead and say it out loud: you own more fly rods than I do, you've written more novels, you've traveled to more countries, you've married more women, tasted more wines, earned bigger bucks. Down with dissimulation! Let the competitive declare victory right smack in our faces! Tell me exactly in which ways you are beating me, and don't let all that competition fester.

Matt's dad, in other words, carries a lot of baggage around when it comes to the college issue.

It was a relief, after our quick trip to New York, to get back to pure soccer. (Matt hears a rumor that Rob, commuting between his camp and practice, has already gotten two speeding tickets.) A relief, because at least in sports the competition is explicit. Being on a team is said to be good for a young person's soul because it teaches cooperation and selflessness and teamwork and all those things that are anticompetition. But the fact is that in today's high school, you have to have done pretty well with competition (the tryouts) in order to be in a position (on varsity) in which you can go beyond competition (via teamwork) in order—are you still following me?—to beat the competition. Why sports may actually be good for a young person's soul is that it takes, or at least should take, a more natural approach to inherent competitive urges that would be there even in a culture that had a more relaxed attitude toward winning. Toting up winners and losers in life is harsh, and for most people, the answer is almost always wrong, but saying "Who won?" in sports is the most natural question you can ask—as long as you don't care too much about the answer.

I don't envy Rob his job, or this part of it: when he has to decide whom to cut and whom to keep. The first round of cuts came on the second morning, when the obviously unfit were gently released to the JV or reserve teams. After that, it became much harder, particularly with the five seniors, who, if they were cut, were not allowed to play on any lesser team. Matt had played with most of them at some stage of his soccer career; each had poured a lot of time and energy into the game and become a good friend of his; and when I asked him who would make it and who wouldn't, he found the subject too painful to more than grunt. To make the decision even more complicated, three of the boys developed injuries and had to sit out the next round of try-outs, so what was Rob supposed to do about that? Cut them because of their injuries, or put them on the team and alienate the kids who had wholeheartedly taken part?

We had been through the agony of this during Matt's sophomore year, when Chris Cheney was still head coach. Matt had done well his freshman year on JV, but varsity was stocked with talented seniors, and it wasn't clear whether there would be room for him there—as the expression had it, he was "on the bubble." All summer I had bugged him about running more, but it was an uphill struggle, and it wasn't until a week before tryouts that he started training in earnest—and then surprised us by running three miles at a stretch. Right from the first moments of tryouts, he played like a man on a mission, and it was this intensity that caught the coaches' attention—other fathers began telling me he was a "lock" to make the team.

Or was he?

What made the suspense and agony even worse was that Coach Cheney kept postponing his final decision. Originally, the final cut was supposed to have been made during a Saturday of scrimmages at Camp Pemi; when I picked Matt up at the end of the afternoon, I could barely bring myself to look at him.

"Well?" I finally managed, as he climbed wearily into the car.

Matt frowned. "What's wrong with your face? You look weird."

"Well?"

"Coach decided not to make any decision until Monday afternoon."

"How did you play today?"

"Pretty good."

"Did the coach notice that?"

"Yeah, I suppose so. He patted me on the back when I came out."

Sunday and Monday morning don't bear thinking about. Like my imaginary Norman, I wanted only the best for my kid, and this was a team loaded with talented seniors who were determined to win the state championship. Like any father, I was proud of my son, wanted him to rise to ever-higher levels of achievement—another year on boring JV might turn him off soccer forever. His best friend, Eric Barthold, was certainly going to make the team, and it would be a heavy hit for Matt if he wasn't there with him. We tried keeping our minds off it, but never had I seen Matthew so tense, and never had Matt seen me so tense—and as for Celeste, she found numerous excuses to absent herself from the house.

Monday afternoon I drove Matt to practice. We didn't talk on the way down, though I had a what-will-be-will-be speech all prepared in the danger zone right behind my teeth. To drop someone off at Huntley Meadow, you drive down a steep dirt road—and who should be waiting there when I did, sitting on the back of a pickup happily kicking their heels, but Chris Cheney and his assistant Rob Grabill. I tried hard not to make eye contact with them—Matthew ducked over to busy himself with shin guards . . . but there was no choice. With no other space available, I had to drop Matt off right at their feet.

Matt got out. It's hard to make a three-point turn without look-ing to your left, but somehow I did it. My window was open, and I heard, or thought I heard, the words, "Aren't you going to tell your dad?" coming from the mouth of what sounded like Rob. I drove up the road, trying to convince myself that what he had said was indeed "Aren't you going to tell your dad?" and what he meant by that was that Matt had made the team. But with the window open, a lot of white noise streamed in, and it was entirely possible my credulous ears had heard wrong.

I drove toward downtown, thought about it, felt the agony clutch at my throat, headed back toward the field, parked on a pull-off, watched the pulse throb alarmingly in my wrist, gently touched it, turned on public radio, waited an agonized ten minutes without hearing any of the words, drove back to Huntley, and parked behind a tree where no one could see me. Matt was down there on the field kicking a ball around with four or five fellow sophomores; some were surely on varsity, but some were just as surely not, and it wasn't clear by this or any other grouping which boys were on varsity and which were on JV. I drove off again, deciding this was stupid and immature, headed for home . . . got about two miles, slammed on the brakes, turned around, drove so fast I got flashed at by a police cruiser, and screeched to stop back at the field.

This time Matt was in a different group, a smaller one, gathered in a circle near one of the goals. Chris was talking to them, Rob was nodding in emphasis, and as my eyes skimmed the players I realized they included the best seniors . . . and it was this glimpse that did it for me, and I felt an exultation, happiness, and relief that would be embarrassing to admit to if I wasn't trying to be honest. The group split apart to begin some running, but just before it did, I saw Jory Kahan, the senior cocaptain, go over and shake Matthew's hand, welcoming him to the team—a magnificent gesture, and perfectly timed, at least for me. Norwich is a bad town for pay phones, but I finally found one in the inn and called Celeste waiting at home. "He made it!" I yelled, then—since there's no exaggerating the depth of my pessimism and caution—said, "At least it looks like he did."

There's an important point that can't be stressed enough, not when the discussion veers toward competition, the good parts and the bad. Soccer, more than any other sport, has failure built into its very nature. Its inventors, ruling that only feet and head can be used on the field, saddled players with a handicap that even the most talented never fully overcome. Watching a team play, you realize the overwhelming majority of their chances come up empty. They probe down the sideline one moment, then up the middle the next—short little exploratory crosses that bounce off someone's shin guard or long Hail Marys that sail wide of an outstretched foot. A winger makes a brilliant little back heel to an overlapping back who scuffs the kick; a striker on a breakaway lifts his head too soon and sails it twenty feet over the bar; on a corner kick, everyone jostling for position, the ball sails behind the goal, and all the activity is wasted. Most of a team's chances flat out fail, a soccer field is drenched in failure—and yet again and again, they go back to probing, they never give up, so, watching, your hope is renewed the very instant that it's shattered.

Disappointment. Hope. Hope. Disappointment. The roller coaster never stops.

The complaint you hear about soccer is that there's not enough scoring, but this is precisely its chief fascination: the fact that goals are so hard to score. It can even be relaxing if you're a fan—you know even the opposition's best, most threatening chances will probably not amount to much in the end. And it makes success all the more enjoyable when it comes. It's not for nothing that soccer, once a goal is scored, sees the most exuberant celebrations in sports, to the point that "celebrations"—the current styles therein, the way someone pulls his off—is a subject openly discussed and analyzed, with some celebrations being even more memorable than the goals that prompted them (e.g., Jürgen Klinsmann's swan dives through the mud).

I suspect this is the main reason soccer hasn't taken the American psyche by the jugular—it's all about failure in a culture that isn't interested in even admitting failure as a possibility, let alone paying good money to watch it in action. How you surmount failure, at least in soccer, is largely through patience, and again, this is not among the favorite U.S. virtues. (Any dramatist, filmmaker, or novelist will of course tell you that failure is far more interesting than success.) Success in soccer comes from failing slightly less often than the other team—perhaps failing once less often in a tight game—and rooting for a team to somehow by some miracle do even better than this is what brings the avid soccer fan back for more.

But it's something to think about, when you first sign your child up for kiddie soccer. For all the competition, you'll be teaching him that most un-American of lessons: how to fail beautifully.

4

Ticket to the World

Coach Grabill scheduled eight scrimmages, or "friendlies," before the season started, an ambitiously large number. He wanted to play the boys into shape, test them against tougher competition than they're liable to see during the regular season, try out various combinations, take a last look at those he may have to cut . . . in other words, take care of the preparatory preseason business any good coach wants to address. They've played these games now and the results are . . . mixed.

The defense looks tight. A goateed Ben Harwick returns in goal—a feisty, even angry Ben Harwick, who, along with shouting at his defensemen to shape up, yells frequently at the refs. A little temperament in a goalie is probably not a bad thing—a lot of temperament in a goalie is probably not a bad thing—but Ben plays better when he focuses that energy into blocking shots.

Ahead of him is our defense, which is strong all the way across. Over on the left is speedy, long-legged Sam Peterson, a sometime starter last year. In the center, Matt Wetherell and Cal Felicetti are the same duo that started for the championship run, and their veteran competence and coolness should be tough for other teams to shake (last year, the defense only gave up nine goals). To their right is Trevor Barlowe, a redheaded junior whose natural position is in the center. There were some questions about his speed (your outside back should be fast, to shut down the other team's winger and to overlap on offense), but he seems to be settling in well; if he doesn't play with Sam's panache, he plays with even more reliability.

So, no worries on the defense. The midfield has Angus Kennedy in the center, our star, and with him Aussie Cyrus, a free-spirited African American kid from Texas, who is very smart with the ball and has that low center of balance coaches like; but he's been nursing a sore knee through preseason, and there doesn't seem to be anyone to replace him. Out wide is Ben Rimmer, full of healthy manic aggression, and over on the other side, Eric Barthold. Big things are expected of Eric—he played defense on last year's team, but he's been moved up to help out the offense—and his response so far has been a bit worrisome. He's playing . . . worried, like he has too much weight on his shoulders. He's fast and plays with a brio that makes you want to laugh out loud—not so much running downfield as swooping, gliding, flying. But watching him in preseason, no one is laughing or even smiling, especially not Eric. Everyone is certain he'll snap out of this minor funk once the real season begins, or is at least hoping he does, since twelve or thirteen goals from Eric seems the minimum requirement if the team is to go very far.

Scoring goals is going to be the big challenge. We're thin in strikers, with only Casey Maue and Yosef Osheyack having any varsity experience. Last year, Rob had five strikers he could shuttle in and out like lines in hockey. This year, sitting on the bench, there appears to be nothing but question marks. Casey has looked solid in preseason, Yo-Yo has struggled, so it's likely that the season will be filled with many 1-0 games.

Weaknesses and strengths were particularly noticeable in two of the scrimmages. On a brisk August Sunday that had a lot of autumn in it, we traveled down to Manchester, the state's largest city, for something called the West High School Soccer Jamboree. A taste of bigcity glitz, at least by New Hampshire standards: the stands at Manchester West overlook the sprawling red brick Amoskeag mills along the Merrimack River. Built in the late 1800s, this was once the largest industrial complex in the world, and, after years of neglect (the textile industry having moved south to avoid unions, then offshore), they're being used again, for IT offices, corporate headquarters, weight-loss centers, and even an Amoskeag Bingo Center. New office buildings rise beyond the riverbank with a deep red color that responds well to the style of the mills; church steeples, pewter colored, add an interesting sharpness to all the rectangles, though it makes it seem that spirituality, in booming Manchester, is slowly sinking out of sight. Not really a skyline, but close enough for New England, and when the game got boring—which it quickly did—I found myself enjoying the way the autumn-hard clouds streamed past the mills, lending them motion, spryness, even youth.

As for the soccer, it stank. By some mix-up, a JV team showed up from Londonderry, not the varsity; but instead of an easy laugher, they completely showed us up. Rob kept his first string in the entire first half, but all they could manage was a 1-1 tie, and it wasn't until the second half subs went in that we pulled ahead. A classic case of a team dumbing itself down to the level of weak competition—maybe. But we did no better in the second game, this one against the Blue Knights of Manchester West High. They're a Class L team, which includes the high schools with the largest student populations (we're Class I, the second largest), and while we stayed with them in an unimaginative first half, the second half we came unglued and lost 2-0, with Matt being burned by a chunky striker wearing ugly chartreuse cleats.

Rob was visibly upset with the way the boys played. He paced hard during halftime, out in the middle of the field where he could be alone, scratching his chin, shaking his head, the very image of a pissed-off, not-bothering-to-hide-it coach. It hadn't been a good day for him; that morning the *Valley News* ran an article about Hanover's quest for an unprecedented third championship in a row, and not only is he worried that this will jinx us, but it sends exactly the wrong message to his kids. He wants them to focus on the season-long process, not the ultimate result—tells them, on the bus ride home, that if they get confused about their priorities, they may be in for a major disappointment.

The four parents who make the drive down ("We're the diehards," we tell each other) aren't happy either, and those championship dreams, by the time we leave for the ninety-minute drive home, have taken a serious hit.

If Manchester represents old industrial/newly resurgent New Hampshire, then Exeter, down by our short coastline, represents the genteel/slightly eccentric side of the state. It was our capital during the Revolution, and three hundred years of uninterrupted affluence has made for a handsome and stately town. Some historians trace the beginnings of the Republican party to a meeting of abolitionists that took place in October 1853 at the Squamscott Hotel in town; Lincoln came in 1860 to visit his son, Robert Todd, who was attending Phillips Exeter, the famous prep school (where that fine old classic *A Separate Peace* is set). The town's war memorial was sculpted by Daniel Chester French, who did the Lincoln Memorial in Washington—another Lincoln link. And in pop culture, Exeter was the home of

Dan Brown of *Da Vinci Code* fame and the spot where, in 1965, two local cops made a notorious UFO sighting, one that led to the best-selling *Incident at Exeter*.

And Exeter has another claim to fame: it's the home of Hanover's only rivals as the best high school soccer team in the state.

They're in the Class L division, so we never play them in a regular season game, though last year we met in a preseason scrimmage and Hanover won 1-0. Rob has scheduled another match this year, sort of an early, unofficial state championship. To make the challenge even more formidable, what is generally considered the best high school team in Vermont, Champlain Valley Union, has been invited along, too, so the boys are faced with a doubleheader: CVU first at 10:00, Exeter second at 2:00, this on a day of ninety-eight-degree heat and 100 percent humidity.

It's a two-hour drive from the Upper Valley, and, again, only the real diehards make the trip: Ben's mom, Casey's mom, Angus's dad, both Wetherells. Exeter High is brand spanking new, a sprawling building on a filled-in wetland a long distance from downtown. Chris Kennedy, who's an architect, is not impressed with the design and is even less impressed by its location. It's so far from the town's center that it seems to reinforce the idea of the teenage years being a totally separate experience from the rest of life, something that must be exiled and hidden—and then, of course, a pretty stretch of meadow-land had been paved under. But it's a luxury facility and probably the only high school in New Hampshire where the Hanover boys can feel like disadvantaged kids.

The soccer field is state of the art—artificial turf, lights, high-rise stands—but it was being used for a football scrimmage, and so the first game against CVU was played on an adjacent grass field, giving one parent (me) a chance to mouth off about the quasimilitaristic rites of football, the over-the-top macho posturings, the . . . (at this point, everyone stopped listening). The nice thing was that the stands, rising so high, provided plenty of shade if you sat directly beneath them, so we could watch our boys take on CVU in relative comfort, albeit with football coaches screaming at our backs.

After an even first half, we gradually start getting on top of them and end up winning 3-1 (take that, you insufferably smug granola-eating quasisocialist Vermonters!). Matt plays poorly, whiffs on a few kicks, whiffs on a few headers, and seems to be having trouble with the sun and the heat. Eric Jayne, one of the very few freshmen ever to make the Hanover varsity, scores his first high school goal on the very last kick of the game, which earns wild cheers from the five of us watching. Toward the end, a CVU ruffian cynically tackles Angus Kennedy well after he's passed the ball off. "Goddammit!" someone yells—a noble "Goddammit!" a "Goddammit!" so loud and imperious it can only come from a head football coach—but no, it turns out to be from Rob over on the sideline, furious that the referee has let CVU get away with it without even so much as a whistle. And, as is the way with Rob, his anger immediately turns on himself; he puts his hands on his head like a prisoner, strides off toward the woods, exiling himself, red-carding himself, furious at getting furious. "There's a Dark Rob," he will warn his players at the team dinner later in the week, suggesting that testing him on the honor code they've all signed will not be a good idea . . .but that there's a Dark Rob, they already suspect.

The Exeter parents host a cookout between games, and it's all very sociable. Chris, the architect, takes Celeste and me into town to visit the Phillips Exeter library, designed by one of his heroes, Louis Kahn, and then after grabbing cold Gatorades for the boys, we're back for the second game. Hanover is still exhausted from the first match; they go through warm-ups with a pathetic amount of lethargy, while Exeter looks as if they have just sprung newly freshened from the shower. Many of their players wear Seacoast United T-shirts, which is the local elite travel team—not just any elite travel team, but one of the best endowed and most successful youth teams in the country, based in a soccer complex with four artificial turf fields and a dormitory for boys who commute long distances to play.

So, they're a classy bunch, and I'm not feeling optimistic as the game starts, not with two of our stars, Ben Rimmer and Aussie Cyrus, sitting out hurt. And yes, Exeter is on us right from the opening whistle, displaying technical skills that are much better than our own, and a patience and precision that are unusual in high school soccer. They manage ten, twelve, even thirteen touches at a time before we get a foot on the ball, and only rarely is the action ever out of our half. Their number 9 looks particularly dangerous—he's big, strong, and aggressive, and it seems only a matter of time before he turns Matt (who, to give him credit, is playing much better this game) inside out.

But something funny happens. They don't score. They work the ball across the field, they find each other, they overlap, switch directions, play the ball into space, but somehow, just before they get to the penalty area, it all seems to collapse. It becomes apparent that they are overcoached, overtaught, overly tutored and refined—and not just by their loudmouth coach who yells at them constantly. No, it's the system that's responsible; these are kids who have been playing elite soccer since they were nine or ten, who know just what to do in every situation, and yet they're hamstrung by their own expertise. They're far too mechanical and predictable, and there is no improvisation in their game, no creativity or flair. Their style of play mirrors perfectly the complaint you hear about the current style of overachieving teenager, the kids who go on to Princeton or Stanford—that all their academic lives they've been successful regurgitating back to their teachers what their teachers feed them, and as a result, all their creativity has been stifled.

It's overeducation that hampers the Exeter team—overeducation and Angus Kennedy.

Angus, nicknamed Goose (his teammates having fun with his name's second syllable), has played wondrously well all through preseason. He has that marvelous ability all the best players seem to have: just when you think he can't get to a challenge, that there is simply too much space between his feet and the ball and not enough time to bridge it, his foot will dart out in an action too quick to analyze and gather the ball in. He's good with his head, likes nodding the ball downward to his cleats; he sucks in opposing players with his seeming nonchalance, then beats them; he's laser accurate with his free kicks; he's the only player on the team who really knows how to slide tackle. He doesn't say much on the field. During free kicks, waiting over the ball, he'll stick both hands against the small of his back and squint goalward like a farmer appraising his cows. He keeps his fists balled with energy while he plays—like many good midfielders, he's tricky with his arms and shoulders, uses them for fakes. "All the best footballers have some kind of wit about them," Nick Hornby writes in his classic *Fever Pitch*—and Angus plays with a savvy, visionary wit.

It's a talent that stands out all the more conspicuously against Exeter's frigid competence. Angus breaks up their attacks, leads us on increasingly bold raids into the offensive end, and almost earns us a goal as Matt heads one of his crosses goalward only to see it headed off the line by a lunging defender.

The game ends 0-0—not a bad result in the unofficial state championship. Our boys are obviously pleased, though exhausted, and Rob circulates among them with water bottles, urging them to drink. The Exeter players, equally exhausted, lay on the artificial grass and get yelled at by their coach.

We got back to Lyme just as a line storm broke across our meadow, shredding leaves, knocking down branches, putting out the lights. Celeste and I were sitting by the window staring out at the lightning when Matt, rehydrated and rested, came upstairs and handed me three sheets of paper.

"What's this?" I said, or something equally obvious.

Matt made his shy little trademark grin. "You think you're the only one who can write about soccer? I'm keeping a journal of the season, and here's the first part."

This is what I read, holding it near the window to what twilight was left.

It's funny. Since I started playing at HHS, we have always had upper-classmen to look up to and lead us, and I definitely have noticed their absence. In preseason we have been constantly reminiscing about funny incidents and quotes from the last few seasons. But our team chemistry and closeness are much better than last year, when we had some cliques. . . . Being a senior brings mixed feelings. I love the leadership, the playing time, the friends, and the fact that this really seems like my closest friends' last year to show what we can do. But it also seems like the pinnacle of my soccer playing career, which is a bittersweet realization for me and adds a lot of importance to the team's success. Coach always has us write our hopes for the season down. For me, the list has been growing more ambitious every year. First, win the championship. Second, become an all-state center back. Finally, have some fun, which will be the easiest to fulfill. But there are worries to go with it. In terms of soccer, will our offense score enough goals? Can our defense prove ourselves with shutouts? And, most of all, what would happen if I got injured? My final goal is not to take anything for granted, focus on one game at a time. The biggest game for the majority of teams in our division is playing against us, and we can't worry too much about a three-peat.

Our first regular season game is against a brand-new high school, Redford, and they will only have freshmen and sophomores on their team. Coach uncharacteristically said, "We are going to go down there and grind them into paste," which made us all laugh. Coach's use of the word "disingenuous" in the Valley News *article was pretty funny, too. Even funnier was stopping on the way back from Exeter for what Rob said would be a "healthy snack," and Ben Rimmer running in to buy himself four Dunkin' Donuts.*

It's going to be tough to balance academics with sports this year. I would honestly be content to just give all my energy to the soccer team, and I would honestly (maybe not quite so) be content to give all my energy to preparing for SATs, working on college applications, and doing homework. Two of my friends, Angus and Eric, seem determined to play soccer in college, both of whom I've played with since the start. They did lots of camps this summer,

both seem to have a few offers to work with, and I am a little envious.

I had a talk outside school with one of the boys involved in the breaking

in and cheating scandal. He said he knew it was dumb while he was doing

it, but he was supposed to be their lookout. He's so smart, it's hard to figure

out why he did it. He said his father is trying to get his trial postponed, so

he can apply early decision to college and not have to say yes on that line

about did you ever get convicted of a crime. No soccer players are involved,

at least not so far.

Hanover's final tune-up was the annual alumni game, and although the mood was more relaxed than in Exeter, the play was, if anything, even more intense. Rob had ruled that only alumni who had graduated in the last two years could play—in previous encounters, the older grads, twentysomethings filled with bottled-up sporting aggression, had played so ferociously that several varsity players were injured. So, Rob wasn't taking any chances. Some familiar faces were missing because their college seasons had already begun—Jimmy Alexander at Bentley, Jory Kahan at Wesleyan, Ben McKinnon at Williams—but there was enough alumni talent on hand to give our lads a real tussle. It was a treat to see Jeff Levin in action again, last year's all-state midfielder—no one, at any soccer level, has such economical feet, able to distribute the ball just about anywhere he wants to put it with the most imperceptible of flicks. He had been recruited by NYU, but he was putting off college for year, heading to England where he hoped (he even had an agent for this) to hook on with a pro team.

The match ended 1-0 alumni after a speculative cross bonked off their surprised striker's head (he wasn't even facing the goal). The man of the match was Dan Bendette, the alumni goalie. He had captained the state champs in 2002 (so much for Rob's no-older-guys rule), then gone on to be a three-year starter at Pomona-Pitzer—and for a New Hampshire soccer player to go out to California and wow them was a remarkable feat. He made spectacular save after spectacular save, and all the while kept up a stream-of-shouting that made any other goalie I ever listened to seem mute. I talked to him after the game; he had used his soccer connections to get a job at next year's Olympics in Beijing, and that was going a long way to easing the withdrawal pains from soccer.

The alumni game—and then the final preseason ritual of parents' meeting and the varsity team dinner.

Parents of all four boys' teams came to the meeting in the high school gym, a considerable crowd, but Rob is the kind of public speaker who has it all—good body English, expressive hand movement (he likes to tick off points with the fingers of his right hand flicking the flattened palm of his left), little cha-cha steps back and forth—and he manages to pack a lot of information and positive energy into the strict twenty-five minutes he allows himself. Celeste and I have sat through these meetings before, but even for us there are some surprises. Rob mentions that last year the Hanover soccer team came in third in the entire country for teams boasting the highest cumulative GPA, and he's hoping this year to win. He has the team stand up to show off their new practice T-shirts; on the backs are imprinted concentric rings, a target, the kind you might use for archery. "We're the targets this year," he says, "everyone is gunning for us," which is funny—or is it? The T-shirts give his next point a certain irony.

"Our overwhelming first priority in Hanover soccer is safety," he says. "Safety in playing, safety in training, safety in transportation."

The moms and dads all nod—safety, for sure. But it strikes me that this is a very interesting and revealing thing to say, culturally speaking. I don't remember what my coach in high school told parents—I have a hunch there was never a parent meeting at all—but if he did list his top priority, it would surely have been fitness or exercise or teamwork, and safety would never have been mentioned. (Safety from what—Russian bombers?) Rob is no wimp, but he has a real sensitivity to parents' concerns, and so if he mentions safety as his top priority, you can be sure that safety is already the top priority of those listening.

The common sense aspect of this can't be argued—there are rules about riding to practice in students' cars, procedures to follow in case of injury, and so on. But clearly there are larger safety concerns, unmentioned concerns, that, welling up from the depths of everyone's fears, have created an entire generation of scaredy-cat parents, even here in Hanover. War in Iraq. Terrorist threats. Economic uncertainties. Columbine killers. Global warming. The threat of AIDS. A soccer coach can't do much about these, but he has his ear to the ground, he knows what emotions are out there, and so, when he lists a team's priorities, "safety" naturally comes first to his lips, just as it does now to a car salesman selling you a van.

On August 29, with only one day left before the start of the regular season, I went down to White River Junction to speak with the Hanover High alumnus whom soccer has carried farthest out into the world: Dr. Tommy Clark.

His story is an inspiring one. He's the son of Bobby Clark, the famous Aberdeen goalie who went on to become a legendary college coach in the States—the same Bobby Clark who, teaching ball control to a bunch of freezing kids in the early eighties on a Dartmouth field, first alerted me to the fact that youth soccer in this country was on the ascendant.

Tommy was raised in Scotland, took to "football" early, and was already playing with the Aberdeen youth team when his father moved the family to Zimbabwe so that he could coach. After dour, rainy Scotland, Africa seemed wonderfully colorful and exotic; young Tommy fell in love with the landscape and people right from the start. But political conditions soon worsened, his father had the opportunity at Dartmouth, and so the family was on the move again. Tommy ended up going to high school at Hanover, where he became an all-American midfielder (a very rare honor in high school) and captained the state championship winning side of 1988. He played four years at Dartmouth after that (I remember with pleasure watching the intelligent way he led their midfield on, in years when Dartmouth had a nationally ranked team), then went back to Zimbabwe to play as the only white player on Highland FC, the top professional club in the country.

He enjoyed this immensely, but then something started to go wrong. Teammates were dying under mysterious circumstances, and no one was saying why. "I knew they had died of AIDS," Tommy remembers, "but the obituaries didn't mention it, and the families didn't either."

He came back to Hanover to attend Dartmouth Medical School, working toward becoming a pediatrician, trying—though the idea was slow to form—to somehow combine his passion for Africa with his soccer playing and his medicine in a way that might make a difference.

"I really can't remember when I came up with my idea," Tommy explains. "I know it was before medical school. My notion was to use the fame and cachet of Africa's top professional soccer players, real cultural heroes, to impact the community around HIV, to get the subject out in the open. And I figured if I could get these soccer stars talking about the disease, it might have a good effect."

The organization that he founded, Grassroots Soccer, trains professional soccer players in Africa to teach twelve- to fourteen-year-olds about HIV and AIDS prevention. Clark built this from scratch, talking to curriculum expert and behavioral change theorists to get a grounding on how best to get health messages across, using his contacts from Dartmouth to begin fund-raising, and, as part of his pediatric residency, designing a community project for Bulawayo in Zimbabwe, the country's second-largest city and his former home.

In Grassroots, the soccer stars are brought into villages, where they explain to the kids who they are, why they're involved with Grassroots, and why talking about AIDS openly is so important. They then lead specially developed games and role playing, which encourages the kids to talk about what happens in their community when someone is HIV positive—and this leads in turn to talking frankly about prevention. The sessions end with a formal graduation ceremony. Parents attend, and the students are given Grassroots T-shirts and diplomas.

Grassroots's headquarters is in White River Junction, Vermont: a world—several worlds—removed from Zimbabwe. The office space is donated by Alex Kahan, the Hanover assistant coach, which is another example of the small, mutually supporting soccer community here. Running Grassroots is a full-time job for Tommy, but he still devotes one day a week to pediatrics and serves as the doctor on call if any boys get sick at Rob's camp. Still another link is that Rob has Tommy listed as Hanover's "technical director" in a none-too-subtle hint that his presence would be welcome at practice. But Jeff Cook at Dartmouth also wants his help coaching, and at this point in preseason, the much-in-demand Tommy was devoting a couple hours a day to helping out there.

He's about to leave for the campus when we talk. Having skipped lunch, he's happy to see Celeste has sent along some fresh-baked blueberry muffins, and while we sit there talking, he polishes off all five—no problem for a man in his kind of shape. He's thirty-eight—young to have accomplished so much—handsome, dark-haired, with the kind of large, serious forehead that suggests someone who is not only brainy but good at headers. There's no trace of Scotland in his accent. He thinks carefully before replying to any questions, answers forthrightly when he does. He's taught himself to understand people, what a person's talent is, and how it can contribute to his cause; while I try sizing him up, I have the feeling he's sizing me up, too.

We're practically neighbors, as it turns out. He and his wife, the parents of two toddlers, are fixing up an old rundown house on River Road in Lyme; although I don't tell him this, it had once been owned by reputedly the meanest, most dangerous man in town, so it was good to have someone safer move in. For Tommy, coming back to the Upper Valley to raise a family meant coming back full circle to his roots, or at least to one significant branch.

I'd read quite a bit about Grassroots over the years, so instead of asking him to go through the whole story, I ask him to talk a little about his high school years. I'm writing a book about high school soccer, I explain, and I'm interested in how big dreams form in a young person's heart. Did he, for instance, have any heroes at seventeen?

"My father," he answers immediately. "The players on the Dartmouth team, who I was already practicing with even in high school. A Hanover High teacher named John Lincoln. I was homesick for Zimbabwe. That was definitely going on during high school. My parents were teachers, not just coaches, so I was leaning in that direction instead of medicine."

He seems a little surprised to be revisiting this—clearly, his vision is firmly fixed on the job at hand, eradicating AIDS, not reminiscing. But, in the little he says, it's obvious he fits the recognizable pattern. Some idealistic young men or women go through their high school years not really knowing what they want to do in life, but sensing strongly that they are meant to do something hard and unusual and important. There are some threads, some leanings they're not fully aware of, though they can feel their subtle tug. A mentor, several mentors, influence more by their example than anything specific they say. Yes, it's a pattern all right, and part of the pattern is not knowing it's a pattern, not until years go by and you can see that every little influence played its part. I wonder, talking to Tommy, whether Matt is experiencing anything like this. By its very nature, it's not the kind of thing that would be visible to anyone else, not even a father.

Our time is running out, but I want to ask Tommy what I'm going to ask everyone this fall: what makes soccer so beautiful?

"The understanding," he says. "At least among the players. Playing with guys you've played with for a long time, it's a great thing, to anticipate their moves, to respond to it before they've even thought it through. Even now when I play just for fun with the lads around town. This is a real high for me, when teammates know their roles."

Some of my informants on the Hanover team have been playing pickup soccer with Tommy, as have some of the Dartmouth players, and I'm told that when Tommy wants to get a ball, he gets it; when he doesn't want to give it away, it doesn't get given away. They're clearly in awe of him (just as Tommy himself is in awe of Cristiano Ronaldo, the Manchester United star whose grace and imagination simply blow him away), and I make a pitch about his coming to Matt's practice—just once would be enough to really inspire them—but he laughs, points to his watch, explains again how busy he is running Grassroots, being a pediatrician, taking care of two little kids, restoring an old home, and helping out at Dartmouth.

There is one last thing to ask him about as he gets into his car. He, more than anyone I've met, exemplifies the universal, international aspect of soccer, how it bridges continents, connects privileged kids in Hanover with the poorest boys in Bulawayo. He nods emphatically—yes, that's another part of soccer's beauty. He looks off toward a dusty rec field just past the parking lot, thinks about it for a second, gets into the car—but not without delivering a perfect last line.

"Soccer," he says, marveling perhaps at his own journey, "is a ticket to the world."

5

A Place in the Choir

All good soccer teams are happy the same way; all bad soccer teams are unhappy differently.

Or at least it's tempting to think so, after watching Hanover's first four opponents in the regular season. Each had a burden it couldn't quite lift, didn't even want to lift—you got the impression of eleven weary Atlases who, instead of shrugging patiently under the weight of the world, were actively trying to dump it on someone else. Hanover won these games by a combined score of 18-0, but these teams mostly beat themselves.

Redford was first, an away game down at their brand-new high school in a plush suburb. This was an unusual case; it had been decided that for the first year only freshmen and sophomores would be attending the new school, with upperclassmen left to finish at schools they already attended. By the time Matt scored the second of his two goals, twenty-three minutes into the first half, it was clear that Hanover's only challenge would be to keep from running up the score.

Bennett, our second opponent, played unhappily, too, only here not only did the coach shout at his own players, they shouted right back at him, so, sitting there on the sidelines, it was like watching a bitter domestic quarrel. You wanted to avert your gaze to the surrounding mountains, block all the nastiness out.

It's too bad about that, because until the game started, I was enjoying our morning thoroughly. Bennett is smack in the center of the White Mountains, and the drive over took Celeste and I past some of our old favorites, including Moosilauke, Tripyramid, and Osceola. It was the Saturday of Labor Day weekend, but there were already red bands across the higher ridges, and down in the swamps the maples had spectacularly begun to turn. A perfect day to be out in the woods, and it was a measure of how important soccer had become to us that we didn't give into temptation, park at a trailhead, and start hiking.

I wish we had. It was no fun watching Bennett, I got myself into a spot of trouble, and as easily as we won, there was some disturbing Hanover news. Leslie Henderson, Case's mom, met us in the parking lot. "The restrooms are across the road in the Laundromat," was the first thing she said, Leslie being an experienced soccer mom from way back. The second thing was, "Case has mono. He'll be out for a month."

We were shocked. We commiserated with her, talked about the chances that all the boys might be infected, and listened to her explain what the doctor had said, worried that without Case, the team would be in serious trouble.

As for my own misbehavior, I'm not proud of it. It was one of those minor stupidities that almost got out of hand—but if I plead guilty, it's guilt with an explanation.

Bennett is another town with a new high school, but for some reason, we played behind the old one, on a wide meadow between the mountains (intervale is the fine old New Hampshire word for these). The view was Western in breadth—we could have been playing amid the Rockies—and I was settling in on the sidelines when Eric Barthold, on one of his trademark dashes down the wing, was brutally tripped right in front of us, for the second time in five minutes.

A bearded Bennett dad, standing ten yards down the line from me, screamed at the ref, "He's a flopper!" Then, that not being enough for him, screamed at a shook-up Eric, "You're a flopper!"

Now, while I had never heard anyone use the term "flopper" before, I understood that he meant "diver," and by "diver" he meant someone who deliberately fell in order to fool the referee into calling a foul. So—and this calculation took exactly one millisecond to course through my brain—he was accusing Eric of being a cheater. Eric, who—except for my own son—was the member of the team I knew best.

"He's not a flopper!" I said loudly and angrily, in a reflex I simply could not control. "I've known him since he was six." I hesitated, but the anger wasn't quite done with me. "You're a flopper. Shut the hell up."

Stunned silence from the Hanover fans—had Walter actually said that?—and rigid looks straight out toward the field. The bearded man seemed startled that anyone had challenged him, but clearly, in the little duel that quickly developed, it was his turn to fire next. "Go back to the jungle!" he yelled—which was actually a pretty funny line. What he was referring to was one of the infamous hats I wear for the sun—not my usual pith helmet, as it turned out, but a khaki hat with a long sun visor and a protective neck flap. Semiwitty of him, though no one laughed. I had made a fool of myself, I was mad and embarrassed, but the Bennett bully didn't say a word the rest of the game, so I felt I had succeeded in protecting our boys, and that didn't feel entirely bad. But, of course, you should never open your mouth. After the game, when Rob came over, we congratulated him on the win. "How was it on the sidelines?" he asked. Celeste, not really thinking, said, "Oh, one of their parents told us to go back to the jungle."

Rob blanched, looked as if he had been shot in the stomach . . .and it took me one horrible second to figure out why. We have three African Americans on the team, and Rob instantly assumed that these were whom the taunt was directed at—and so we had to run after him and explain before he took matters into his own hands. Moral? Never open your mouth at a soccer game, no matter what the provocation. Never open your mouth at a soccer game! Never open your mouth at a soccer game, repeated, for your weakness, one thousand consecutive times.

Fall Mountain, our home opener, played miserably through force of circumstances. Always before, they had been our nemesis, a rough-tough team (*argy-bargy* is the splendid Brit phrase) who eliminated us in the semifinals Matt's freshman year, then last Halloween took us down to the last thirty seconds of the quarterfinals before Jeff Levin's miraculous goal sent them packing. It was the one game in the season I missed; I was in Pittsburgh on business, and before leaving, I'd worked it out with Scott Barthold, Eric's dad, that I would call him on his cell phone to get periodic updates as the game progressed.

A good idea, in theory, but it turned out to be pure torture. The game was due to start at 3:00. I called from my hotel room at 3:20, and we were up 2-0. "Thanks, Scott!" I yelled, as if he'd scored himself. "I'll check back in ten minutes." Too nervous to stay in my hotel room, I went down to the street, walked toward the university, kept glancing down at my watch. I called a second time, heard what I thought were anxious crowd sounds, felt my spirits drop even before Scott gave me the bad news. "Fall Mountain scored," he said. "They scored twice, so it's 2-2."

I called back an embarrassing number of times, right through the second half, and each time a patient Scott told me the score was still tied. There couldn't have been a more nervous, anxious man in Pittsburgh during the next fifteen minutes, but through a supreme effort of self-control, I kept myself from calling back until I knew the game must be over. (Or was it? Overtime could add an extra twenty minutes.)

"Well," Scott sighed, when I called at last. A gloomy "well," I thought—I braced myself for bad news.

"They won," he said, in his usual calm and even voice.

So. That's that. My heart sunk. The end of everything.

"Yeah, Jeff Levin scored on a spin-around shot with thirty seconds left—it was incredible."

Fooled by a pronoun! When Scott said "they," he meant "we," and never will I let him forget it. My exultation was all the greater for that one moment of despair—and the tensest man in Pittsburgh, as he walked down Forbes Avenue, was now singing out loud.

It was obvious, two minutes into the game, that Fall Mountain had sunk. Last year's team had fifteen seniors, so the heart of the team had gone missing; not only were the newcomers' skills bad, they had very little spirit. Matt sprinted up from defense to notch another headed goal—for the time being, he was the team's leading scorer—and Rob once again had the problem of not running up the score.

With the game virtually over after ten minutes, talk among the parents shifted to discussing the pros and cons of the new artificial field. This was the same field I had visited during construction last winter; originally, the plan was to play three or four home games here, but now Rob and Mike Jackson, the athletic director, had decided that all the boys' games would be on the fake grass, the better to prepare us for the state tourney, which was always played on similar surface.

I was prepared to hate it—fake grass!—but I was gradually won over. The markings were horrible: yard markers for football with big white digits. And four sets of sidelines for various sports—two whites, one red, one yellow—confused things mightily. The coziness of the old field was gone, fans and parents were spread out more, and the space seemed positively hostile to casual, friendly schmoozing. Friends of Hanover Soccer had kicked in $250 to build a fence behind the western goal to keep shots from sailing down into a ravine, but we got what we paid for: a low fence that had balls flying over it all game. But the field is self-contained. It sits at the bottom of a natural amphitheater, and I found this focused the game in a way I liked. With the new stands, you can climb high and get that aerial view that is so important in watching soccer, where geometry, looking down at the geometry, provides much of the game's appeal; sitting high, you can read the game even better than the players. And the smooth fast surface suited our smooth fast game.

I sat up there the next game, during what was supposed to be our first hard test against Milford. ("The boys need to get some real competition," Rob told me before the game. "We're getting edgy with each other at practice. It hasn't all been holding hands and singing 'Kumbaya.'") Again, circumstances did the opposition in before the game even started. The Milford bus driver got violently ill, pulled the bus over on the interstate, and the coach called for help—it was two hours before another driver could come, and the team remained stuck in the bus for all that time, in 90-degree-plus temperatures. By the time they got to Hanover, there wasn't much fight left in them, and we won 2-0 in a game that was never that close. Matt headed in again, but the referee ruled he had pushed a defender, so it was disallowed. My sister Christina was visiting. She had never seen Matt play before, and she oohed and aahed every time he cleared the ball downfield, assuming that the farther you kicked it, the better the play was. I tried to correct her, explained that if he kicked it too far, the goalie would reach it before our forwards, but she refused to listen. "That was a long one," she said, clapping mightily. "Way to go, Matt!"

What I enjoyed was watching the continued partnership between Matt and Cal Felicetti, his fellow center back. They complement each other perfectly—Matt the take-charge guy, the leader, who occasionally gives way to rashness; Cal the businesslike silent partner, who is only impetuous when he has to be and then goes absolutely nuts. Watching high school soccer, you always keep one eye on your son, but when I'm not watching him, I tend to watch Cal, and when I watch him, I always end up smiling, and it's been that way since he was eleven.

He looked like Dennis the Menace at that age, and there's still a trace of that left, even with his early-Beatles mop and slightly pugnacious chin. He looks a lot cockier than he actually is, and when you compliment him after a game, he says "Thank you" so softly and modestly, it's almost as if he's blushing.

Cal's small, and he doesn't look like a superb athlete—not until you see him fight for a fifty-fifty ball, when he dances so fast, spins so wildly and yet with such control, you realize, almost despite yourself, that hey, this guy is good. He's the best dribbler on the team, and sometimes this gets him into trouble, but he always gets out of it again in yet another hairbreadth escape. He gets the bench laughing, the way he dances and dribbles; he probably smiles and laughs more than anyone else on the field. In the air, he's magnificent—he leaps like a wild salmon for headers—there is no other analogy that fits. (Well, one more: his hang time resembles Michael Jordan's.) When he's tripped and falls, he rolls farther and more spectacularly than anyone else; when he commits a foul, he puts his hands on top of his chest, gives the ref an innocent "What, me?" little smile. Early in his career, the coaches had him playing all over the place, never quite sure what to do with him. It was Chris Cheney who was smart enough to plant him back on center defense, even though people warned him that

Cal was too small—and the discipline and responsibility of defending turned out to be the one thing Cal's game needed to fully blossom.

Because both Cal and Matt are good at headers, they run up for corner kicks while the other two defenders, reinforced by a midfielder, hang back. Rob has worked out a good scheme for this. Casey Maue takes up a position on the far post close to the goal line; since he's so tall, the other team's best defender stays there with him, removing him from the center of the box, where the real danger will emerge. Cal positions himself about twelve yards out. Just as Casey's size attracts attention, Cal's smallness makes him anonymous, so he often remains unmarked. Matt lines up on the edge of the six-yard box and runs diagonally across the goal in the direction the ball is coming in from, hoping to nod the ball down hard.

There is something very stylized about corner kicks after the free-flowing improvisation of open play. The two teams, after running so hard, now come to a standstill as everyone walks slowly to their positions in the penalty area. Who is marking whom has to be worked out—and what this resembles in action is two lines of boys and girls at a dance, the wallflowers shrinking shyly back, the macho boys pointing possessively toward the ones they want, and then via all kinds of shuffling advances and skipping retreats, everyone finds a partner at last. A dance—but then, as the player in the corner raises his arm, prepares to launch his kick, things get a little bit rough. The partners don't dance after all, but shove each other with their shoulders and chests. "I'm not dancing with YOU!" they seem to be saying—the lack of manners, after the formal beginning, can get rambunctious pretty fast ("Where are the chaperones?" you have time to wonder). But now the ball is coming into the box, just overhead high and moving rapidly, a perfect trajectory. And suddenly you realize, in a breathtaking instant, that it's a dance all right, but instead of the high school sock hop you thought it was, it's a ballet—and Cal or Matt are often the ballerinas, leaping high over everyone to head the ball in.

The Milford game, though we won easily in the end, had just enough tension that the choir got started in the stands. Bob Maue, Casey's dad, led off as he usually does, with his deep resonant voice that could be a Russian basso. "Let's go, Hanover!" he yells, a basic kind of lyric that is hardly Cole Porter, but always seems appropriate. Cal Felicetti, Sr. and Rick Barth are basses, too, and they triple Bob's lead, really giving our sound a solid floor. Kevin Peterson, Sam's dad, is more of a baritone, and, what's more, he can really sing, so he adds some needed melody. "Let's go, white! Let's hustle, boys!" Chris Kennedy cheerily chimes in, though his voice can be all over the place. Scott Barthold and Barry Harwick are our tenors, but squeaky ones—Scott because he's so quiet normally, his voice cracks when it's forced to soar; Barry, the Dartmouth track coach, because he's hoarse from yelling "Last lap, boys!" for so many years. Matt's dad joins in. The sound really has to be pretty smothering before he'll expose himself, but he comes in somewhere between the basses and the baritones with a "Let's do it, white! Let's turn it on!"

There's a good deal of gruffness in all this—someone listening would be tempted to turn down the switch marked testosterone—and so the women's voices, chiming in now, are refreshingly welcome. Leslie Henderson and Joanie Barthold are our altos, and they really like to sing: "You can do it, boys! Make it happen!" Marcia Kelly, Betsy McClain, and Celeste Wetherell sing soprano, not coloratura, nothing fancy, but a feminine ringing sound that sounds good against all the bass. Celeste has problems remembering she's part of the choir, not a soloist, and her old cheerleading genes sometimes take over, but she's gotten better over the years, as we all have, so when we really get going, the sound is bright and happy and inspiring and paternal and maternal and all those other qualities we soccer parents like to think we epitomize.

Looking back on it now, after our fifteen years of sometimes bemused involvement, the biggest surprise of this soccer-parent business is how social it's all been. Celeste and I have forged friendships with other parents that we hope will last. We've made some enemies, or at least pissed a few people off. We've carpooled with each other, gotten lost together, shared pizzas or tailgated, commiserated with each other after losses, rooted together, celebrated, signed on to the same avid fan club, wished our boys to be happy and successful together, bonded over this in a way that runs deep. If at times this all becomes a little too social—if sometimes you feel, with all the social niceties, the subtle snubs, the subtle pecking order, that you're a character in *Pride and Prejudice*—then that's more than made up for by real camaraderie and good fellowship, the kind that in our culture is in very short supply. Soccer is our Masonic Lodge, our VFW chapter, our fraternity—and, speaking personally, I wouldn't have much of a social life without it. A loner, a borderline misanthrope, a novelist who likes to think his only true friends are his characters (demanding friends, but patient, and it's hard to piss them off), being a part of this unique soccer-parent subculture, not to mince words, has made me a nicer, more tolerant kind of man.

My education in all this (my conversion? my reformation?) began back when Matthew was six or seven, playing little-kid soccer here in town. We parents watching oohed and aahed a lot when our sons or daughters managed to get their foot on the ball. There were a lot of pictures being snapped, lots of encouragement; the mood was about the same as at a Christmas concert or a dance recital or any of those other little-kid events parents make a fuss over. Most of the parents knew nothing about soccer, and the cheering from the sidelines was of the order of "Good kick, honey!" or "Way to go, Mikey!"

Kid stuff, being a parent at little-kid soccer, and I wasn't prepared for the upsurge in intensity that came when Matt began playing travel-team soccer in sixth grade. "Travel team?" a wise and knowing friend said, when I told him Matt would be playing—a friend whose son had already gone through the program. "Be prepared for the line business, that's all I can say."

The line business? I soon found out what he meant. At most travel-team games, there are no bleachers to sit in, no stands, so you spread your blanket or open your chair on a patch of grass along the sideline opposite the players' bench. This seems pretty straightforward, but it turns out that there are all kinds of considerations to take into account before actually planting yourself down. A spot near midfield would be nice, but the opposing-team parents are already sitting there, and because, even in a mild way, they seem like the enemy, you decide to move downfield, avoiding one woman who is already shaking cowbells. But careful, now. You don't want to sit next to the boors who spend the whole game sideline coaching ("Lob him, Omar! Lob him!"), nor do you want to sit next to a parent who hardly cares for soccer at all and chews your ear off about too much homework in school or the latest Red Sox collapse.

You move down a few yards more, spot someone you don't particularly like, call out some hypocritical pleasantry, then suddenly "discover" that the ground is really too wet near him/her, and so, with apologies, you back off again toward midfield, deciding to take a chance with the opposing parents after all. But then, the game begins. Right away, one of their endomorph loudmouths starts screaming at the ref, and so, leaving your chair there, you stroll down to where it's quieter, but end up standing next to a parent who's chattering away on a cell phone, driving you nuts.

You find a friend, someone who pretty much has the same intensity toward soccer that you have, not too much, not too little—but then, with a straight face, perfectly sincerely, he or she reminds you that last time you stood next to each other, the boys lost, and it would probably bring bad luck to have the same juxtaposition again. Finally, with no other option, abandoning your wife, you go off to the far end of the field, where at least there's some shade, but then the referee hollers at you for sitting too close behind the goal, and you're off again on your perpetual soccer-dad migration in search of a place to enjoy watching your son play soccer where no one will piss you off.

The Whys and Wherefores of Watching Youth Soccer: The Strategy of Placement—what a great thesis this would make for a PhD in sociology, if it hasn't already been done. The sociologist could talk about the not-so-subtle pecking order, the class system, in which parents of stars tend to stick together, not only for obvious reasons (their sons get invited to play in the same tournaments and join the same Olympic Development teams, so you travel more with them, see them more), but because snobbishness influences "the line" as it does any human grouping. Likewise, parents of marginal players tend to be marginalized on the line. No one likes saying, "Oh, your son is playing like shit," and it seems hypocritical to say anything else. Experienced parents know that these kids probably won't make travel team next spring, so why even bother putting the energy into making friends with moms and dads who will vanish?

Petty stuff? Yes, there's plenty. But over the years, with a core group of parents, real loyalties and friendships form, especially with a group that is as supportive and enthusiastic as the parents have been on Matthew's teams, both Lightning and Hanover. It's the only in-crowd I've ever been even casually a member of, so I owe them some gratitude just for that. I remember watching a game with our boys on the weekend after 9/11, the referee solemnly leading the two teams out to the center of the field for a minute of silence, which the parents shared. Glancing around, I saw that most of them were sobbing. Yes, we're human, and for all my amusement and irritation, I'm proud to have stood on the line beside them, and I'll miss them intensely when the season, and my soccer-dad career, is over.

Let's stay with the sociological focus for just a few more paragraphs. This year's varsity parents are a surprisingly diverse lot. Occupations represented include nurse, novelist, surgeon, architect, town finance director, zoning administrator, tennis pro, charity director, ornithologist, traffic engineer, physical therapist, emergency room doctor, arborist, snowmaking engineer, obstetrician, car salesman, med school professor, chemist, track coach, college disciplinary officer, drama professor, and dormitory repairman. The average age must be forty-eight or forty-nine, judging by all the jokes about the big 5-0. Most are in good shape and exercise seriously. Five couples are divorced, but the ex-spouses seem to get along well enough, at least at soccer games, the battles and the heartbreak having been more or less resolved by this point. All are affluent, though some are more affluent than others; we don't seem to have any trust funders or Internet billionaires. We are all, in the modern way, far too invested in our kids.

I know most, but not all, of these forty-six parents, will stop and chat to maybe fifteen of them by the sidelines, will end up standing near five or six. I have yet to meet the parents of two or three players, parents you never see at any game. I wonder about this a lot. Are they simply too busy to ever come? Is it because of their disdain for soccer, something they only grudgingly tolerate because their son is good at it? If this is so, it's newsworthy—that in our sports-obsessed culture, there are still some holdouts who think it's all a waste of time. When I was young, this type of parent was much more common. (Think of Lou Gehrig's mom in *The Pride of the Yankees*: "Lou, Lou, you must study, get a good education, and here you are wasting time always playing this baseballing.") Sometimes rumors reach us of strong parent-son conflict (someone doesn't play because he missed practice, and the reason he missed practice is that his father refused to drive him there), but, by its very nature, most of this conflict is invisible. Some boys come alone to games, come alone to team dinners and awards banquets, and the mystery of this never gets explained.

(Not long ago, parents in Europe would never watch their kids play soccer. They dropped them off at the pitch, then adjourned to the nearest bistro or pub. But now, judging by a report I heard last night on the BBC, overinvolved soccer moms and dads are springing up all over England, and parent misbehavior at games has become yet another sign of the decline of British civility.)

The good things about Hanover parents is that they behave impeccably at games, don't yell at the ref, don't abuse the other team, clap when our opponents play well, and serve heart-healthy snacks to the visitors before they get on their bus for home. This is a norm you absorb when your son first makes the team. It's in the cultural air, no one spells things out—though now and then you get a sharp ethical reminder. We had one dad last year who didn't quite get it; after his son was roughly tackled, he started heckling the ref. Scott Barthold, Eric's dad, stood it for maybe twenty seconds, then yelled, "Will you shut the hell up?!" It startled us—Scott is the softest-voiced dad on the team—but it had shock value, and it kept the offending dad quiet the rest of the season.

Are we too decorous? Sometimes I think so. On Matt's Lightning team was a father who had grown up in Greece, and hurling abuse at the other players, at the referee, at his son, was all part of the fun for him. Normally, I'd stand as far as I could from such a type, but I grew to like him—he was passionate about soccer, he wasn't about to hide that passion, and every now and then, I'd hurl some abuse right along with him, and it felt pretty good.

As for soccer moms, I'm a bit reluctant to use the term, so trendy is it, so vaguely demeaning. In contemporary parlance, soccer mom is a thirtysomething woman who drives a minivan with plenty of seat belts and cup holders, votes for the party she thinks is strongest on security, picks sports for her children based on which are the safest, multitasks, does aerobics, and in her harebrained femaleness knows hardly anything about soccer at all. Maybe it's where we live, maybe because the stereotype is a ludicrous oversimplification anyway, but the women I meet whose children play soccer hardly fit this model at all.

Joanie Barthold, Eric's mother, blasts it completely apart. She's become one of our closest friends, and we love her dearly, so it's not easy writing about her—but in the interests of responsible soccer journalism, I feel I should make the attempt.

Joanie is ageless, but if I had to pick a number, I'd guess forty-eight. She's average height, or perhaps a little shorter, and there's a compact balance and strength about her that suggests the world-class skier she once was. Her eyes flash at you in stereo—common sense from one eye, compassion from the other—and it's impossible not to like her at first sight. She often looks sleepy from too many nights on call or from the hangover from her last epic adventure, and sometimes her smile comes at you disguised as a surprisingly sad frown. There is absolutely nothing in her face or expression to tip you off that beneath her friendly, easygoing exterior lurks the most competitive person I've ever known, though with Joanie, the competition is not so much with other people as competition against her own limits—competition, for that matter, against human limits.

She's an obstetrician who is much in demand at the hospital. I've told her I'd like to be a woman just so she could deliver my baby; her combination of professionalism, compassion, and you-can-do-this optimism would guide me safely through all my fears. If someone on the team is injured, she's often the first one to rush out on the field— Joanie, our ob-gyn doc, gently testing a strained knee or consoling someone who's taken a shot in the groin. When Angus Kennedy got his head gashed open during the quarterfinals last year, Joanie was the one who rushed him home, sewed him up with stitches, and rushed him back again in time to play the second half—so all those cesarean sections she's done over the years played a key role in our state championship.

On the sidelines, she's fun to stand beside, though you have to be willing to let her do her thing, which is to keep up a running stream of sotto voce commentary that lasts the entire game. "Why doesn't he pass the ball that's it oh shoot come on Eric look alive out there buddy make it happen make it happen that's Angus for you Angus to the rescue only how come he didn't see Rimmer running down the flank okay here we go shoot it Casey why doesn't he he does!" (Voice rising now.) "Nice job I really need to learn to keep my mouth shut good stuff that's it boys MAKE IT HAPPEN!"

Watching travel team together, we had a little routine going where she had to stand exactly two steps to my left and a foot or so back of me or god knew what would happen, and we managed to win the boys seven or eight games that way before our mojo fell apart. During Eric's and Matt's sophomore year, new construction was going on beside the high school field, and a rule was made that only a parent could be a ball boy on that side because it meant being admitted to a "hard hat" area. Joanie volunteered, of course—if any dirty job is on offer requiring running, she's your man—and all the parents have happy memories of watching Joanie racing after stray balls amid all the construction debris, hopping over girders, jumping up on cement blocks, coated in dust now, desperate to find the ball and fling it back over the fence toward the field.

As for her competitive side, it's so strong, it's a little frightening. She was brought up in the White Mountains, took to downhill racing early, skied competitively at Dartmouth (and played soccer, when those early women's teams needed recruits), was on the bubble for the Olympics, and won a U.S. Master's title a week after giving birth to Eric. If anything, her need for competition has only grown as she's gotten older. Last year, after not having time to adequately train (for Joanie, adequately is a relative term), she entered her first full marathon down in Texas and did very well—but that's nothing compared with the informal marathons she and her husband Scott complete weekly at home, where bicycle sprints the breadth of the state or running up and down Mount Lafayette or all-night mountain-bike races are the kinds of things she relaxes with—never mind the things she does when she wants to get a little exercise. In other aspects of life, she's not competitive at all—they live in an old farmhouse here in Lyme, raise sheep, drive cars even older and more battered than ours—but if it comes to testing your limits against a punishing physical challenge, Joanie wants in. Burning lungs? Joanie finds truth in them. Aching muscles? In her, they bring solace and joy.

How does she accomplish so much? In that respect, she fits the soccer-mom mold perfectly: she balances career, family, community activism, and sports in a superhero kind of way. When her kids were younger, she was infamous in Lyme for her shamelessness in cadging her kids rides to school and soccer practice; "carpool," for Joanie, meant that you drove ninety percent of the time and the Bartholds hardly ever. Just when you got sick and tired of this, someone would bang on your door late at night, and who would it be but Joanie, with a freshbaked loaf of "Barthold Bread" and some homemade raspberry jam.

Joanie once said something very funny to me. "I feel inadequate," she said—and I'm afraid I laughed out loud. The poignancy—that even a Joanie Barthold feels inadequate—only struck me later on.

She wins it easily: Queen of the Soccer Moms. And there's one more award to give her, while we're dishing them out. We were talking on the sidelines before a game, a bunch of senior parents who have been watching her longest. It was unanimous—we voted in a block. Joanie, we all agreed, was the one parent most likely to lose control of herself, run impetuously out on the field and start playing, should the boys in a tight and vital game ever tire and need fresh legs. "She'll do it, too," Celeste said—and so we decided to make the award a silent, honorary one. We didn't want to give her any ideas.

6

THE BORDER PATROL

We have two kinds of autumn in this part of the world. Both can take your breath away; both can break your heart. One decorates September, the other dominates October, but our seasons are all mixed up now, and sometimes we get the two versions of heartbreak on the very same afternoon. This happened this year on September 15. I was driving home from the Oyster River game with Celeste and Kevin Peterson. We were on the boring stretch of Route 4 with nothing but third-rate antique stores to look at, and I'm afraid I wasn't doing much to hold up my end of the conversation. We were trying to brainstorm a nickname for Hanover's four stalwart defenders, who had just shut out our rivals as the best Division I team in the state. I liked "the Untouchables," but we decided the boys wouldn't know what that meant. Celeste liked "the Enforcers," but we thought that was a bit too muscular and stern. Kevin took a bit longer to come up with an idea, but it turned out to be a winner. "Let's call them 'the Border Patrol,'" he suggested from the backseat. "No one gets through."

In a two-hour drive, that was the high point. All day the weather had been perfect, with the kind of burnished summer feel that makes you feel it will go on forever. A light southerly breeze that wafted monarch butterflies across the playing field. Wildflowers still in bloom, clumped in ready-to-pick bouquets. Fleecy clouds that looked fresh off an Impressionist's easel. It mimics spring, this softness, it makes you want to laugh, dance, and sing—the realist in you, the Puritan doubter, is simply overwhelmed. But it's not spring, your spirit is apt to feel wistful, and that's the heartbreaking part of early fall, knowing it's far too perfect to ever last.

And it didn't last, not even through the rest of the afternoon. When we came to the rugged hills that separate central New Hampshire from our home in the west, the clouds, so soft in the morning, had darkened to the color of tarnished brass, and we could feel the temperature drop even inside the car. Celeste put the heat on, and it was clear that not only had real autumn arrived—our old-fashioned New England autumn that speaks of foliage, pumpkins, cider, and Pilgrims—but an autumn had come with an undertone of winter, a winter of the spirit, that thing about fall that rests uneasily on the heart.

Too much to read into a simple cold front? Perhaps. Or maybe I was just grumpy after seeing our fine effort against Oyster River only result in a 0-0 tie. We played two overtime periods without a winning goal. Last year, miraculously, we won four games in golden goal over-time, those Grabillian "pig-pile games," and not having that happen this time made me worry that our karma might have been exhausted. It took a while for my spirits to bounce back again, and when they did, it was autumn, good-cop autumn, that did it—autumn, the season I was born in, the season I like to think of as my season, the season when soccer is meant to be played.

Soccer has always been the autumn game for me—never mind that it's now played all year around. When I was growing up, baseball had summer to itself; July and August were thought to be far too hot for a running game like soccer, and it was only with the first buffering chills of September that boys started playing (girls, of course, didn't play at all). Soccer had a tang to it, just like autumn did—it was a bracing time to play a brisk sport. Players would return to their New England prep schools, and the leaves might already be turning by the time their first game came around. Down in the New York suburbs, the public high schools would be playing now, too, including mine, on what was already an overcrowded, overdeveloped Long Island. But even here, autumn could get the blood stirring, with cold fronts blowing down from Canada over the sound, pumping us full of an energy that, with few other acceptable outlets, made its way to our feet. Autumn weather was my Walden, my Adirondacks or Sierras. There was nothing else so intoxicating around, and while the other players stood listening to grumpy Coach Steen, I'd be off to the side staring up at the clouds or reaching down to examine a leaf, trying to soak autumn into my senses like a soccer-playing Shelley or Keats.

And it's funny: although most of my high school memories have faded, those cold, brisk practice sessions under adamantine autumn clouds remain with me as something worth treasuring. You'd come out from the locker room to practice, surprised there was still so much warmth in the sun, but then, by practice's end, the light would have slanted sideways, and if a distant tree hid the sun's disk, you might need to move a few yards to get back into the sunlight, never mind that the coach was screaming at you for being out of position (2-3-5—a prehistoric era!). The cold would feel good in your lungs, which is to say it hurt like hell, doing sprints, but later, at home, you could take some pride in having toughed it out—it was like coming in from duck hunting or fishing for steelhead. The cold soccer ball could hurt, too, those heavy leather balls that smashed against our shins like ice balls or ricocheted off our foreheads like cannonballs from the Revolution. But that was okay, too, since what was really going on, though none of us was smart enough to realize it, was that memory was making sure we remembered all this by using the half funny/half horrible pain that is often its most reliable weapon. Goose bumps under shin guards; frozen drool on our jersey collars; shivery snot; burning fingertips; rain-sodden hair. Autumn's methods weren't always pretty, but at least you knew you were alive.

I can barely remember the names of my teammates now. They come to me in halves: there was a midfielder named Tobias, but I forget his first name; an outside right named Paul, whose last name escapes me; but I remember everything connected to autumn, and how huge and pleasantly eerie the sky looked as our season stretched closer to Halloween. Autumn is said to be football season, and that was part of it, too; the thuds of linemen slamming into each other at the adjacent practice field was a good autumn sound, like geese honking, something I appreciated without ever wanting to honk myself.

At one practice, trick-or-treaters ran past the goal, ghosts and little goblins, and the first one in their line took it in his head to slap the goalpost as he dashed past, and all his friends decided they must do it, too, a line of maybe fifteen kids, fifteen slaps, and Coach Steen becoming more apoplectic with each one. He ordered our goalie (Pete? Jack?) to chase them away, but our goalie just went over and slapped the goalpost the same affectionate, playful way, and one of the little kids, in gratitude, turned around and threw him a Milky Way.

The danger of getting caught up in high school sports, of course, is the danger of living vicariously through your son or daughter—but there's a good vicarious part that's often neglected. For me, the thing I enjoy reliving most, through Matthew, is the fun of being a young man outside on a day that is much colder than the day before but warmer than the day that will come after, knowing you're alive every time the ball stings or with each burning breath that expands and exhilarates your lungs, sensing, in the sky, a bittersweet bittersweetness you'll never experience quite so intensely again.

That's what I was thinking about as we drove home from Oyster River. And that is why, as autumn settled and deepened, I fell in love with soccer once again.

Oyster River was the first of back-to-back games against Hanover's traditional rivals, although "rivals" in a very different sense.

Oyster River High School is near the coast in Durham, the home of the University of New Hampshire. As in Hanover, there are lots of sports-obsessed parents with disposable time and money that they can pour into their sons' sports. Between them, the two schools have dominated New Hampshire Class I soccer since teams started playing fifty years ago (an anniversary that was celebrated before the start of the game), and no two teams have accumulated so many state championships, Hanover winning four in the last ten years, Oyster River three. Because Oyster River does not have a football team—football, like cheerleading, became politically incorrect here in the eighties, and the sport was dropped—their teams get the fast shifty halfback types who would not otherwise have a fall sport.

Rivals—but there's nothing going on viscerally. It's a decorous, respectful rivalry between teams from totally different parts of the state. Matt's freshman year, a shoving match broke out between players after a very chippy game, but that seems like a long time ago now, and I doubt anyone on the field except Matthew remembers it occurred.

As for this year's game, it turns into the tight battle everyone expected. Oyster River has lost several gallons of spirit from the team we beat in last year's semifinal; they're a quiet bunch, and they may be confused and bothered that they can't get behind our defense, no matter how hard they try.

This is not totally surprising, since our defense has become unshakable—seven games into the season, and we haven't allowed a goal. Matt and Cal are solid as ever in the center, and over on the outside, Trevor Barlowe and Sam Peterson have proved all their doubters wrong. Trevor, who some thought didn't have enough speed, absolutely refuses to let anyone get past him down the right side; he has a bulldog determination that gets his moppy red hair shaking, and when his moppy red hair starts shaking, you know the attacker is toast. He's learned to use the sideline cannily; it becomes, in effect, his partner, so time and time again he forces the winger to go out of bounds; either that, or he spins and whangs the ball off the attacker's knee for a Hanover throw-in.

Over on the left side, Sam plays a bit differently. He holds his body canted at a 45-degree angle to the sideline and forces attackers inside, onto his natural, right-footed side, where he can then dart in and strip the ball away. He's also learning to overlap more on offense, get crosses into the box. There had been some grumbling among teammates about Sam during preseason, that he wasn't pulling his weight. Though Sam has a sleepy kind of look and a deceptively lazy style of running, he's silenced all his critics.

But there are still some worries in the 0-0 result. Our offense again looks suspect—they get few chances, and Yo-Yo Osheyack's best effort is stopped point-blank by the acrobatic Oyster River keeper (Oyster River goalies are famous, like a rare kind of shellfish—many go on to play in college). Angus, as brilliant as he is defensively, still has this odd psychological reluctance to get inside the other team's box. Disturbing, too, is Rob's refusal to put in any subs, reawakening worries that our bench is dangerously thin. But we undoubtedly have the better of play, we outshoot them 19-4, and we come away with what might be a small but significant psychological edge, heading toward a likely rematch in the playoffs.

Aussie Cyrus, our expat Texan, played a fine game in midfield. He's been nursing a sore knee all season, and when it stiffened up late in the second half and he had to come out, our game lost much of its creative flair. He's built solid, with the low center of gravity so many good soccer players employ; not only does he have a soft touch with his feet, he uses his chest as a kind of pinball cushion, absorbing the hardest of high balls and letting them meekly roll down to the gutter of his cleats. Southerners moving to New England can have a hard time adjusting, and young men of color, in New Hampshire, can feel lonely and out of place, but at home games, Aussie has more friends rooting for him than anyone, and a lot of his tricks—his fakes, dekes, and stutter steps—seem designed just to make them laugh.

He's particularly good with his arms and hands. Standing over a ball, he likes to make a little up-and-down motion with his right hand—the motion a Grand Banks fisherman would make jigging for cod. It's reflexive, random, but it always confuses the defender, and Aussie often follows it up by letting his arms drop slack to his side and dipping his head, like a marionette whose strings have suddenly been severed. What's this?—you can see the defenders look puzzled—and before they can figure out what's happening, Aussie has dished the ball off to an overlapping winger, and it's too late to stop him.

Somewhere among Matt's soccer flotsam downstairs is an old VHS tape called *Soccer Dog*—and the title explains the plot. The little fox terrier that joins his kid's team is pretty good with a soccer ball, though it becomes obvious, a half hour into the film, that the goals it scores are the same one recycled over and over. It may well be the worst soccer movie ever filmed, but like all atrocious classics, it has a classic line. The nerdy, know-nothing father who is dragooned into coaching his son's team, addressing the lads on the first day of practice, stares them straight in the eyes, deepens his voice.

"Boys," he says sententiously, to the eager, upturned faces. "The first thing you need to know about soccer is that the importance of the feet is totally exaggerated."

Funny stuff—but what is not exaggerated, what is in fact vastly underexaggerated, is the role of arms and hands in a sport that except in special circumstances (goalies and throw-ins) strictly prohibits their use. Watching Aussie do his puppet moves got me thinking about this. I started paying closer attention, and I realized that arms and hands provide an expressive, decorative side of soccer that is often overlooked.

Something should have tipped me off to this sooner. Over the years, boys on the team have sprained their wrists and have soldiered on with plastic bubble wrap around their forearms—have played, in effect, armless, at least on one side. Brave of them, selfless—but the truth is, even the best player, hobbled this way, plays terribly. Their feet aren't affected—theoretically, they should be fine—but without that forearm swinging up in a natural, unhindered way, they play as if the weight were shackled to their ankles, not their wrists.

Partly this is a balance issue. Watch players when they warm up, and you'll notice that as they kick a ball with their right foot, the opposite arm (the left arm) swings naturally upward in a counter-weight reflex they're totally unaware of—it just happens. If that same player leans back to put more power or loft into his kick, the arm on the right side, the foot side, will elevate, too—and it's this arm motion that gives a balletlike grace to what otherwise would be merely brutal, clodhopper kicking.

And that's just for starters. If a cross is coming in high, a player is apt to throw his arms up high to get enough lift in his foot to bring it down (Matt does this well; picture an old-time preacher throwing his arms jubilantly in the air and shouting "Hallelujah!"). On headers, the same thing happens, and often, if you watch closely or study a photo, you'll notice the player's hands are tightly clenched, absorbing some of the shock. Hands come up to protect the face if you're standing in a wall before the other team's free kick (picture a see-no-evil monkey); hands protect the groin, too, in that endearingly modest pose even the hardest of players will assume as an attacker stands ready to blast the ball ten yards from where they're standing.

And then there are throw-ins, the one part of the game when field players are allowed to handle the ball legitimately. To me, there's something vaguely comic about it, the way you have to keep both hands on the ball, square yourself to the field, bring it back over your head before flinging it . . . you can't see this without picturing the player saying "Phooey!" or "Bad cess to you!" as they let it go. A charwoman flinging a chamber pot out of a second-story window? A Scotsman tossing whatever it is they toss at Highland games? A two-handed javelin thrower at the Olympics? I'm still trying to find the simile that fits, but throw-ins partake of all these motions. There's something ludicrous and slightly vulgar about it that I can't quite pin down.

Players taking a free kick or corner will often raise one hand just before they kick, letting the other players know to be ready, and though everyone does this differently—there are stern, Episcopalian benedictions; the formal "How!" gesture Indians make in old-time Westerns; oddly wistful waves, as if the player is leaving on a train; the "Fire!" sort of gesture you'd get from an artillery officer standing beside his cannon—the suddenly uplifted hand definitely catches your attention. Then, of course, there is the outward spreading of the arms with uplifted palms you see when an easy shot is scuffed, the famous "full Jesus" gesture (looking up to heaven), or the quicker, more subtle "half Jesus" gesture when the arms don't elevate as high and the palms stay limp.

Players challenging hard for a ball or sprinting like mad down the sideline will sometimes windmill their arms about, perhaps from excess energy that has to be discharged or rupture them. And there's plenty of touching, grabbing, and pulling, too—not as much in high school as there is in the college or pro game, but enough. A defender will reach out to touch an attacker's jersey just to know where they are, keep tabs on them, and this is often a tentative, tender gesture, since no one wants to be called for an obvious foul. When a cross comes into the box, the pushing and shirt pulling can become frantic, the defender counting on the mob to hide this, but clearly the hands are very important now, nasty hands, sneaky hands, hands that grab, poke, and cheat. "Keep your hands to yourself!" Celeste used to yell, when the boys were little—the mother in her simply couldn't take this lying down.

The goalie can always use his hands, of course (what stroke of genius this was, from the game's inventors!), and there is lots to be said about how various keepers use theirs. Ben Harwick, the Hanover goalie, has one very characteristic habit. A long ball will be played behind our defense, he'll run out to scoop it up, and when he does this, he leans down very close to the ground (think of a slinking Groucho Marx) and holds one hand out in front of him with the palm bent stiffly back. "I've got it!" the gesture says, but it comes across as much more imperious than that—it's the gesture of an emperor who simply doesn't accept disobedience as an option. I've seen strikers who would otherwise have a chance for a breakaway stop in their tracks and let Ben have it, unable to penetrate the force of that simple gesture.

It's a two-hour drive from Oyster River back to Hanover, then another half hour back to Lyme. Matt was wiped when we got home, understandably, but he was cranky, too, which wasn't like him. The pressure is getting to him, we decided, the way modern parents do—pressure being the word that explains everything. But it could just have easily been autumn he was feeling, the sad, bittersweet part I used to feel so strongly when I was his age; we could use autumn as our buzz word, and it would explain just as much as pressure, which is to say explain hardly anything other than that the human heart, the young human heart, is often miserably troubled.

The next day he snapped out of it, and we got the second of our two Matthews: the one who can snap, crackle, and pop from sheer energy. He had surprised us by starting in again with his autograph collecting, after not bothering to send any requests out for two years. That day in the mail he hit for two: Edwin van der Sar, Manchester United's Dutch keeper, and Martin Sheen, the famous American actor, who generously included a long personal note. Matt all but ran around the room with them, he was so pleased (interesting; when he's happy like this, he'll unconsciously start calling me Daddy, not Dad). That morning's *Valley News* had his photo in it, going up for a header, and he was excited about that, too, to the point I told Celeste I'd almost prefer the moody Matthew—it was easier on the nerves.

The truth is, the senior-year business, all the warnings we'd heard about how crowded it was, how "pressured," was turning out to be true. Soccer season was always ridiculously busy, and taking five honors courses meant a homework load that was crushing. But it was the added burden of searching for colleges that seemed liable to sink us. We hadn't visited enough campuses, there weren't any windows during soccer when we could fly anywhere, Matt kept adding and subtracting schools on his list, there were two rounds of SATs to get through and at least fifteen application essays to write (the big one that the "common application" requires, then "supplemental" essays for each college), and almost every day the guidance department was sending home reminders of upcoming deadlines.

One of Matt's courses was Great English Novels, and one of the books they were reading was Mary Shelley's *Frankenstein*. The teacher, who was turning out to be maddeningly unpredictable, gave them a predictable enough assignment: to create a Frankenstein monster of their own, one who would exemplify the moral conundrums raised in the novel. Matt's creation was "Joe Perfect"—a specially engineered seventeen-year-old designed specifically to be admitted to any college in the country. His brain would be genetically wired to insure perfect SAT scores; his skin would be a blend of Caucasian, Asian, and African American, the better to play every race/minority card; his muscles would be pumped full of designer steroids so he would excel at sports; and his brain would receive injections of DNA taken from strands of a disinterred George Orwell's hair, so "Joe" could write the perfect admission essay.

"Take my word for it, Matthew," I told him once he finished. "Joe Perfect? Some lab is working on him even as we speak."

(College pressure isn't just felt by boys. In Matt's World Religions class, the teacher invited in a woman who is a self-professed witch, a follower of Wicca. After class, one of the girls took her aside, asked her to come into the library, then, where no one could overhear them, begged the witch to read her future and tell her which college she should apply early decision to: Princeton or Yale.)

What Matt is up against this year is the classic anti-learning dilemma faced by every smart senior: risk taking a class that is interesting but hard, or play it safe in an easier course in which you know you can get an A. He'd taken a risk with Great English Novels, and he was finding it tougher than calculus and physics combined. The required reading list, for a one-semester course, included *David Copperfield*, *Pride and Prejudice*, *Frankenstein*, *Jane Eyre*, *Great Expectations*, *Middlemarch*, *Lord Jim*, *Sons and Lovers*, *To the Lighthouse*—more than four thousand pages of demanding world-class prose.

"*Middlemarch!*" I said, when I saw the list. "That's child abuse, assigning that. I feel like reporting your teacher, Mr.—"

"Mr. G."

"To the authorities. There can be no novel in the entire canon where the sentences move so sluggishly. It's a half hour to get through two paragraphs. It's not reading, it's coal mining."

"Thanks for the encouragement, Dad. We got that *Pride and Prejudice* paper back today."

"The one I helped you on? Did he like my point that Jane Austen is all about sex? Never is the word mentioned, it's all very decorous, but what these characters are endlessly debating is who they are going to spend their adult lives making love to."

"I got a C."

People tell me I'm a leader out there, but I don't know. Maybe. I'm always trying to be aware of what's happening on the field and trying to adjust my position accordingly, and I guess I'm telling other players to do that, too. I've played so much center back by now that everything I'm doing feels automatic. If we clear the ball, we step. If an opposing player has the ball and picks his head up, we drop. If the ball is on the left, we shift that way. These are the principles we focus on, and all I'm doing is shouting to remind everyone to keep an eye on our shape. But as far as leadership goes, it feels like that's what my job is out there, and it's felt that way forever.

Maybe I shouldn't admit this, but I like trying to intimidate the other team through little things. Before the game, I stand with my arms crossed and stare right at the other players' eyes, and when the game starts and the strikers are near me, I shout really loud to the other defenders, get my voice out there as something they've got to deal with. I like to establish myself as a presence as early as possible. Muhammad Ali taught me this, not that I ever saw him, but I've read his autobiography, seen films. I even have his autograph, which is really hard to get now. A lot of strikers trash talk, call us "faggots." You can't play soccer in high school without being called that. You'd think they would call us "rich kids" or "cheaters" or "jerks" just for variety. Nope. It's always "faggots."

Many of my classmates involved in the cheating stuff are on the football team, and there was an article in the paper in which their coach implies that football helped them learn many important lessons and develop into men. I have some trouble with that reasoning; something is wrong about it, but I can't quite figure out what. I went to the big football game last Friday night against Lebanon, and there were teachers there and administrators and students, and we all cheered the "cheaters" when they made a good play. I can't figure that out either. But now it turns out the cocaptains have been "fired" by our AD Mike Jackson because of the cheating, so at least there are the "consequences" everyone is talking about.

I haven't told anyone about this, not even Dad, but I e-mailed some college coaches, or at least filled out these online recruitment forms they have, asking you where you played, how your team is doing, what your grades are like. I just did this without really thinking, and it surprised me how fast coaches got back to me. It's going to complicate the college search. As much as I don't want to be a full-time athlete and a part-time student, I think that soccer is such a positive influence in my life that I should really consider continuing to play. I like how when I'm playing, all of life's anxieties and stresses disappear with the opening kickoff. I like the friendships and opportunities soccer has brought me. I like the "status," small as it is. It would be hard just to blow these off.

The whole soccer team did the five-mile Crop Walk yesterday to raise money for farmers, and Rob was in fine form. He jokingly encouraged us to "take out" the ninety-seven-year-old man leading the march so we could finish first. So far this season he's worn the Barcelona "third" jersey, a Manchester United "away" jersey, and the Croatian national team jersey with a matching set of shorts. Rob likes to arrive at practice with the windows down in his little car, listening to a Wyclef Jean remix of "Another One Bites the Dust," which always gets us laughing.

Apart from being funny, I have come to really appreciate Rob as a coach this year. At practices, he rarely "coaches" for all of practice. Instead, he's thought out a variety of drills, which he tailors to what we need to work on. During games, he takes care of substitutions and will occasionally offer some advice, but mainly he trusts us and puts control of the game into our hands. He doesn't overcoach. I love it when he leaves us alone at halftime and goes for a stroll over to where the spectators are, just so he can chat with them while we figure things out on our own. Down the line from us, the opposing team's coach will be yelling and screaming at his players, and there Rob is in his Croatia jersey, way over on the other side talking to Dad or getting Mom to laugh.

There was a nice article in the Manchester paper about Yo-Yo, how his parents were killed in Ethiopia when he was seven and he was brought to the U.S. He didn't know he was deaf until he was taken to the hospital and given hearing aids. The amazing thing is, he reads the game really well, stares into our eyes and figures out what we're going to do, or reads our lips even when we're a long way away. And now we've learned that he's been selected as a member of the U.S. Deaf Soccer team, which will play in the World Deaf Football Championships in Greece next July.

Giving up our first goal of the season, when and if it happens, will be traumatic. Maybe it would be better if I deliberately scored an "own goal" just to get it out of the way. Only kidding . . . I think.

September's second big game was against our traditional blood rivals, Lebanon, a ten-minute drive down Route 120. For many years, Lebanon was the blue-collar mill town, whereas Hanover was where the rich kids lived, and it was rare to have a football or basketball game between them where fistfights didn't break out in the stands. Even as recently as Matt's sophomore year, there was genuine bad feeling between the soccer teams, and the classic quarterfinal that year, which Hanover won in a penalty shootout after one hundred minutes of incredibly tense and exciting play, saw several players injured in challenges that grew rougher and nastier as the game wore on.

As mentioned, the economic and class differences between the two towns has evened out over the last ten years, with the Lebanon mills now turned into upscale boutiques and the Dartmouth Medical Center having migrated south over the city line. Coach Grabill has made it his personal mission to reduce tensions on and off the playing field—many of the Hanover-Leb soccer players play on the same travel team in the spring, so they've become pals—and he's been, if anything, too successful.

"The Lebanon team is like my family," Rob was quoted as saying in the paper, the morning of the game. He went on to talk about how clean the play always was, how brotherly all the players felt, and how Lebanon was one of the top teams in our division. Come on, Rob! I felt like saying. We weren't joining hands before the game and singing "Kumbaya," but it was pretty close to that now, and there was at least one fan along the crowded, surprisingly quiet sidelines (me) who thought that a little more in the way of old-fashioned-good-clean Lebanon-Hanover bad feeling might make for a lot more interesting and passionate game.

But I wasn't immune to this new Era of Good Feeling. Lebanon High often invites me down to speak to their students about writing, and they always make me feel welcome. The school itself sits just north of downtown, and its soccer field is right in the middle of things, which always guarantees a good crowd. Best of all, their parents include Sue and Larry Higgens, old friends from Lightning, where their son Mackenzie played with Matt. I went over to say hello. Sue is the earth mother of soccer moms. She sits in her folding chair, dispensing goodwill and wisdom, and the only thing that ever worries her is whether Larry, standing with his camera a few yards farther down the line, is going to explode at the refs. This must have happened once upon an ancient time, but Larry, big and bearish as he looks, is the gentlest soccer dad imaginable and spends most of the game whispering "Oh boy! Oh boy!" as the play surges back and forth. Nevertheless, Sue views him as a loose cannon, and her worried admonitions to him—"Larry! Careful now!"—form one of the funniest, most reliable husband-wife routines in Upper Valley soccer.

The game, once it began, was as tight as everyone expected. Lebanon had lost its best and roughest players to graduation, and there was something a bit tentative and sluggish in the way they played. Through a strange soccer chemistry that is very common, they dumbed us down into playing the same way. The refs, perhaps responding to rough Lebanon-Hanover games of the past, blew their whistles at the slightest contact, so just as play began to flow, everyone would have to stop for yet another free kick. Angus Kennedy broke in alone on goal, but the Leb keeper, Andrew Kelly (another old teammate from Lightning), made a great sprawling save. In the meantime, Mackenzie Higgens, playing out of position in midfield (he was born to be a defenseman), won ball after ball in the air, which was something we weren't used to, play in the air being one of our strengths.

It was the pride and joy of Pinnacle Hill Road in Lyme, Eric Barthold, who finally scored. This came off a Ben Rimmer throw-in that skipped past a defender and came to an unmarked Eric waiting eight yards out to the goal's left. This had become Eric's spot, the spot, and this was his fifth or sixth goal taken from the exact same position. Eric had long been dealing with a medium-bad case of a disease that can be all too common among talented young soccer players. He was so good so young that in middle school he was capable of dribbling around five or six defenders to get an unassisted goal. Naturally, when the competition stiffened, this became impossible, and yet that same instinct remained: to do it all by himself. Eric—and you could see this very plainly—was in the process of crossing that line that separates the solo soccer superhero from the outstanding, integrated team player. Finding the spot—the spot, the place in the box where so many nice things can happen if you arrive there in time and wait—was an important milestone in this transformation. When the cross came to him, he kept his head down, concentrated, and made no mistake. 1-0 Hanover.

In the meantime, the Border Patrol was cleaning up any problems in the back, all but frisking the Lebanon attackers, demanding passports, and refusing them entry. Cal got a little rough with this—put his shoulder into a Lebanon striker inside the penalty area and was lucky not be called for police brutality—but other than that, Lebanon could not mount any credible threats. Matt led from the back, calling out instructions, pointing, waving, cheering, and it was his voice, as usual, that dominated the on-field chatter.

The half ended 1-0, which wasn't a commanding lead, but there was enough confidence in our style to make me feel the game was in the bag. I walked down the line opining as much to some fellow dads, walked on to the port-a-potty, then, as long as I was that far from the field, decided I had time for a little stroll.

I ended up sitting on a bench outside the school. A small group of students played Hacky Sack near the gym, silently, dreamily, like mimes in training. Beyond them, freckle-faced field hockey players laughed with each other as they hurried toward practice. Back over the field, the cumulus had widened to let in the sun, and the crisp autumn light seemed to shrink players and spectators alike, so they appeared much more distant than they were in fact. Or perhaps something in my own mood made them seem distant; a few seconds ago, I had been part of it, as passionately involved as anyone, and now I seemed to be looking down at the experience from another planet.

Well, maybe I would be, this time next year. Having the last of my kids go off to college loomed like retirement looms for those with conventional careers, a decisive turning point I wasn't at all sure I was ready for. Certainly, I was rapidly approaching a point at which the multiple demands of child raising (harder now than ever) were wearing me out—not the normal daily wear and tear, but the deeper, more essential exhaustion you reach when you realize that nature simply does not equip us to burn the same parental fuel forever. But one of the things I really enjoyed about being a father was that it gave you a very direct connection to every young person you saw, a paternal investment, a cross-generational bond. Having a son still at home made me feel that not only was every seventeen-year-old I saw of immediate interest and concern to me, but so was every kid younger than this, every toddler, every baby. I was still an active, hands-on dad, and that meant somehow a dad to everyone. Maybe this connection would continue as Erin and Matthew grew older—they would undoubtedly keep me up to date on what twentysomethings were thinking—but the intensity of the link wouldn't be the same, nor the softness, the tenderness drawn out of me in the course of a normal day.

I knew myself well enough to suspect that I would probably never attend another high school soccer game once my son stopped playing.

This is what I was a little sad with, as I sat there watching the way I probably would always watch soccer in the future, or watch childhood for that matter—from the distance, in passing, from the far side of nostalgia.

But as long as I was feeling some distance, I decided I might as well put it to work. There was still plenty of parenting to do, speaking locally. Hanover High's cheating scandal had become a major national news story, with not only the *New York Times* and the *Boston Globe* doing stories on it, but *People* magazine, *Good Morning America*, and even the *Wall Street Journal*. Students had become used to seeing TV cameras and reporters waiting on the sidewalk (or fed up with seeing them—a Coke bottle had been hurled at an NPR reporter's feet), and with the eight Democrat presidential candidates in town for a debate and a trailing press corps, the story fed on itself in the usual over-the-top American frenzied media way. Not since two Dartmouth professors were brutally murdered in their home six years ago had Hanover received such unwelcome attention. Affluent, Ivy League town that takes academic honesty seriously. An organized "ring" of cheaters. The break-in aspect. Yes, the story was juicy. It may even have been significant, but seniors and parents of seniors suddenly felt themselves drafted to fight on an ethical battleground they would have preferred to dodge.

"Did you hear what the *Valley News* did?" Matt asked, when we took a break from Great English Novels to talk it all through. "Their reporter called up all these admissions directors at all these colleges and asked them what their opinion was. Now every college in America thinks of Hanover students as cheaters."

This was my own fear, of course, but one I needed to keep hidden. "Nah, they're smarter than that, these admissions people. They know a good student when they see one. Anyway, I called up your guidance counselor, and he says he's going to stress the academic integrity of those who weren't involved."

"Yeah?" Matt frowned; he wasn't quite ready to let go of it. "I think it all stinks."

"It's called being tarred by the same brush."

"I wonder about coaches, too, whether they've read the stories or seen us on TV."

Something in the way he said this made me glance across the table at him.

"Coaches?"

"I had an e-mail."

"From a soccer coach?"

"Three of them. Three different college coaches I mean. I had a phone call, too."

This was big news. I felt the wary surprise you get when a possibility that has been tamed, neutered, kept under wraps, suddenly escapes again—but I decided that while we were on subject, it might be best to keep on subject.

"You've been talking anymore to any of these kids? The cheaters?"

"Don't call them that. They're not all bad."

"The alleged cheaters?"

"They hang out together, they move through the hall in a huddle. They're football players. Two guys on our team were questioned, but the police didn't charge them."

"You mean the soccer team? Does Rob know?"

Matt had been learning a lot from reading the papers. "No comment," he said. Then, in an even more puzzled voice, "Hey, in *Frankenstein*, how does the monster learn to speak such perfect English?"

Local reaction to the scandal has been all over the map, from some people saying, in so many words, that the alleged cheaters should be hanged, to others who are ready to lead a march on the town hall protesting police brutality. One response is so old-fashioned that it's almost endearing. "Well," more than one person has told me, after we've talked about the incident, "boys will be boys."

How boys will be boys is one of the dilemmas everyone is struggling with these days. You can hardly pick up a magazine or turn on the television without hearing yet another report on the crisis among boys, how poor their performance is in school, how ambitionless they all seem, how listless or hyper or medicated or stoned. Even carving away the ugly fat of hyperbole, there seems to be much truth in this, speaking solely from what I can observe here in town. We live in as favorable an environment to raise a child as can be found in the United States; we have good schools, involved parents, beautiful countryside, cultural and recreational opportunities second to none; and yet, out of the fifteen boys who graduated with Matt from eighth grade, at least nine seem to have come crashing down in various kinds of emotional/behavioral flames.

One boy, a sweet kid I coached in basketball, has been arrested for car theft and vandalism. Another has struggled through a mysterious case of male anorexia. Two others have been sent at the town's expense to one special school after another, trying to deal with (in one case) his absolute refusal to accept even the mildest form of discipline and (in the other case) a depression that puts him at risk of suicide. Another boy has twice crashed his parents' SUVs. Another steals wine from the supermarket and slinks away into the woods to sullenly chug it down. Another . . . but it's too sad to go on. These are boys we've known since they were infants. Things are not going well for them, and it's hard to know exactly who or what to blame, aside from the usual suspects.

Divorce. Absentee fathers. The changing roles of the sexes. Additives in food. Economic uncertainty. Cynicism/dishonesty/ nihilism trickling down from on high. Drugs, legal and illegal. The spiritual side effects of capitalism/imperialism/militarism/hedonism. Celebrity worship. Video games. Rebellion against the absurdity of today's world. You can add your own reason, or close your eyes and throw a dart at my wretched list, but the overall conclusion is the same in all instances: that our contemporary culture makes it very difficult for young men to come of age.

If the cheating scandal has done nothing else, it's given people with even the slightest claim on moral expertise a platform from which to pontificate about the "boy crisis"—but I'm not going to join their ranks. When it comes to solving the problem on a national level, I have absolutely no suggestions whatsoever. On a more personal level—what I can do to help my son grow up—I have lots to say, have perhaps said most of it already. As hackneyed and vague as the phrase is, I try to be there for him, not just at soccer games, but when it comes to plowing through *Middlemarch*. I try to give him values and interests that are not just those of his teenaged peers. I continue to work hard at marriage. I am passionately involved in my vocation and avocations and try to include him when I can, but I hope most of all that he finds his own. I try, when it comes to politics, to keep a lid on my growing cynicism and despair. I try to be happy—how fiercely do sons want their fathers to be happy! I try to say yes more than no, but make the noes count. If I often have to be the voice of reality, I try to make it a soft and honest voice. I watch my weight, wear my seat belt, go easy on alcohol, and keep an eye on what emulation might be teaching on the sly.

If that translates into a prescription for bringing up a twenty-first-century son, then it's one that will never be widely available—reading George Eliot together!—but perhaps the problem is so overwhelming that it can be answered only at the level that counts, between each son and each father, if not exactly the way we've done it, then by something commensurate. Matt and I have been lucky; I'll say no more than that. I'm too superstitious, too frightened of forces I don't understand, to claim Matt is through the worst, most dangerous years when so much in a young man's life can go wrong.

As for the "Hanover 9" and what should be done with them, I'm afraid I'm in the suspend-their-butts camp. They have done real measurable harm to the school, the community, and my son—there is simply no other moral conclusion I am able to grasp—and if I feel protective and angry and vindictive, then it's a natural, gut-level response I don't apologize for having. And yet, when I remember the little boys they were such a short time ago, I want to hide my face in my hands and sob.

Soccer—judging by the sudden whistle, the crowd sounds, the grunt of the ball—had started up again, though it felt so distant I had to stare and squint to get it back. It was past 5:00 now, the sun had dropped low enough on the horizon that it was giving our goalie Ben Harwick fits, and I realized I needed to add another characteristic hand gesture to my list: a goalie standing with his hand against his eyebrows, peering into the sun—a prairie kind of posture, the silhouette of a cowboy or a seer.

Even with the big crowd, my absence had been noted. "Hey, where you been?" Chris Kennedy said when I walked back to the line. "Same old same old!" Sue Higgens called cheerfully/ruefully, pointing toward the scoreboard. Joanie Barthold came over for the little hug she always gets when Eric scores a goal. "Is that really tea in there?" Larry Higgens asked, pointing to my thermos, resurrecting an old standing joke. "Good to be back," I felt like saying. My little hundred-yard stroll could have been to the North Pole.

Hanover was in the process of taking control of the second half. Angus put on a one-man show in midfield, breaking up every Lebanon attack before it could get started. If our four defenders formed the Border Patrol, he was the zealous state trooper, pulling people over before they could cause trouble. I realized, watching him, that his true talent resided in his creativity in destroying the opposing player's creativity. Case, his cocaptain (miraculously cured of his mono), was playing with the same kind of intensity, though, as always, there was a comic undertone to it as he battled gallantly with his endearingly clumsy feet. He won the battle for a crucial three seconds—he sent a low grass cutter past Andrew Kelly's right for what obviously was the winner.

2-0 Hanover, full time. Not too much in the way of celebration, from either players or fans—a rematch was coming in October, and there was a strong possibility we would face them in the playoffs for the third year running. The talent was clearly on Hanover's side, but the odds were swinging toward Lebanon, and surely their time would come.

It was the Border Patrol's seventh shutout in a row—a remarkable feat, but in the way of these things, it was starting to bring a certain pressure. Would it be possible to go the entire season without being scored upon? Chris and I, glancing at the schedule, realized there were only three or four teams left that had a reasonable chance of getting a goal against us. Last year's team had allowed only nine goals, nearly a record for stinginess, but had any Hanover soccer team managed to be unscored upon for an entire season? We talked it over, decided to ask Rob. Greatness—in the very limited but nonetheless glorious high school sense of the word—seemed like a real possibility.

I went up to our defenders after the game intending to congratulate them, but two things held me back. The first was the realization that all our players helped mightily on defense—it wasn't just the back four. The second was the unaccountable shyness I always felt the first minutes after a game, when the players, even my son, seemed enveloped by an aura of glory I was too timid to penetrate. Go over and shake everyone's hands after a victory like this? It was like getting up the nerve to shake hands with the 1961 Yankees after they had just won the World Series; it required a chutzpah I simply didn't have.

The players were in the bus now, the fans had packed their chairs and driven away in their minivans, until it was only me left on the field like a last piece of litter, staring toward the west and the keyhole of light left by the sunset. It didn't take a particularly introspective man to understand what was written in those clouds—it was a plain and chilly enough script. Time to put snow tires on, stack firewood, insulate the windows, wrap the house up snug. Time to look toward bigger things, too. Winter is coming, softness can't last, and whatever it is you want to do in life as regards compassion and tenderness and pity and love, better do it soon, time is passing, do it now, time is cruel.

7

MIDTERMS

The season picked up speed as October deepened, and everyone wanted to hold it back.

Coach Grabill wanted to savor the team's accomplishments, hang the experience on the wall, and marvel like a connoisseur, but there was always another practice to organize, another minor crisis to surmount, details needing attending to in a way that made time blur. The parents felt again the bewildering pace that comes with getting older, a month flying by like a week, a week passing like a long afternoon. The seniors lived in the moment, as seventeen-year-olds should, but that moment seemed more fragile than others in their lives as they began to realize that what they were racing through so fast was their final season together, and they would soon be facing their first senior year lesson in saying good-bye.

The regular season comprised sixteen games, and each one, printed boldly there on the schedule, acted like a protective wall separating all that was soccer from all that was not. PLYMOUTH loomed like a pyramid on an empty plain, and when that pyramid crumbled, there was MONADNOCK, as square and solid as a fortress, and when that disappeared below the horizon, there was SOUHEGAN, a castle inside a protective moat, and when those turrets sank, there was always the second LEBANON game, the reassuring roadblock that would surely stop time in its tracks. "I can't believe we've played six games already!" became "I can't believe the season is half over!" became "I can't believe next week starts playoffs!" Believe, I felt like saying—but I couldn't believe myself.

We were having two styles of games, depending on geography. Our games to the southeast toward Massachusetts were at new high schools built by affluent suburbs to house-exploding enrollments— these games were evenly matched, suspenseful, tight. Our games to the south, directly below us along the western edge of the state, were always blowouts, played against undermanned teams in aging high schools where the student population was often in decline. Temporary classrooms, built in the go-go eighties, were still in place at the back of the gyms, so the schools resembled old-fashioned New Hampshire farmhouses with an ever-diminishing, ever-shabbier series of back buildings attached to the original house and barn. The soccer fields were so lumpy with neglect that the soccer ball, in protest, would take on a life of its own, skipping randomly off damp hummocks or sinking deep into flinty divots and sulking there until a boot drove it out.

Rob would keep the starters in for thirty minutes just to give them some exercise, then, with the score 6-0, in would come the reserves. He tended to keep the Border Patrol in longer than he might have otherwise, saying, in public, that he didn't care about our unscored-upon record, but he was obviously starting to be seduced by the whole romantic notion of coaching a team that goes the entire season without being scored upon at all.

Outcome-wise, there was no reason to make the long drive to any of these games, but having seen every minute of every match so far, it seemed a nice streak to keep going, and maybe it would be important to Matthew someday to say his father was always there through the course of his final season. But the truth is, I greatly enjoyed these games, or at least enjoyed traveling down to those half-forgotten towns: Swanzey, lost in the scrubby woods south of Keene; Charlestown, the old French and Indian war outpost along the Connecticut River that seemed, in the autumn twilight, a lonely outpost still; Claremont, a faded mill town that was fighting hard to reinvent itself. This was solid blue-collar small-town America, America as it once was—or at least it seemed like that, and although it may have been an illusion, it's one I took comfort in—my season's guilty little pleasure.

At all these games, there would be moments of happiness and poignancy both. At Fall Mountain, who should be dancing along the sidelines but the school's cheerleading squad in their little ski hats and mittens. Their football cheers didn't really work for soccer, but they kept up with them anyway, and the worse their boys played, the louder they cheered. At Monadnock, it was Senior Day. All the parents of senior players got flowers, but the game started at 3:30, the parents obviously couldn't get out of work that early, so the boys handed the flowers to each other. At Claremont, there were more cheerleaders, the stands were full of supportive fans, and they had a gutsy little midfielder, the team captain, who exhorted them on with such never-say-die spirit that Rob wanted to adopt him onto our team, the way Iroquois once adopted their bravest enemies.

There were two problems with these easy victories. Aesthetically, they didn't bring out the talent in us, the art; the boys knew they were going to win, knew it wouldn't take much effort, and so the games became a passionless display of technical competence without much heart. Morally, the team hadn't been tested yet. Things had been far too easy, and the lessons that come with falling behind and struggling back again, or losing at the last tragic second and rebounding in the next game, had yet to be learned. And physical challenges—we had yet to meet a team that played dirty and rough. This made Rob uneasy, it worried the supporters, and it made everyone feel that even with an eleven-game unbeaten streak, we still had lots left to prove.

The chance to play beautifully finally came against Hollis-Brookline at home. It was a cool, crisp Saturday—"football weather" they call it, those benighted souls who persist in the delusion that football is America's game. Dartmouth was playing Princeton in their refurbished stadium three hundred yards away, and roars from the crowd, shorn of passion, were breezelike whispers by the time they reached our stands. In warm-ups, it was obvious the boys were "on," though the signs of this would be hard to explain; suffice it to say, for someone who had been watching them since they were six, it was clear from their body language and their laughter that they were going to play extraordinarily well.

"It's in the bag," I told Joanie Barthold.

"Yeah?" she said, wanting to trust me, but not quite sure.

Jeff Cook had come to the game, the Dartmouth coach, along with Chris Cheney, who had coached most of the boys in Lightning, and their presence was noted; the boys, as the game started, seemed to preen, putting extra little flourishes into their headers or hustling top speed to save balls from rolling out of bounds. Hollis-Brookline had an odd record for a good team—they had dropped the first three games of the season and won everything since—but one of our parents knew from another parent who had a friend in the south of the state that several of their key players had been suspended for some unspecified disciplinary issue, which explained those early-season losses.

We won 2-0, but it wasn't as close as the score suggests. Ten minutes were gone when Yo-Yo got open for a header, and while their goalie saved it, Eric was waiting in the spot to slot it home. Exactly one minute later, Angus drilled in a grass cutter from twenty yards out, and that was that, with the Border Patrol refusing to give the Hollis-Brookline strikers even a peek at goal. Aesthetically, our play was all anyone could hope for. Our passing was imaginative and beautifully creative, the field seemed to sizzle with understanding and thought, and if a defender faltered for even a second, there was a teammate behind him to bail him out and often a third defender waiting as a last-ditch reserve. In the air, we were unbeatable—I counted a series of five headers that brought the ball all the way from our deepest corner to their goalmouth without it ever touching the ground. It may not have been the team's masterpiece, but, in the gallery of beautiful high school soccer games, it was definitely a keeper.

The team's first moral test came on the afternoon of a "test" morning. The SATs were on October 6, and our kids, like millions across the country, trudged into the gym to try and figure them out, just as I had myself forty years earlier. Matt, when he came out again four hours later, was one of those smiling. "I think I aced it," he told me, when he was sure no one else could hear. I handed him his sandwich, asked him if he had his mouth guard, wished him luck, then waved as he climbed into the team bus for the two-hour drive to Dover on the coast. Celeste and I were right behind them in the car; it was her fiftieth birthday, Erin had come up from Mount Holyoke to join in the celebrations, and between teasing about the big 5-0 and getting caught up on what was happening in college, what can be a laborious drive went by very fast.

St. Thomas is one of the few Catholic high schools in the state, and rather than playing sports in a parochial league, they're incorporated into the public school system. In other years, they've been patsies, but they were much improved now, with only one loss going into the afternoon's game. On a hillside overlooking their field, someone had planted signs with blown-up copies of a newspaper article that had appeared at the start of the season predicting who would be contenders for the state championship. Hanover was listed there, Bow, Souhegan, and Lebanon, but not St. Thomas—and through all but the first of these names, someone had drawn a heavy black slash, marking another upset St. Thomas victory. A nice Jesuit bit of psychological warfare—and, to add to the pressure, Hanover had a long tradition of playing poorly after SATs and had lost that day the last two years in a row.

Tradition continued. The boys started sluggishly, while St. Thomas played fresh, hungry, and confident—had they done better than our boys on verbal and math? Their fans were the first semiobnoxious ones we'd encountered all year; they were on the ref immediately, particularly one little cluster who, as they picnicked on the hillside, gesticulated angrily with their chicken wings. Hanover fans, in the meantime, stood on top of the hill and looked worried—never had a team jumped out at us with such energy, and never had we been so dull in response.

But soccer can be a funny game that way. Five minutes in, just when it seemed we were fainting from ennui, Angus Kennedy, with his newfound willingness to shoot, put in one of his patented grass cutters from thirty yards out. That seemed to restore us—for all of fifty-three seconds. After the restart, one of the St. Thomas wingers broke clear on the right, centered the ball over the top of our defenders, and found an onrushing striker who headed a looper that found the back of the net. St. Thomas, who knew full well that Hanover hadn't conceded a goal all season, celebrated like they had just won the state championship.

Eleven games without being scored upon. The dream, the illusion, of going an entire season without giving up a goal—gone, in a brutal instant, and the boys looked stunned. Parents, stunned likewise, immediately confabbed. Not a bad thing, we quickly decided. Now the pressure was off, the burden was lifted, and the boys could relax and concentrate on soccer basics.

Or not. Clearly, the goal had rattled our boys badly, and Matt worst of all. Again, an over-the-top cross came in from the right, this time landing at the striker's feet. He was one on one with Matt—the other defenders had been lured out of position, so for once there was no backup—but all the Hanover fans relaxed, knowing it was dependable, unflappable Matt Wetherell who had him covered.

What Matt would usually do in this situation is crouch down like a guard playing defense in basketball, ready to shift this way or that in response to the attacker's moves. What he actually did do (and watching from the hillside, this looked as inexplicable as it truly was) was to stroll past him the way a pedestrian strolls by someone on the sidewalk, heedlessly, casually, not giving him a second thought. The striker, quickly overcoming his amazement, blasted a shot on goal that Ben didn't have a chance for—and thanks to my son's error, Hanover was losing a game for the first time all season.

In England, soccer writers call such lapses moments of madness, and that's exactly what it seemed. Had Matthew gone nuts? Not since that disastrous own goal in Nashua when he was thirteen had he made such a glaring error. I knew he felt terrible about it, because the embarrassment drained right down through his legs to his cleats to the ground through the grass over to me. It hurt! Hurt terribly. Play resumed, he began flying around like a dervish trying to atone. St. Thomas fouled Angus just inside midfield, Matt stepped up to take the free kick, put it right where he wanted to in the box, and their goalie dropped it onto the feet of a waiting Eric Jayne, who punched it home. A vital goal, coming just before halftime, partly redeeming Matthew, partly redeeming us.

We had a soccer-mom-and-dad birthday party for Celeste during halftime. Blueberry muffins, a candle, fake champagne. All of the guests were far too polite to mention Matt's moment of madness. Tests of character in sports are different from tests of character in ordinary life: they almost always occur in public in a very short period of time, whereas the trials life throws at us usually have to be overcome in private over the course of many years. Hanover, experiencing adversity for the first time all season, had forty minutes left to prove itself. Could we take a punch? Spring back off the canvas? Come out swinging?

The answer was . . . yes. The instructions Rob gave them in his forty-five-second pep talk (the rest of halftime he spent over on the sidelines wishing Celeste a happy birthday) had immediate effect, as we were on them right from the kickoff, our SAT doldrums a thing of the past. In the first half, we were sending lone rangers forward, not an organized posse, but now possession passes were being exchanged at midfield, building the attack with more patience and craft; Angus and Aussie were laying balls off to an overlapping Trevor on the right or Sam on the left, and their crosses were asking questions of the St. Thomas defense that were being awkwardly addressed. It seemed inevitable Hanover would score, but, in soccer, the longer it seems inevitable that someone will score, the more likely it becomes that no one will score. So, we were surprised and not surprised when, with only five minutes left on the clock, Case headed a shot that their goalie misplayed, and Eric, waiting in the spot, side-footed it home for a 3-2 Hanover victory.

A character builder, no doubt about it. Adversity practice. A test that, in the context of what the boys hoped to achieve this season, was of more immediate relevance than those hated SATs. Matt coped well with his moment of madness; he appeared mature enough to understand that shit happens, and rather than shaking his self-confidence, it made him more eager than ever to prove himself—and prove himself on a larger canvas. The biggest surprise of the season for Celeste and me was that perhaps it would not be our son's final year of soccer after all. He had received several e-mails from college coaches as word of Hanover's extraordinary defense spread; two coaches had actually called the house, and we were all scrambling to understand what this meant.

Playing in college was never Matt's dream. Making high school varsity, starting there, winning state championships—those were what we focused on, as worthy, within-reach aspirations. As talented as he was, there was that matter of pace, which, although adequate for high school, seemed to rule him out of playing further—but then (and this is where the surprise was) his pace, thanks to all the running he had done in the spring and summer, had considerably improved. He'd had an extraordinary season, he was the leader of a defense that might very well turn out to be the stingiest in New Hampshire history, former teammates were already doing well on college teams, and so playing another four years suddenly began to seem not like a strong possibility, but at least a possible possibility.

Whether we should pursue this was another question. One of the reasons I had never encouraged Matt to think about playing college was that I had lots of doubts on that score—not just whether he was fast enough, but whether it was a good idea even if he were. I'd met various Dartmouth players over the years, knew how single-minded and monkish they had to be, to the exclusion of much that was valuable in the college experience. College was about focusing on the future, sports was about living in the moment; and I thought the former should begin to be his priority. I also felt a bit like my father or grandfather would have if their sons had wanted to play. "Soccer schmoccer! Go to college to play a silly game in shorts? And for this we shell out fifty Gs a year?"

But now that we were possibly at this point, I began to look at things a little differently. Matt loved soccer, he was having more fun now than ever, grades had never been a problem for him, he had lots of interests outside the sport (music, politics, marine biology, and film, for starters), so monomania wasn't an issue, and, quite naturally, he felt sad to think his playing days would soon be over. Wanting to postpone this parting for a few more years was perfectly understandable.

In terms of concentration and focus, it was probably a good thing that Hanover's next game was against Souhegan, a tough opponent from the south of the state. This year's team had a reputation that preceded them: trash-talking prima donnas who grabbed and pulled in the dark, secret corners of their poorly lighted field. An exciting game—but I'll let Rob Grabill tell the story for a change. After every match, Rob writes up a game report, posts it on the team's soccer blog, and sends it off to the local newspapers, which often print it verbatim, including Rob modestly quoting Rob.

The Hanover boys took another important step toward postseason with a hard-fought 2-1 road victory over a strong Souhegan squad on Saturday night. Goals by Casey Maue and Matt Wetherell and superb Hanover defense paved the way for Hanover's thirteenth victory of the season, extending their two-year unbeaten run to twenty-one games and maintaining their hold on top of the table in Class I. The game, pitting two of New Hampshire's perennial powers, had a playoff feel to it and produced glorious soccer on both sides of the ball.

Souhegan's 9–5 record entering the contest was deceiving.

The Sabers play the toughest schedule in the division, facing every top team, most of them twice. Although their regular season record sometimes suffers as a result, few teams will be better prepared for postseason play, and no one will want to see Souhegan in their playoff bracket.

Hanover took their task seriously, however, and was more than ready for every challenge they faced from the Sabers. Hanover's best chances came early on from the outside, with Angus Kennedy (a two-way monster all night) grazing the crossbar on one free kick and blasting a second restart into the groins of the Souhegan defensive wall.

The Sabers spent less time in Hanover's end, but one foray was dangerous, with striker Tim Eagen breaking for a shot that should have found pay dirt. With the half winding down, Casey Maue (aka "The Wildebeest") had his hustle rewarded when he won a ball in the box and worked free for a shot that rippled the onion bag and gave the Marauders a 1-0 lead with less than a minute to play in the half.

Hanover anticipated a strong push from S'hegan in the second half, but it was the Marauders who turned up the heat on their hosts, generating a number of good scoring chances in search of their second goal.

Back in the Hanover end, the back four were ruling the air and doing a great job containing Souhegan's attack, particularly speedy all-state midfielder Jonathan Harris, whose father was coached by Hanover's Rob Grabill in prehistoric times twenty-five years ago.

As the game wound down toward the ten-minute mark, it looked as though Hanover might be content to play out the string and claim their first 1-0 victory of the year.

Harris had another idea, however, breaking free on the left flank and coming in clean on the Hanover goal. Ben Harwick slid out and made a sliding save on Harris, but the ball popped free, and striker Jess Anderson was first to the ball, tying the game at 1-1.

With every reason to be frustrated, the Marauders wasted no time in regaining the lead.

Thirty seconds after the restart, a foul gave Hanover a free kick forty yards out. Angus Kennedy lofted a ball into the Souhegan penalty area, where a determined Matt Wetherell, leaping highest in a crowd, headed it home for his fourth goal of the season and a 2-1 lead.

The one-goal advantage seemed safe, and as the clock wound down, it was again Hanover pressing for more.

"The win was a very satisfying one," Coach Grabill said as his weary troops headed back to the bus and three waiting jumbo-sized boxes of

Dunkin' Donuts, "and gave us confidence that we'll be able to handle
whatever the postseason hands out."

Everything was soccer that fall—soccer was the majestic triviality that
kept meaner trivialities at bay—and yet it wouldn't last much longer,
so everything about the experience came coated in poignancy, and yet
even poignancy couldn't slow time down. I had stayed ahead of events
with my writing, but now they were out in front of me. I was writing
not about games that happened that week, but games from the week
before that or even further back.

I kept a notebook, something I'd never done before, but all it was
now was a flat, rain-smudged monument to futility, a catalog of
scenes, events, stories, and images I would never have the space to
write about properly. The second Lebanon game, for example, Leb at
home before 750 people, when Rob pulled off what was meant to be
a wonderful surprise, rewarding the boys for the four thousand dollars they raised in the Crop Walk by buying them blindingly bright
yellow uniforms in the latest European style to unveil just before
kickoff when the boys peeled off their warmups—uniforms bought
with Gold Club bonus points Rob had earned by buying so many
replica jerseys for himself through the mail—and yes, they were
blinding all right, but distracting, too, with the new socks hanging
loose on the boys' calves, so they were constantly reaching down to
pull them up, undoubtedly a factor in a game that after two overtimes

resulted in a disappointing 1-1 tie, so at practice the following day, when Rob asked his grim, discouraged players sitting in a circle at his feet if there was anything they would like to get off their chests, Cal Felicetti immediately raised his hand and said, "Coach? Can you promise us we'll never have to wear those uniforms again?" ("Cal," Rob later said, when trying to sum up for a reporter how gutsy he is, "was the only one of my players with the fortitude to tell me my uniforms were crap.") . . . and then, after writing about how the tie felt like a loss and how psychologically that was not necessarily a bad thing at this stage of the season, I'd include a quick update on what the parents were doing, Celeste joining with five others to operate an impromptu concession stand to do a little fund-raising—chili, hot dogs, hot chocolate, and lemon squares—and how this immediately became a big hit, a gathering spot on the terrace above the field where students, parents, and fans could socialize before, during, and after the game, our alcohol-free version of an outdoor pub, where we talked, among other subjects, about the outstanding way those seniors who weren't starters played when they got their chance, Dylan Riessen, Erick Barth, Oliver Horton, Paul Burchard, whose unsung value to the team wasn't just a coach's cliché, a contribution recognized on Senior Night, which was a tearjerker if you stopped to think about it, Rob making an appropriately moving, uncharacteristically brief speech over the PA system, the parents meeting their sons at midfield to be handed bouquets, and, for once without embarrassment, hugged—and a quick tangent slipping in mention of our favorite soccer movie, *A Shot at Glory*, wherein a star player well past his prime (played by Ali McCoist, the famous Glasgow Rangers striker), down on his luck, needing the money, signs on for a lowly second-division Scottish team and leads it to the finals of the Scottish Cup—a movie featuring a brilliantly over-the-top Robert Duvall doing a prolonged imitation of Sir Alex Ferguson, and, if that wasn't enough to wow us, the movie ends on a salmon river with Duvall showing McCoist how to fly fish—a tangent that probably wouldn't lead very smoothly into a paragraph about getting to Matt's game early and watching the last half of the girls' game, looking for the differences in style, enjoying these thoroughly—the girls' efforts more visible in their expressions, the individual personalities stand-ing out with more distinction than with the boys, the rooting and cheering louder from the bench, the speed not faster but faster look-ing, the wheels spinning with more fury, the pigtails streaming, the surprising roughness combined with a certain tiptoe confusion that made them look, just in flashes, like very little little girls—and then, coming back to the boys again, darkening the mood just slightly, certain sudden and surprising signs of disquiet in the team's morale, Rob acting, for the first time anyone could remember, like a typical coach, getting mad at small things, snapping out at players, and then, feeling terrible about it, coming over to their house to talk things out, making us wonder if there were strains and fissures we didn't know about, ones that could crack the team apart just before the challenge of the playoffs, a worry interrupted only long enough to point out that once you get past the first five hundred pages, *Middlemarch* turns out to be pretty good—all these things, and then those random moments of beauty I tried to press between the pages of my notebook: a full hunter's moon rising over the playing field so we hardly needed lights; the spray kicked up by cleats when we played in the rain, each boy the centerpiece in his own private fountain; headers, volleys, and flicks that almost went in, wonderfully struck, just high or just wide, not quite goals and so neither honored nor commemorated, except by half-illegible scratches in the notebook of an aging writer trying to get it all down, every flash, every happening, before time swept it away.

The regular season ended with the team undefeated at the top of Class I—and, as a result, we were seeded number one in the state tourney, with our first playoff game scheduled at home the following Tuesday night. Several records had either already been achieved or could soon be achieved if the boys played as flawlessly as they had all season and had a little help from fate. They were the first Hanover team to go undefeated in the regular season for fifteen years. They had scored more goals than any Hanover team in more than thirty-five years (so much for my preseason worries about offense). They had thirteen shutouts, which meant, if they managed to play all four possible playoff games without giving up a goal, they could tie the state record for season shutouts at seventeen. If they did this, gave up no playoff goals whatsoever, then they would hold the all-time record for fewest goals allowed during a full New Hampshire season—four—a truly remarkable achievement. If they became state champs, it would be the first time in fifty years of Hanover soccer that the team had won three championships in a row—a state championship that would also put us ahead of Class M Gilford for the most in state history—and, for that matter, give Hanover more state championships than all but four high schools in the entire United States.

If. It seemed, watching the boys practice, that this is what they were preparing themselves for—to scale the treacherously sheer, dangerously icy cliff of If, where fate, just before the top, could hurl you into the abyss just for laughs. They had already accomplished much that was memorable and special, but no one had any illusions about how cruel sports can be that way—do poorly in the playoffs, have one irredeemable moment of inattention or bad luck, and all that would be forgotten. (Every state final for as long as anyone could remember had been decided by a one-goal margin.) How far skill and passion could take them was very much the question, but they had raised the stakes themselves, and if perfection was within reach now, the word itself seemed the one thing standing in their way, making the possibilities too melodramatically stark: perfection or failure, with no room in between. Not for nothing had Rob printed targets on the back of their practice shirts when the season first started. Sixteen teams were in the playoffs—the argy-bargy, the cocky, the confident, the contenders—and they all had Hanover in their sights.

8

FINALS

Rooting for an undefeated season in soccer is like rooting for impossibility. In no other sport is superiority so tenuous, are upsets so common. Football has its juggernauts, baseball its big red machines, basketball its dynasties—but in soccer, thanks to the difficulty of scoring, the most dominant team often loses. The U.S. amateurs stun England's best in the 1950 World Cup; the minnows from Greece humble the glamour teams at Euro '04; an English second-division side knocks Manchester United out of the Carling Cup; the Faroe Islands, on its peaty home turf, gives fits to any team in the world. There is no sure thing in soccer, which is simultaneously its allure and its torture, particularly for a fan like me, whose pessimism increases the better his team performs.

To say I was nervous going into the playoffs is the wildest understatement this book contains. I couldn't sleep. I kept tossing and turning, weighing good outcomes against bad ones, letting them fight it out in the torturous middle ground of my pillow. To go undefeated all season was asking too much of fate, I was convinced of that on philosophic grounds, whereas my more pragmatic side recognized that defending a title is one of the hardest feats to pull off in all of sports. We were clearly the best soccer team in the state, but I worried whether chance, luck, or fate would allow us to prove it.

Nemesis, the Greek goddess who allots to men their exact share of good and bad fortune, the goddess in charge of divine retribution, had gotten a lot of ink that autumn in op-ed pieces wondering whether America's foreign adventures had tempted her once too often. Did Nemesis act in small corners of life, not just in big ones? I wondered—and, if she did, did she understand that these Hanover boys were friendly, homebody, nonpartying intellectual jocks who hadn't harmed anyone in their march toward perfection?

I also worried that the writer in me, the one who was putting together a book about the season, might be subconsciously rooting for a loss in the finals, the tragic end a novelist is drawn to with every imaginative molecule in his body. A loss in the first round would all but sink the book, a defeat in the quarterfinals would be very hard to put a good spin on, failure in the semis might take some explaining, but the writer in me knew he could find a way, a fatally good way, to deal with a loss in the final—and so to have a novelist in the stands is not something a team particularly needs. Fate, having long since taught him how ironic and bitter life is, might feel, after a season of pure happiness, that he was due for a fresh lesson.

I fought back against my worries in ways I'm not particularly proud of. One was by readying messages of comfort and condolence that, prepared beforehand, would be available when Hanover's luck inevitably turned sour. You can't win them all—there was always the old classic, as valid now as ever. Wait until next year!—which wouldn't cut much ice with the seniors. It was a great season, and of course you're disappointed at the ending, but the pain won't last—that might work better, but I felt guilty about the whopper in the last clause. We're all so proud of you no matter what the outcome, you'll always be champs to us—true enough, but, at night in the worst of my insomnia, the words, when I pictured delivering them to my tearfully brave son, didn't soothe him quite the way they should.

One day to playoffs now. What I needed was a role model of upbeat buoyancy, total sunniness, unshakable, positive, nothing-but-blueskies, we-can-do-this optimism. Not for the first time that season, I wished I was Rob Grabill.

Luckily, I had another, more effective way to cope besides stockpiling condolences—but it takes some explaining.

High school soccer games, so often scheduled at six o'clock, present challenges when it comes to dinner. For the first half of the season, I usually took my chances on finding something to eat at our opponent's field, but, before driving down to Souhegan, I stopped at our minimart and assembled myself a picnic: a turkey sub from a local sandwich maker called Ewas, a small bag of Madhouse Munchies potato chips, and a slice of blueberry coffeecake from Steve's Snacks up in Maine. Total cost was $5.97, which turned out to be the best investment of the season.

We won at Souhegan—I was swallowing my last piece of coffeecake when Matt headed in the winner. The next game at Fall Mountain I brought the exact same picnic, and we won again. Against Lebanon at home, feeling far too cocky, I bought a chicken salad sub, pretzels, and carrot cake, which turned out to be a big mistake. We didn't lose, but the tie felt like a loss, and I blamed myself most of all.

"Sounds like you've got a little superstition going," Scott Barthold said after the game, when I confessed my responsibility.

"Yes, I knew you were going to say that," I said, "but the truth is it works; it isn't a superstition at all."

And the truth is it wasn't. Next game, against Monadnock, I brought the original combo, and we won big-time—case closed. Whatever happened during the playoffs, I was going to make sure my dinner consisted of those lucky ingredients, and I wouldn't worry myself about how exactly, through what obscure but infallible law of physics, the good vibes from my picnic were translated into good moves on the pitch. The carbs calmed me—for most of the playoffs,

I sat quietly, watching fate operate—and you can't ask more from a turkey sandwich than that.

As long as I was going in for this kind of thing, I decided I'd better keep on the alert for any omens or portents out in the larger world that might spell trouble. I noticed with alarm that the championship game, assuming we got that far, was scheduled for Saturday, November 3, which was another SAT morning—nothing could jinx us more. Adding to my worries was that on a river trip just before Halloween, I caught the largest brown trout I'd ever caught in twenty-six years of fly fishing here—a twenty-four-inch, six-pound monster that came from nowhere to attack my fly. I played it tentatively, nervously, half hoping it would escape—there was no way I could put a spin on it that was favorable. To have that kind of good luck, and then to ask fate for even more luck within that very same week, was being far too greedy. As I reached down to release that gorgeous butter-and-steel-colored fish, I felt, on the boys' behalf, a foreboding flush that makes for funny reading but was very real.

Omens—but living up here in the country, my meteorological perspective largely local, I missed the most significant one of all. Toward the end of October, perhaps at the very same moment I was letting go my fish, a dust devil spun up from the Sahara desert, gained momentum, towered upward, gained intensity, took on shape and cohesion, then, hungry for moisture, started west toward the sea. Seeded first in the playoffs, Hanover drew the team that was seeded last, Coe-Brown, who had come in sixteenth out of the twenty-four teams in Class I. It's a high school in Northwood, east of Concord—the kind of small, nondescript place you pass through on the way to places more important. Route 4 there is called Antique Alley, and it was nice to see that the town produced young people, not just knickknacks and old wicker. I happened to be standing on the walkway that leads down to our field when their bus pulled up. As the boys filed past me, I could see them looking at the artificial turf field, the stadium, the lights and big crowd, with wow, we're-not-in-Kansas anymore expressions they tried unsuccessfully to hide.

If our boys had shown any signs of hubris, the first playoff game would surely have been the place fate could chasten them best—but our boys had never shown any signs of hubris. The young Coe-Brown team played with spirit, but it was clear from the opening whistle they were out of their depth. Against the wild and windy rain, they could make no impression—there seemed to be an impenetrable wall stretched across midfield—and you had to concentrate a little before you realized the wall consisted mostly of Angus Kennedy, proving, if there were still any doubters, that he was the best defensive midfielder in the state.

Weather was a factor at the other end, too. The rain was warm and enervating, and our offense took a long time to get unglued. With twenty-eight minutes gone, Casey finally rounded the Coe-Brown defense and rammed in a shot, but it wasn't until the second half and a wonderful Angus free kick past the Coe-Brown wall that Hanover got its second. By then it was obvious we could play all night and Coe-Brown would never elude the Border Patrol. Rob sent in the reserves to mop things up, and they played with more energy and brio than the starters.

Room for improvement, we decided on the terraces; 2-0 against a very weak team. But at least we hadn't peaked too early.

During the course of the game, people would arrive with news of the Lebanon versus Souhegan playoff game taking place a few miles down Route 120. It was tied at halftime, and things looked good for Leb because the Souhegan goalie had lost his cool and punched a Lebanon striker in the ear, earning a red card and putting his team one man down for the rest of the match. Unfortunately, this handicap energized S'hegan, and they scored two unanswered goals to win, thereby knocking Lebanon out of the playoffs in the very first round. We have friends there, and their coach Rob Johnstone is a fine man we all respect, but we were overjoyed not to have our traditional rivals waiting to upset us in a deeper playoff bracket.

Meanwhile, over the Atlantic just west of Africa, the desert sand-storm, now forming a low-pressure center, began drawing up warm, moist air from the ocean's surface. Cooler winds, blowing in a circular whirlwind pattern, rushed into the chimneylike low-pressure center to replace the rising air, so the storm was now a cyclone.

The quarterfinals had always been a stumbling block for Hanover—there was a tradition of losing there or just winning by a whisker. Two years ago saw the double overtime, penalty-shootout against Lebanon, and last year came the last-second victory over Fall Mountain, the game I listened to via cell phone from Pittsburgh. This year's quarterfinal opponent, Merrimack Valley, had already won some big upset games and were ranked sixth in the state; an old-time fan in attendance (well, Rob) remembered that it was Merrimack Valley who had beaten Hanover in the fluke quarterfinal of 1978, thereby ending that team's attempt at the three-peat we were now trying to pull off ourselves.

I watched them carefully in warm-ups, trying to judge whether they brought anything to the field that should concern us. Usually, the other team is strangely anonymous, bodies with faces that never quick click into focus other than as obstacles standing between your team and happiness. When a personality manages to emerge, it's usually because he's (a) terrific, (b) rough, or (c) weird. Merrimack Valley had a player who fit into the (c) category big-time, if you define weird as unusual and interesting. I noticed him in warm-ups—a boy who was even smaller than our freshman Eric Jayne. He was clever with his feet, he seemed to have a nice caressing touch with the ball, but his tininess was remarkable.

"See that number-27 kid?" I said to Chris Kennedy, as we leaned over the fence watching. "Am I wrong, or does he look twelve years old?"

Chris squinted. "More like eleven."

"Is he their mascot or what?"

He came in toward the end of the game and played quite well—feisty, smart, aggressive—and after the final whistle, as Merrimack Valley walked back to their bus, I stopped the coach and asked about him.

"Yeah, he is twelve," he said, with a little laugh. "He's a senior, and he's going to MIT next year. Genius at math. Genius on cello."

The coach deserved credit for answering me—his team had just lost 8-0. Hanover, as if to exorcise once and for all the ugly demons of quarterfinals past, absolutely blew Merrimack Valley off the field, with as flawless a display of total soccer as any of us had ever seen—and goals galore. A Felicetti header off a corner; a brilliant long-range lob from sub Kevin Dade; a pretty feed from Dylan Riessen to Eric Jayne; a corner that went from Lyme's Eric Barthold to Lyme's Matt Wetherell to Lyme's Henry Caldwell into the net, allowing one writer in the stands to instantly compose the imaginary headline he'd been waiting for all year: SUB-LYME!!! These were goals to remember, but none of them would be for very long, because the team's accomplishments only served as the pedestal on top of which was displayed the most brilliant personal exploit of the season.

The Merrimack Valley quarterfinal saw the apotheosis of Casey Maue. Readers who have come this far with me know I've had some fun with Casey's "clumsiness," which was never real clumsiness, but the name we gave to the ongoing battle between his athleticism and his slightly challenged feet. "The Wildebeest," Rob called him, for his size and his gentleness. No one we saw all year had a higher work rate than Casey, or more heart, and now, after twelve years of playing soccer, all this effort was splendidly rewarded.

Casey, in the course of the last six regular-season games, had managed to spread his upper body coordination downward to his knees, shins, calves, ankles, feet, and toes, so they now joined in a totally coordinated package that spelled trouble to the other teams. This showed up best with a trick he had suddenly perfected—the striker's trick of cushioning a cross against your chest, then, with your back still to goal, twisting your shoulders suddenly sideways, so the ball deflects around the defender, allowing you to get past him with a unstoppable head of steam. Again and again this trick had worked for Casey, since it was beautifully calculated to take advantage of his greatest strengths: his six-foot, five-inch height and his inspiring determination. Casey was, we all agreed, *en fuego*—on fire.

Ten minutes into the game, Angus made a run down the channel and blasted a shot that the keeper dropped, and Casey pounced on the rebound for his first goal of the night. Eight minutes later, Eric made the same kind of run Angus had, slipping the ball off to Casey, who buried it for goal number two. Goal number three came off a rebound of an Eric Jayne shot, and goal number four came eleven minutes into the second half, on another Barthold dish-off. Four goals, a hat trick plus one, and there was no one watching that night who doubted that, had Rob left him in longer, Casey would have scored six or seven.

As the Hanover players happily, modestly celebrated, the quarterfinal monkey finally off their backs, thousands of miles eastward the cyclone moving off the African coast had now reached the Cape Verde Islands, taking on a resemblance to a dark and cloudy donut with a calm, clear hole in its center. With its rotating gales now reaching a sustained force of seventy-five miles per hour, it was now classed as a full-fledged hurricane, a Cape Verdean hurricane, with two thousand miles of warm, nourishing moisture to feed upon as it crossed the ocean toward North America.

It was at this point in its development that meteorologists gave it a name, a curiously gentle and Christmaslike name. Noel, they called it. Hurricane Noel.

The semifinals were held at Bill Ball Field in Exeter on Tuesday night. This was new. Before they had always been at Stellos Stadium in Manchester, but B'Ball was better suited for soccer: the sight lines were clearer, the stands were a bit closer to the field, and the scoreboard was the glitzy, up-to-date kind that flashes messages at you all game. Rob's having brought the team there for that preseason scrimmage in temperatures approaching a hundred degrees now seemed a stroke of genius. The field was familiar to the boys, they had done well there the first time ("Playing there in August," Rob e-mailed me, "we discovered that we had unusual courage and amazing depth. Who knows what we will discover this time?"), and the cold November evening, compared with what they had faced last time, made it feel like booster rockets had been strapped to their shin guards, pushing them on.

Our opponent was Hollis-Brookline, the canvas we had painted our masterpiece on back in September—but they were reinforced now by a star midfielder who had been absent that first time, and everyone expected a harder match. Playing a team you've beaten in the regular season can be tricky psychologically; though your coach warns you about it, you tend to get a little overconfident, whereas the other team is out for revenge. In Matt's first season, Hanover's only losses during the regular season had been to Souhegan and Bow, and when the playoffs came around, we beat them in succession for the championship.

When we got to Exeter, the first semi was under way with those same teams, Souhegan and Bow. It was a chippy, rough game; no sooner did we get there than the referee ran over to Souhegan's hotheaded center back, stared at him for a long grim second, reached back to his hip pocket, and brought out a vividly red red card. Bow, with the resulting man advantage, had no trouble slicing through the Sabres defense, led by a fast, opportunistic striker named Ryan Obolewicz who scored three goals to book his team into the finals.

It was the roughest game we'd seen all year, with an undercurrent of nastiness just barely under control. The state playoffs can be that way. Last year, in a Class L final between little Lisbon and tiny Pittsfield, a Lisbon player had his leg shattered by the deliberate foul of a Pittsfield player who then stood over him screaming down curses and taunts—and when the Lisbon player was stretchered over to an ambulance, it was ringed by Pittsfield parents screaming even fouler abuse. The referees doubtless remembered this—and blew their whistles with increasing frequency as the game wound down.

Bow, I noticed, played with two sweepers on defense, thereby conceding lots of space on the flanks. They had a big, strong midfielder who would obviously try to split us down the middle, but this is exactly where our strength lay—bring him on! Except for him and Ryan O, their offense seemed one-dimensional. What worried me most was their roughness—the gratuitous, argy-bargy shoulders shoved into opponents when the ball was clearly going out of bounds, the late tackles delivered just for emphasis. The one criticism you heard around the state about Hanover was that it was a technical team who couldn't handle being roughed up—and while I sensed this was jealousy talking, our soccer virility hadn't yet been tested.

The Bow team, after celebrating, took seats in the stands to watch the next game—a game that doesn't take long to describe. We won 2-0 in a match that was very similar to the September meeting, with Hollis-Brookline totally unable to dent our defense while we generated just enough offense to finish them off. The most encouraging aspect was that Ben Harwick played well in goal, making a vital save on the big HB middie. It had been an odd season for Ben. He had been in goal for all those shutouts, but the truth is we could have played those games without a goalie and still won most. He had been getting on the refs a lot, probably from sheer boredom, and some fans worried he would be rusty and stale in the playoffs. Ben needed excitement to play his best, high tension and drama, but these were fueling him now, and he seemed ready to handle, in the final, what would be the sternest test of his soccer career.

That's on the positive side. On the negative, Eric Barthold only played five minutes before limping off with an injury. In practice two days earlier, he had rolled his ankle, and there was ligament damage that needed time to heal. Henry Caldwell, his replacement, played well, scoring our first goal early in the first half and then setting up Casey for the second with only a few seconds left in the game (a goal that sent an emphatic message to the Bow players sitting in the stands trying not to be impressed). But Eric was a vital part of the team; his running drained defenders of their oomph, and even if he didn't score, he was always good for a key assist or a game-saving

tackle. We had been extraordinarily lucky with injuries all season—
except for Aussie's chronic knee, we hadn't lost a starter all season—
and to have Eric doubtful for the finals made those of us who were
studying all the omens start to wonder if fate hadn't jumped ship at
the last minute.

On Wednesday, Hurricane Noel slammed into the Bahamas, fifteen
inches of rain falling in the space of twelve hours. Flooding was
widespread, houses were destroyed, beaches eroded—and then, having proven what it could dish out in the way of damage, Noel headed
northeasterly toward the U.S. mainland.

*I have completely mixed emotions as we head into the finals. The first
part of me is certainly a little bit cocky, certainly a little bit nervous, certainly pretty excited; if we win, we go undefeated, so we will have won
the threepeat, and I will leave high school never having lost a playoff
game.*

*But along with this anticipation comes certain reflections. I try not to
dwell on it too much, but this is the last important game I will ever play
with my fellow seniors. The guys on the team have been my best friends
through high school, and it's sad to face our last game together, the end to
a (so far) great season. I would imagine for guys like Aussie and Cal, this
is a bit tougher, to be "hanging up their boots" after Saturday. Some of us
perhaps will continue to play in future years, and others have other sports*

teams to look forward to playing on. For those guys, though, this is probably the end of their careers in a sport they are really good at.

Back to just looking at Saturday as a game. Bow impressed me when we watched them play. They have a striker, Ryan Obolewicz, who has scored thirty goals this season, and he will be a test. They have another big striker from Germany with bleached hair, who is fast for his size. So we'll have our hands full!

Before our last practice, coach took me aside and said, "Matt, I've been watching you in practice all week, and you're going to have the game of your life tomorrow. One thing to keep in mind. No rash tackles early when you're all pumped up. Their strikers feed on that. Let your adrenaline settle, then play your normal game."

Which is Rob's way of coaching—deliver some real confidence boosters, then gently remind you of what to do.

Speaking of Rob, he had some good Grabillisms at our team dinner. He goes around the room saying things about each player, and he roasts them pretty good. "If I'm not being mean to you," he says, "then it means I don't love you." He mentions Ben's always getting on the ref. "Well, he paid for it with that yellow card," he says, "and besides, he could have had five or six." Still on Ben, referring to his beard, the way after a game he wears a towel wrapped around his head like a pirate. "I used to teach him in Sunday school, and now he's turned to Satan." On Trevor Barlowe, our junior back: "He's a championship game virgin." On Dylan: "He had the third-sweetest assist of the season." On Oliver

Horton: "You ever seen him tap dance? This guy has major tap dancing chops." On our cocaptains: "Angus was the Dad all season and Casey was the Mom."

He stands by each player as he says this, takes a deep breath, thinks, sighs, grabs his head, as if there is so much to say! Without breaking his spiel, he bends down to tie his shoelaces, walks around some more, grabs kids by their shoulders, adds asides to the parents sitting nearby ("You should have known you were getting into this, but think of it this way: you're not paying for babysitting."). What a performance!

So, we're all trying to stay loose. In the huddle we have at midfield before games, just when everyone in the stands is thinking we must be saying something inspiring to each other, we always try to say something funny, which is a tradition Jeff Levin started last year when he was cocaptain. Before the semifinal, totally at random, Cal deepened his voice. "If any man would go to law with thee, and take away thy coat, let him have your coat also." The Bible! And Cal of all people! It cracked us up.

Before I stop writing, I have to mention Eric's injury, the ligament over his ankle. I'm absolutely praying he will be able to play this Saturday, not only because he is one of our best attackers, but also because we have shared soccer experiences for the last ten years, and out of any guy on the team he is the one I admire most as a person and a player, and he deserves being in the final. I can't imagine winning on Saturday and him not playing, and both things are going to need to happen for me to be truly happy.

Other than that, the team spirit seems high. We always manage to make the trip down to games fun, and on the way down to Bill Ball we will probably half watch a movie, pass around a Playstation Portable for a Tony Hawk skateboarding trick competition, tell stories, and make fun of each other. About halfway to Exeter we'll pass under the sign for the Bow exit, and that's exactly where we intend to send them—straight to the exit!!!

The hand of fate, having worked so subtly, now took hold of the future and gave it a significant Hanover tweak. Hurricane Noel, finishing up with the Bahamas, now moved north, weakening, dropping from hurricane status to something meteorologists called an extratropical cyclone. The last forecast Thursday night mentioned the possibility of gale-force winds and torrential rain along the New England coast for Saturday. When I woke up Friday and turned on the weather, the prediction was much more definite. Flood tides, strong winds, and a lashing rain for the Portsmouth-Exeter-Hampton area, the worst of it peaking in late afternoon.

Rob had kept us all abreast of developments, and about noon came the e-mail saying the state soccer association had postponed the final game until 4:30 Sunday. Yes! I wanted to shout. The benefits of the delay were obvious. It meant we wouldn't be playing in atrocious conditions that could only help a scrappy, physical team like Bow. It gave Eric one more vital day to rest his injured ankle. It avoided the dreaded

SAT day jinx and gave the boys who were taking it on Saturday morning time to relax after their ordeal. It meant the game would be played after dark (for no obvious reason, Hanover played better under lights) because daylight saving time now ended on November 3, not the last weekend of October—and with clocks falling back, that gave the boys an extra hour of sleep on game day. The storm, as it developed, spread inland as far as Bow, messing up their practices, while here in the Upper Valley there was nothing worse than clouds, giving our boys two excellent practice sessions to sharpen up. And since our previous two championships had come on Sundays, not Saturdays, the last possible obstacle to our success was removed in a stroke.

Perfection, the boys were learning, needs perfect luck.

I had my lucky picnic with me when I got out of the car in Exeter on Sunday evening, Celeste carried enough blankets to hand out spares, Erin tugged along her homemade posters (MATT IS PHAT, one read—PRETTY HOT AND TEMPTING), and by the time we reached the stadium's entrance ramp, we were part of a long train of Hanover supporters, most of them burdened just like us. The girls championship game was in its final minutes, Oyster River was up 1-0 over Hollis-Brookline, and the crowd noise came across the parking lot in a series of amplified whispers, whines, and whoomphs. The final whistle sounded—and this time the roar was solid enough to make us stop walking and look up. Girls in white ran toward the stands with their arms jubilantly waving while girls in blue slumped in tears on the grass—the stark, clear-cut alternatives awaiting our boys could not have been illustrated more explicitly.

At least the weather was perfect. Noel was now Nova Scotia's problem, and the sky above Bill Ball Stadium, even with the arc lights, was so clear I could make out Andromeda and Pegasus in a line that exactly paralleled midfield. The storm had stirred the tides up enough that the smell of the sea wafted over the concrete—it could have been a clambake we were hurrying toward, or a stargazing party on the beach.

I dropped all my gear by the ticket kiosk and groped in my pocket for my wallet. In a generous mood, I not only paid for the three of us, but the four Hanover students waiting in line just behind. (I was feeling pretty good about this—at least until I looked at my ticket stub and found I had received the senior citizen discount.) The boys arrived before us, but they had been confabulating with Rob in the locker room beneath the stands, and it was only now that they emerged on the concrete ramp leading toward the field, filing slowly, confidently (to my eye) toward their date with destiny. Oyster River fans, among them members of the boys' team who had crashed out of the playoffs in an early round, caught sight of them and began chanting "Overrated! Overrated!" but a little halfheartedly, as if they couldn't convince themselves to really mean it. Matt gave them a cheeky thumbs-up, and the other boys ignored them. Descending a last little step, their cleats touching turf, they made twisting, pirouette moves to avoid some equipment bags, then began jogging easily toward the bench on the field's far side.

The spectators from the girls' final climbed down the risers on their way out, and it was easy to tell, standing underneath the stands, which was the winners' side, which was the losers', just by the weight of their footsteps on the metal. Their place was immediately taken by Bow fans, congregating to the lower right nearest the field, while the Hanover fans, always striving for the larger view, climbed higher toward the center.

Bill Ball was festive enough, if you could get past your nervousness. It must have been a brave sight from the air, all those lights tucked in tight against the blackness of the Atlantic. I remembered on various trips flying over the lonely expanse of the continent, starting our approach to the airport, seeing out the little window one of the few sights that are clearly comprehensible from the air: a high school or college sports stadium, a horseshoe, oval, or bowl of yellow-white lights ringing neatly its illuminated rectangle of grass. It was a bold, a happy, a very American kind of sight that always made me wish I was down there, a part of it, caring intensely, cheering my head off—and now here at last I was.

Celeste, Erin, and I climbed the risers to the very top, where the press box formed a backrest against which leaned our fellow parents, plus a bonus helping of grandparents, sisters, significant others, well-wishers, friends. Here waited Chris Kennedy, staring out toward the field with his optimistic squint; Joanie Barthold, with her ready-to-laugh-or-cry expression, ready to laugh or cry; Barry Harwick, watching over things with his coach's seen-all-this-before, anything-can-happen bemusement; Bob Maue, Casey's dad, our basso cheer-leader, hitting the deep notes already; Casey's mom and Angus's mom standing a few rows to the right where they could watch alone, too nervous to sit still, too honest to hide it; Cal Felicetti's dad, outwardly relaxed but all topsy-turvy in the eyes. Once again—and for the last time ever—our little traveling village formed around its common center: our love for our boys. Without anyone saying it explicitly, we knew what they had the potential for, and we knew, without saying it explicitly, how hard it would be to convince destiny to let them have it.

I'd like to say that my own mood, sitting higher and farther away from the field than anyone, was serene, writerly, detached—it was anything but. One of the problems of having a son play defense in soccer is that a back has major opportunities to fuck up. A pass across the goalmouth picked off by a lurking striker. A mistimed tackle that allows an attacker to break in alone on goal. An own goal as an attempted clearance finds the back of your own net. Make one mistake, cost his team a championship its undefeated season, and it would be something Matthew would agonizingly remember all his adult life. Watching him finishing his stretching and tug on his white game jersey (Hanover, as the top seed, was the home team), I envied those parents whose boys were on the bench, as Matt had been his sophomore season during the championship run. They could enjoy the game's drama without worrying about scars.

On the field, after the preliminary announcements and the national anthem, it was time to introduce the players, each of them stepping forward as their name boomed out from the stadium's speakers. Now—why hide it?—my romantic, over-the-top awe of them reached its peak, and I saw them not as boys I had known since their infancy, but as heroes ready to add to the legendary exploits they had already achieved.

Here steps forward Number 0, Harwick, our unbeatable goalie, so pumped for this one his chest throws off sparks. Number 2, the fearless Felicetti, he of the miraculous last-second interventions, the nimble, jitterbugging feet. Number 4, the modest Barthold, his ankle heavily wrapped, still fragile there but never fragile in the heart. Number 7, Aussie Cyrus, injured likewise, wincing just to step forward, but a gamer to the last. Number 8, Ben Rimmer, often benched, but not for the big one, when his drive and passion down the right is irreplaceable. Number 9, Yo-Yo Osheyack, the fastest, shiftiest runner on the pitch. Number 12, the redheaded Barlowe, an outside back for all seasons. Number 13, young Kennedy, our deconstructing midfielder, the best player in the state. Number 15, Sam Peterson, the unsung hero of the left touchline, winner of every single battle he fought there all season. Number 19, the indomitable Wetherell, the brainpower at the back, waving nonchalantly now toward the stands. Number 23, the indefatigable Maue, huge in size, huge in spirit, giving the fans the biggest, happiest wave of all.

The team huddles at midfield. Who's telling the joke, and is it a good one? we all wonder. On the other side of midfield, the Bow players, sleekly dressed in dark power blue, give an exuberant war cry while our boys separate silently, almost negligently to their positions.

The crowd sucks in its collective breath, then expels all that nervousness in a huge roar as play begins. Almost immediately, the contrast between the teams' playing styles becomes apparent, the drama taking on the dynamic it will have all game. We are the superior team technically, with better ball control, better touches, better headers; they are nearly as fast as us, but are considerably more physical. Still, within five minutes I sense that Hanover is in almost every important respect superior—and yet superiority in soccer is such a tentative, fragile thing that this gives me no confidence whatsoever.

Most of the early play is in midfield, where Kennedy and Cyrus attempt to impose their dominance with some marginal success. They not only defend well, they're holding onto the ball long enough to mount a coherent and threatening attack. Maue immediately establishes himself as a presence in the Bow penalty area. Yo-Yo, bloodied in a hard collision, shakes off the cobwebs and narrowly misses a longrange shot. Barthold moves well, but a little stiffly, and it takes a few minutes for him to trust his ankle on one of his patented end-to-end runs. Cyrus, Wetherell, and Felicetti all have good shots from the top of the penalty area off corners, and Wetherell, rushing up again from defense, snaps his head just beneath a cross to the far post. Bow looks dangerous on counterattacks, but their roughness produces a series of Hanover free kicks that look increasingly promising, with our dominance in the air already an established, unshakable fact.

Bow's roughness is increasingly the issue. Obviously, the Bow players are pumped with enough high-octane adrenaline to explain and partly excuse some of the aggressiveness, but much of it seems calculated; you can picture their coach telling them before the game that Hanover is a team of technical wimps who don't like to mix it up. The referee begins blowing his whistle with more frequency, the players that are falling wear mostly white shirts, and the Hanover players that seem special targets are Yo-Yo and Aussie Cyrus. On one play right below us a Bow midfielder decks Yo-Yo with a flying tackle that puts a cleat right against his chin. No card is issued, no foul is called, though Yo-Yo writhes on the ground in agony. When play stops, Rob races straight across the field to minister to him ("I wasn't going to let some rent-a-trainer move him with a broken neck," he explains after the game), and we're all surprised—not that Rob would do that, but that a man his age with bad knees can run so fast.

So. Bow is rough, physical, borderline dirty. I'm willing to give them the benefit of the doubt—it's a semilegitimate way to play soccer—but there's an undertone that seems suspicious, even sordid. I notice something now that I'm not sure anyone else catches. Behind our goal is a dark walkway that leads from the brightly lit stands on one side to the brightly lit stands on the other. Standing alone there, ten yards behind our goal and slightly to its left, stands a man who, judging by his seedy posture, upturned collar, and black coat, looks to be a flasher. Ben keeps glancing around at him—the man is obviously yelling something at him, though it's impossible to hear what. ("You suck goalie!" is what he yells, we find out later—which is actually the sweetest, nicest, least-foul thing he says.) A Bow parent deliberately stationed there to distract our keeper? Ben says something to Sam, Sam yells over to Rob, Rob goes over to a security guard and points—but by the time the guard starts over, the Bow dad has slunk away.

The referee, after letting much of the rough play pass, now decides to regain control of the game. With five minutes left in the half, Trevor Barlowe is clattered down just past midfield—a late tackle that earns us a free kick from forty-five yards out. I'm not the only Hanover fan who remembers this is exactly the spot where a similar free kick, finding Wetherell's head, won the game for us at Souhegan. Matt and Cal obviously remember, because they hurry up now from defense and take up positions in the box, along with the target man Maue and the ever-opportunistic Barthold.

Goose Kennedy stands over the ball, peers up once, then, with deceptive casualness, strokes the ball toward the penalty area. It's a perfect cross—high and soft and near enough the goal to tempt the goalie into springing for the ball, but far enough out that he can't quite get it. He stretches, strains, misses, falls. Maue, with the goalie now totally out of play, manages to get a head on the ball, which pops straight up into the air. The white shirts of Hanover, with the goal totally undefended, swarm into the box. Wetherell makes a run at the floating ball, cocks his head back, leaps mightily, just misses, but draws two defenders away from the goalmouth. The ball is still in the air, seemingly on its way back upfield out of the scrum, but then, with unscriptable symmetry, Barthold and Maue get their heads on the ball almost simultaneously, Maue's head directing it up, Barthold's head directing it goalward—and somehow, in a high curving arc, it floats under the bar into the net.

A joint goal. A team goal. A collaborative effort.

Hanover players, jubilant, go rushing back to their positions like those kung-fu warriors in contemporary Chinese films—elevated, defying gravity, flying. As for their fans, it as a fascinating goal to watch, it happened so slow. Some of us, sensing how perfect Angus's cross was, stood up the moment the Bow goalie came out. Others, more cautious, waited until Case got the initial head on it. The rest, now sensing the goal was open and unprotected, rose to their feet even later, but by the time the ball left Barthold-Maue's head and but-terflied into the net, the slow building wave had reached its apogee, foreplay was over, and we were all standing and screaming our heads off as delight crashed over us in a joyous climax.

Halftime. Time, if I could manage it, for a little stroll.

I filed down the risers, took my place in line for the men's room, then went over and stood a little way out from the snack bar where no one would notice me. Soccer might still be a little foreign and exotic here, but the smells were American enough—fries, hamburgers, and ketchup. The hot chocolate was selling well, too, since it was much colder out now, and most people, when they took their paper cups, held them near their cheeks for warmth.

Before me, I realized, was what would surely be forty minutes of incredibly tense soccer. Before me, I understood, was the last forty minutes of my son's high school career. Out of these two certainties, I tried squeezing a moment of distance, of perspective. A fellow parent had said something to me at practice two nights before, a remark that, delivered casually, had kept me thinking.

"Of course we want them to have a perfect soccer season because we want desperately to have perfect kids."

My first impulse was to tell him/her that he/she was wrong. For me, the pleasure taken from an undefeated season would be very similar to the pleasure parents took from their son's undefeated season in, say, 1957. The brave immaculateness of the word itself: undefeated. The roller-coaster ride that led to it. The emotional history of rooting/cheering/caring—and having this, against all odds, rewarded. The pride in your son and his team. Our 1957 mom and dad would have known all about this.

But maybe there is something different about our twenty-first-century versions. Perhaps more than any generation of parents before us, we want our kids to be perfect, work hard to try and insure this, and keep setting the bar higher—all but whipping them toward ever-higher honors and achievements while driving ourselves crazy worrying whether they will reach perfection after all. Hanover's parents weren't immune to this charge, and I couldn't escape it either, not after this fall. Was I overinvolved in my son's soccer? No question about it. Was I overinvolved in my son's life? Possibly—but then we are all overinvolved in our kids' lives, except for those—the other fifty percent of our generation—who aren't involved even the slightest.

Sociologists who study this often say it's because middle-aged people are now terribly frightened of the future and want to ensure our children are never harmed. ("Safety," Rob had said back in August, listing the season's top priorities.) I think this is true, but with a significant emendation. What parents are is guilty about the future, which isn't exactly the same as frightened. We feel guilty that for virtually the first time in this country's history, we're going to hand our children a world that is in many measurable ways worse than the one we inherited ourselves—and it's this guilt, our effort to smother it, that makes us think that perfection in our sons, perfection in our daughters, is their ticket to safety.

No one knew better than I how cruel sports could be, in a dozen obvious and not-so-obvious ways. But at least in sports, perfection is sometimes achievable—for these boys, all it would take was forty minutes of concentrated effort—and it's no wonder all of us sitting at Bill Ball were so involved. But it was my sense of what might be awaiting these boys later in life—a worry I could hide while I watched them but that was always lurking there just beneath my pride—that made me root for them so fiercely—root for them to withstand what would be coming at them in the second half and achieve their three-peat. To have that in life, at least. To be able to say, no matter what their futures, for one season we were a perfect team.

Rooting for this, even as I stood there leaning against my cold concrete pillar, tugged so hard it all but choked me. Two minutes left now before the second half began; fans took their hot chocolates and snacks and headed back up the ramp toward the field, the bright light at the end of the dark tunnel making me feel I was on my airplane again, starting our approach . . . but I lingered for another few seconds, telling myself to be prepared for their losing, but not being able to convince myself even an inch. Defeat simply could not touch these boys. I like to think I'm realist enough to recognize inevitability when I see it, which is usually bad inevitable, but at the same time I like to think that my hope isn't so atrophied that I can't recognize good inevitable when I see it—and good inevitable was what had possession of Bill Ball Stadium. If I was about to watch my son's last half of soccer, I knew, in my deepest being, that it would be to watch him win.

Everyone in B'Ball knows Bow will come out flying, determined to tie it up. They haven't been shut out all season, and total aggressiveness has always been their style. Rob has surely warned our players about the coming storm—but even so, the first ten minutes are murder. Bow manages three corner kicks and four hard shots in those first ten minutes, and several of these are hangers that should have been goals. Ryan Obolewicz, the Bow striker with the big rep, has been marked out of the game by the Border Patrol, which in the first half had taken his passport, denied him entry, stripped away his citizenship, and rendered him stateless. Still, Bow's big midfielder, picking up the slack, gets a look from just outside the box and rips a shot toward the goal's lower left corner that is clearly, from my angle, on its way into the net, when a diving Ben Harwick, who had leaned right, recovers his balance, dives left, extends his arm, and pushes the ball past the far post out of danger—a save that in one quick lunge justifies all the hours Harwick, since grade school, has put into learning how to play goal right.

That's the first ten minutes—Bow rampant. And yet we somehow withstand it, and not only withstand it, but in the next ten minutes go on the attack ourselves, with Maue, Barthold, and Osheyack all having chances that just barely miss. This turns out to be the game's turning point. We don't score, but it gives us time to regain our composure, gives the defense time to rest.

In the close-packed swarm of play, in what seems a gradually dimming light, it's hard to pick out any one player, but, as always, I can instantly find my son, just from the shape of his shoulders or the way he holds himself when he runs—a trick of recognition I learned when he first started playing at six, so, like a father emperor penguin, I could always locate my boy in a mob. I've always felt connected to him watching him play, actually connected, as if his muscles couldn't contract without mine contracting likewise, so inseparable were our bones, sinews, and nerves. Connected—but never has it been this intense. Would our stamina make it together to the end? His half could—he's playing well, his best game ever—but my effort to stay with him out there, like so much of fatherhood now, was leaving me exhausted.

Bow has more chances, but most come now on the periphery, unsupported, where Barlow or Peterson can deal with them safely. And yet the tension only increases. The clock is down to ten minutes, and it's clear that Hanover will be faced with the job of holding a 1-0 lead, something we had failed to do not once but twice earlier in the season, against both Lebanon and Souhegan. Bow is more dangerous than either—but with the game on the line, the undefeated season, the all-time state records, the Hanover defense reaches deep into itself and finds its finest hour. Again and again, Wetherell or Felicetti clear

the ball upfield, not being choosy about where it goes, but just getting it out of danger—and if they don't get to the ball first, then it's
Kennedy, playing well back.

Bow has one more rush left in them, but Ryan O, exhausted now,
trips over the grass as the ball rolls over the line for a goal kick.
Harwick takes his time with it—I try to remember if there's a penalty
for delay of game in soccer like there is in football—and so Wetherell
(impatient, his eyes rimmed with sweat, so, to one fan watching, he
looks twelve again, wearing the sports goggles that always made him
look like a spaceman) steps up and takes the kick himself, knocking it
far past midfield into history.

You can watch the minutes tick down in high school soccer, but you
can't count down the seconds—the scoreboard clock stops with two
minutes left, and the referee decides exactly when those two minutes
expire. They like to blow full-time after goal kicks, but this ref waits
a few more seconds, just long enough for Bow to gather themselves
at midfield for one last attack—but when the ball comes into our
box, Kennedy makes a spectacular full bicycle kick to clear it away.
Suddenly, though we can't hear it from the stands, the whistle sounds,
the Bow players slump to the ground, and our boys are running with
their hands held high above their heads toward midfield where they
find each other, form a joyous, jumping, hip-hopping swarm, and
then—joined now by the reserves erupting off the bench, everyone
tugging off their shirts and waving them like banners—race for the

stands, where their supporters, parents, and fans are leaning over the fence trying to reach them.

I tried picking out Matthew, but it was impossible this time, the boys were so tightly pressed together—so now, more than ever, it was impossible to think of them as anything but one solid, indivisible team. The season had been team, the winning goal had been team, the celebration would be team; if anything, the boys seemed embarrassed and apologetic when, once the award ceremony began, they were called forward individually to accept their medals. I looked for Rob, spotted him over by the empty, neglected goal where he could be alone for a moment. He watched his players celebrate with quiet enjoyment, but he wouldn't take part in it himself, not when his pride in them was so strong it must have choked him. And that was funny—funny sweet, funny sad. That the only time anyone sees a quiet, subdued, withdrawn Rob is just after his team has won a state championship.

Me, I was quiet, too, at least after that spontaneous, unstoppable shout when the boys raised their hands to the referee's whistle. My thoughts weren't exactly solemn, but close enough to keep me in my seat when everyone around me was jumping up and down. So. They had won. They had their undefeated season. They had their three-peat. Whatever lessons they would learn about failure, about heartbreak, about disappointment, about coming oh-so-close would have to be delivered in another way, at another time. It would be delivered, of course—that's the part that made Rob and me so quiet—but soccer wouldn't be the messenger. For these boys, soccer would be the three strokes of perfection they could toss in the balance when heartbreak finally came.

And then Celeste was hugging me, Erin was too, I was getting hugs from everyone in sight and giving out my share, and we all rushed down to the fence and cheered as Casey and Angus, holding either side of the championship trophy, led the team in a victory spring across the field. Reporters were collaring Rob, photographers were snapping pictures, and then someone had the idea of letting the eleven seniors pose by themselves for a final photo. I watched them press together, then, only moments later as is the way of things now, someone already had the picture downloaded and printed, so we parents could pass it around. I got it last, and moved apart from the others so I could see in a better light.

There is Rob, standing to their left in his warm-up suit, much the shortest, still pensive looking, still proud. Sam stands next to him with his curly wet hair, the winner's medal looped around his chest, his expression more distant than the others, quieter, dreamier, as if he's focused on something far beyond the field. Matt comes next, holding the three-peat poster Erin had painted that morning tempting fate—his smile is probably the widest and happiest, but there's a new something in his features I can only describe as cragginess, or ruggedness, or character, something I swear wasn't there eighty minutes ago. Around his neck is draped Casey's arm with three fingers extended, while Casey himself, movie star handsome, stares toward his friends in the stands or the bright, limitless possibilities of his future. Angus is scrunched in next to him, staring the camera straight in the eye, cocky as always, ready to play a second game or a third or whatever it takes to keep all this going. Eric sags happily, wearily, between Dylan and Oliver, flashing what, for a quiet boy, must surely be the first charismatic smile of his life, so wide and dazzling that it's obvious there are plenty more where that came from. Next to him stands Paul Burchard and Erick Barth, quietly content just to be with their friends, a part of it all; and below them on the turf sits Aussie, with three fingers spread on either hand, his mouth wide open as if he's yelling from happiness. Beside him is Ben holding the winner's plaque, already a pirate again, a towel draped over his head emphasizing the swarthiness of his beard. And last of all is Cal, looking surprised and stunned, as if whatever he expected from life, it was nothing as good as this.

I stared down carefully at the picture, just as I stare carefully down at it now on my desk as I finish writing. And it's funny what I saw there at Bill Ball and see there now. Always before, whenever I studied pictures of the team that year, the sentimentalist in me always rushed backward, time blurred into reverse, so what my hopelessly sentimental eyes saw were team pictures of the boys when they were eleven, twelve, or thirteen, smack in the center of boyhood, with their moppy hair, missing teeth, giggly expressions, braces, and glasses. Now, for the first time ever, my imagination and memory weren't strong enough to do that. Somewhere between the moment the photographer called them over and they struck up that happy pose, a final transformation had taken place, perhaps at the very second they had put their arms around each other's shoulders. I scanned the photo from Sam to Cal and back again—yes, there was no mistaking it now. Eighty minutes had been enough to do it. The boys were gone, there was simply no trace of them. The faces I stared down at were the faces of men.

9

FAREWELL

Route 25A is one of those roads that climbs steeply out of the present, takes a turn or two through the past, then levels off onto a plateau of timelessness where it could be almost any century at all. It's old New Hampshire, at least past Orfordville, where the hills close in. You pass an antiques store with a closed sign in front that's been hanging there since the last millennium, then a classic Cape with an attached barn, glistening in sunlight, then a stone house, solid as a fortress, ready still for the French and Indians . . . then, where the shadows come back, the first trailers, getting smaller and shabbier the higher over the pass you go. It's not a notch (those hemmed-in mountain roads our state is famous for)—very soon, a quarter mile before claustrophobia, the view spectacularly widens—but there is something quintessentially New Hampshire about it all, the New Hampshire that isn't quite as picturesque as Vermont and isn't quite as gritty as rural Maine but seems content to dream along forgotten and at peace with itself, at least on a still November morning like this one.

At the very crest of the hill comes two notable landmarks. One is the farmhouse of the most infamous of our former governors, dead now these eleven winters—an endearing old codger who won election by traipsing around the county fairs carrying a hatchet and a sign around his neck reading AX THE TAX! A simple enough platform, but good enough to win him election and eight years in office, during which time legends, real and apocryphal, accrued to him like sticky snowflakes. There was the time he tried obtaining nuclear weapons for the state's national guard. His ordering flags be flown at half-mast when Jimmy Carter was elected. The scheme, which he was only reluctantly talked out of, of having toll keepers along our interstates keep track of how many minorities were entering New Hampshire that day and cutting off entry when they reached a certain percentage of the state's population.

Yes, old "Mel" was vintage New Hampshire, just like the "scenic highway" that now bears his name, so it seems fitting that from his farm, if you glance quickly to the northeast, comes one of the finest views in the state: Mount Moosilauke, the most westerly of the White Mountains and only ten miles away here, with no lesser peaks intervening to block its majestic sweep. On this particular morning, the remnants of a passing hurricane had left snow at high altitudes, and not only were the twin summits dazzling in whiteness, but icing ran down the ravines almost all the way to the valley floor. A beautiful sight, but a warning as well, and it made the warmth, the rare and precious November sunlight, seem like luxuries layered atop our flint.

Just below the governor's farm, the road crosses the Appalachian Trail and flanks a rocky body of water named Lower Baker Pond. At the east end of this pond comes the sign for Camp Pemigewasset, and it's there I turned, crossing a plank bridge over the pond's rushing outlet. Back in summer, things were so busy I had to leave my car here at the entrance, but now, deep in off-season, there was nothing preventing me from driving right up to the cabin that serves as the main office. I passed the tennis court where the soccer goals had been dragged for winter, and then the camp beach, where dock sections and floats were neatly piled one atop the other in a way that suggested they had been stacked precisely this way on exactly this spot for the last six decades, covered now in a brown duff of pine needles and a bright topping of leaves.

Rob's little Subaru was parked outside the headquarters cabin, with the proud vanity plate reading PEMI. He saw me out the unshuttered window, pointed apologetically to the phone, held his fingers up: "Five minutes!" That was no problem—I followed a path down to the pond. The water level, this late in fall, was low enough that a ring of rocks encircled the entire shoreline, making me think of Walden with its famous terrace. Across the water rose a hillside of birch, and with all the leaves off the hardwoods, their serried whiteness was blinding—it was a sight made for Robert Frost. I walked down the shoreline, looking for a flat rock to skim—there can't be a setting as tranquil and soothing as a summer camp out of season—then, hearing Rob's voice trail off, cut back through the cabins to his office.

"Hello Class I Coach of the Year," I said, sticking out my hand. "And now I hear you're New England Coach of the Year, too."

He laughed, waved me over to a rocker near the bookcase. At camp, leaning back in his chair, he looked more like Teddy Roosevelt than ever, a young TR, the man with the charismatic smile always ready for any adventure, big or small. "Bully!" I expected him to say—though with Rob, he says it with his eyes.

"They had to give it to someone," he said modestly.

"And the rumor is you guys have won the big one, the state Sportsmanship Award."

"The boys deserve that several times over. Second year in a row, too." He reached across the desk for his morning hot chocolate. "Matt get used to being first-team all-state yet?"

I shrugged. "That's turning out to be something of a problem. He feels guilty about the others not sharing it, that just he and Angus were selected. He knows it should have gone to four or five of the guys."

"Tell him that when he gets to the award ceremony, he's accepting on behalf of all of us. He's struggling to accept the fact that he's one of the best defenders in his state, but that's okay—he'll get used to it."

I screwed the top off my thermos, poured myself some tea to match his cocoa. "So. You ready for off-season?"

"Not!" Rob ruefully laughs. "Soccer coaches are like farmers—always on an agrarian schedule. I'm putting my tools away now, ordering seed catalogs for next year, thinking about what I'll plant. What I miss is the smell in my car from all the equipment, that indefinable soccer odor. It's like having a wet dog back there for three months, and now he's hopped out."

It was my turn to laugh. We talked some more, neither one of us wanting to let the season drop away quite yet, drawing out the afterglow for as long as we could. Rob, in speaking to the parents after the championship dinner, said something I thought was quite profound. "It would still have been a perfect season even if we lost the last game," he told us. "I could have sold the boys on that, I really could have. But this is America. Winning everything makes it easier to explain what a magic season it's been."

He takes this part of coaching seriously: his responsibility to interpret to the boys just exactly what it is they've accomplished, knowing they don't have the perspective yet to do this themselves. How well he accomplished this comes across in the letter he sent all of them the morning after they beat Bow:

It was wonderful for a team this deserving to win, but the team's true triumph went beyond wins and state records. This was a team that established a culture of inclusion, unselfishness, and genuine respect for each other and the game they all love. They had bull's-eyes on their backs from day one and never buckled under the oppressive weight of expectations. They took their responsibility as role models seriously, both in the school and in the community. These are the exemplars that parents in the Upper Valley want for their young sons. This team understood that community membership brings the responsibility to make a difference in helping others and gladly gave their time to help. This was a team that once again put sportsmanship and fair play first on their agenda every day. Whether or not they win another award for this is moot. They consistently honored the game of soccer. They deserve their place among Hanover's greatest teams.

As we talked, I kept thinking, as I did when I visited back in the summer, how well Rob fit into this setting. On a soccer bench or prowling along the touchline, no one seems more at home in his coaching role than Rob—and yet, natural as he is there, it's nothing to how perfectly he fills his role as director of this one-hundred-year-old camp. All the sadder then, to realize that this past summer, Rob's thirty-eighth at the camp, was his last one ever. The owners of Camp Pemigewasset are making changes, and these changes, for reasons no one can understand, do not include Rob.

I've known this for a while—ever since the second Lebanon game, when Rob saw me in the stands and came over to unburden himself, asking me to keep it quiet until the season was over. That he spent the championship run coaching under an extraordinary amount of strain was not something anyone would have guessed. And while he's always had a strong fellow feeling with the seniors on the team, perhaps it was deeper this season than ever, since, after thirty-eight years filling perfectly the perfect job, hoping to go on there for many more years yet, his future is suddenly as uncertain, mysterious, baffling, and frightening as is theirs.

And so I was wrong before to say it was a season in which disappointment couldn't touch us. Rob had taken it all upon his own shoulders, sheltering his boys.

"What's the latest on this?" I asked, hoping something had changed.

"It's over. I take care of camp this winter just like always, but when March comes, I'm done."

"Do the guys on the team know this?"

He didn't answer me at first, then slowly shook his head. "It would have been so selfish if I told them."

"Rob—"

"Those boys got me through it, the season they had. Those boys . . . those boys . . . saved . . . my . . . life."

He leaned forward over his desk, to pick up something, I thought, but then I realized that the motion was more convulsive than that— that Rob was crying. It shocked me at first—it was like watching Teddy Roosevelt cry, or Knute Rockne, or Sir Alex Ferguson—but it didn't last long, he had control of himself again, and if I liked and respected him before that moment, I liked and respected him even more once it was done.

"You'll find something," I said, in the lame way you do.

He pushed his glasses down his nose, rubbed hard at his eyes. "Of course I will."

"You're not going to give up coaching, are you? Not moving from Hanover?"

He made an emphatic *brrup* sound with his lips, rolled his eyes heavenward. "Of course not!" And there he was again, that same old unquenchable Rob.

There wasn't much to say after that—finally, after four months of total immersion, we were both soccered out. Or at least one of us was. On the way to my car, because old habits die hard, Rob took me over to the camp's soccer field and proudly showed off the improvements they had made getting it ready for next summer.

"And over there," he said, pointing to a hill, "is where I make my personal luge run every winter. I start way up there, slide down all the way"—he swiveled and pointed—"right across the pond."

We shook hands good-bye near my car, and when I drove up the road, I could see him in the rearview mirror staring out across the water. In talking to him after a game once, he mentioned that, as a boy, his favorite book had been *Goodbye, Mr. Chips*, that irresistibly sentimental old novel about an English schoolteacher who is beloved by generations of students. At the end of the novel, a dying Chips remembers them all, the bright and the dull, the athletic and the meek, all the boys who had passed through his classroom and come under his influence. He sees quite clearly their faces, remembers their manner, struggles hard to put names to them all, then finds, as age overcomes him, that he is back again in the past, calling off the roll, doing what he was put on this planet to do: to counsel and inspire generations of young men.

Rob isn't at this valedictory stage yet, not by a long shot, but it's easy to imagine him doing the same kind of thing one day. What must be the count now, the boys he's influenced by his life and personality? Thousands, certainly. Like Mr. Chips, he can one day think back in satisfaction on all that he's done for them, but, unlike Chips, he'll remember everyone's names, the names of their sisters, the names of their cats—what goals they scored, the way they celebrated, the sound of their laughter, the shape and texture of their smiles.

I'm writing the last pages of this book in late November. The sun came up this morning well south of Smarts, our local mountain—it was as if the astronomical rules that govern things had been suspended, letting the sun escape toward Massachusetts. The weather forecast spoke of heavy snow working in from the coast, and when I went outside to get firewood, I caught that damp steely odor in the air that means a significant storm.

This afternoon, finishing work, I went around the lawn making some last futile gestures toward summer. I dragged our Adirondack chairs to their winter home beneath the deck, tightened the tarp over our sailboat on its trailer, pulled withered morning glory vines off our rail fence, stabbed at some maple leaves with my rake. These chores eventually led me over toward the soccer goal near the slight rise in our meadow we call Sunset Hill. It looked even more neglected than it had the previous winter; this was the first year we'd had it that Matthew, too busy with soccer down in Hanover, hadn't blasted balls toward it practicing his shot. The net still had those cannonball-size holes in the middle, the upper part was sutured together with twist ties and bits of fly line, and around the base the weeds were junglelike and clingy, having spent the summer grafting themselves onto the twine.

Feeling guilty, I tried raking away all the neglect. Who knows? Maybe the snow forecast was wrong, maybe Matt would get a hankering to play with me, maybe the grass, anticipating climate change, would stay green all winter. But mostly I just needed to putter around, staying in touch with the last faint pulses of summer. There's an autumn mood of loneliness that isn't bad at all, not if you're starting to get up there when it comes to age, not if you know it won't last long and that the family will soon be coming home. So, as I raked, I listened carefully for cars on our dirt road, knowing one of them would be Matthew. Maybe it's different for other parents, but when I'm expecting one of my kids to appear, I always feel a happy expectancy that is as fresh and powerful now as when they were little.

The sun had started its disappearing act again, having hopped the river and slunk its way south along the Vermont ridges, when Matthew pulled in with the van. Sometimes he drives right into the garage and disappears with his homework, but this time, spotting me through the trees, he parked on the far end of the driveway, waved, started over. Not only was I stationed near the soccer goal, there were two soccer balls there, one directly at my feet, the other on the grass right in front of the approaching Matthew. They had stayed in much the same spots all summer—in cutting the grass, my tractor would brush them aside on one pass, push them back again on the other—and the sun had blistered their surfaces in homely black and white scabs.

"Dollar shot?" I yelled, as Matt came to a stop by the first ball.

"Dollar shot?" Matt acted puzzled for a moment, knowing full well what I meant, but pretending not to.

"I don't think you have it in you."

Challenged, he took off his warm-up jacket, tossed it on the grass, picked the ball up with both hands, put it back down on a high, teelike tuft of grass, took three steps backward, and squinted toward the goal, which was a good forty yards away and on an angle that gave him very little obliqueness to play around with. It was a tough shot—it would require him to bend the ball considerably—and I was pretty confident my dollar was safe.

The "dollar shot" originated with me being a crafty little entrepreneur. A long long time ago now, when Dad and I were playing in the field, I suggested that if I could shoot the ball into the goal all the way from where our hammock was, then I would win a dollar. Dad agreed, I aimed, I shot, I scored—the easiest dollar I ever made! But then he made it harder. There were shots that had to go through trees, shots from impossible distances, corners I had to bend in, crossbars to hit, and shots that had to go in on one bounce. Of course, I don't think I ever actually got my dollar, no matter how many of these impossible shots I ended up making. Dad would remind me that I'd missed the previous day, and so we would always come out even. As I got older, the shots became ridiculously difficult. It became double or nothing, quadruple or nothing. But money had nothing to do with it; instead, it was me looking to impress Dad, a way to convince him to stay outside and watch me play for a few more minutes. Playing with him, I always hated to go in.

I hope someday to have a field like this or a lawn my kids can play on. When I think about kids, I like to think I'm going to be a good father. I love working at the child-care center, and I love reffing kids' basketball games, so maybe that's a good sign. How will soccer fit in? I'm not sure, but I would love to have a goal in the yard and coach my son or daughter's teams, but I want to let them choose for themselves what they want to be good at, whether it's soccer or something totally different. Dad was good at basketball, he loves fly fishing more than anything, but he saw it was soccer I loved best, so that's what he put his whole heart into encouraging.

Sometimes I'll listen to the news and it will be about war or global warming or something terrible, and I'll think—no thanks, no kids for me. My friends sometimes say that, too. But it sounds like giving up on the world, and that's the last thing I want to do. My great-grandmother had seventeen kids—and I guess every one was a vote of confidence in the future.

Okay, I don't know what Dad will tell you, but when he called me over from the driveway, challenged me with that totally impossible shot, I deliberately missed the first three tries, hustled the bet up to a hundred dollars, then buried my last shot top left corner. Sweet!

If I close my eyes, really stretch back in memory as far as I can go, I remember being a tiny little kid playing soccer with Dad on the lawn, with two baby spruce trees for goals—trees that must be fifty feet high now. Dad would deliberately let me score—he was always falling over, letting me get around him—and then one day he didn't have to pretend anymore. I could dribble around him any time I wanted to, only he would yell something funny and I would start helplessly giggling, and then he would close in and strip the ball away, score down at the other end where we'd made a goal with our jackets. I would grab him by the waist while he was celebrating and he would swing me around and we would wrestle and hug on the grass.

I think I'll remember that for a long time. I'll remember that even longer than I'll remember the last game in our championship season—and I'll remember that forever.

"Put it on my tab!" I yelled when the ball sailed in.

The problem was, I had no idea what the tab was up to now. With double-or-nothing, quadruple-or-nothing shots, it was probably near thirty thousand dollars now, going back eight or nine years. "I'll include it with your tuition," I was going to say, but Matt, having drilled it, had grabbed his Hanover jacket and was now on his way back to the house. It would have been nice to have him stay a while longer, but it was nearly dark out, and if I played goalie for him like I used to, the chances of my getting a ball in the face or groin were extraordinarily high. He disappeared into the sunset, and I was alone near the goal once again.

Below me on the grass was the second of the two soccer balls, the one Matt hadn't shot. I stood over it, looking down. I realized, with considerable surprise, that the one thing I hadn't done in my season of total soccer was actually kick a soccer ball—that this was undoubtedly the first autumn in fifty that I hadn't.

Well, there was still time. I brought my right foot back and canted it outward, so that the inside of my shoe was facing the ball—I did that, then gently brought my foot forward until it stopped against the ball itself. It was hard from the cold—slightly deflated, but hard—and the cold was immediately transferred to my toes. I tapped it more firmly—it rolled over once and stopped. I took three steps backward like Matthew had, ran toward it, swung my leg back, and realized, even as I did so, that this was a motion that my muscles, having performed it so smoothly so many times over so many years, had now totally forgotten. That would have been okay, but not only had they forgotten how to kick a ball properly, they reflexively shrank back from even attempting it in the first place. So—there was some forcing involved. If Matthew was watching from the window, it could not have been very pretty.

The ball, repelled by my foot, rolled sluggishly goalward. I wish I could say it ripped the net, twinkled the twine, bulged the onion bag, tore the posts off, found pay dirt, buried itself in white. Instead, it rolled to the seam in the frozen grass that marked the goal line proper, thought about rolling across it, stared up at me with a dimpled black and white smirk, then decided that right there was as good a spot as any to spend the winter. And, looking at things from the ball's point of view, why should it bother rolling farther? The ball knew it wasn't Matt who kicked it. The ball knew who kicked it was Matt's old man.

10

D-III Dad: A Soccer Sequel

The long road back begins with a single step.

Twelve steps actually. Six down to the landing, a right oblique turn, then six more down to the basement and Matt's bedroom—his boy cave, his soccer den, and now, if he could reach it, his recovery room, too.

Whether he could reach it was very much in doubt. Three hours earlier, he had woken up from ACL surgery on his left knee and was still groggy from anesthesia and painkillers. Crutches were new to him, and his body, sagging on the grips, seemed heavy and useless. Celeste and I did our best to help him, but now, faced with descending those stairs, we could only fuss impotently about. He braced the crutches under his arms, squinted in concentration, winced from the pain, took that first slow, careful step . . . and immediately fell backwards on his ass.

It was clear to us, as we helped him up again, all three of us near tears, that this was going to be a slow and difficult rehabilitation—and that the chances were only fifty-fifty that he would ever play college soccer again.

His injury was ironic—and it turns out that a person's anterior cruciate ligament is a very ironic part of the body, one that enjoys tearing when you least expect it. Matt, in his junior year at Haverford, had played every minute of every game. Two weeks after the season ended, playing pickup, just-for-fun soccer with some teammates, one of them collided with his knee. The pain was excruciating—there was the dreaded "pop"—and he needed crutches to get back to his dorm room. His ACL was blown—surgery to rebuild it was scheduled for Christmas break back in New Hampshire.

In all his years playing soccer, Matt had avoided any serious injuries. Braces had shattered on a mouthy header in high school; stitches were needed above his eye in a college game; his right hip had a tendency to do weird temporary things; there was a mild concussion that kept him out of a portion of one pre-season. The usual, but nothing that required surgery.

Until now.

It was funny about that, from a soccer dad perspective. Watching him play in person, I hardly worried about injuries at all, always felt that my presence would somehow protect him from harm; it was like I was there at the playground, my eyes on him constantly. Once he went off to college and I couldn't attend many games, I worried about him all the time, and there wasn't a practice or game where I didn't expect the phone would ring, telling us he was hurt.

One full year was what it would take for his knee graft to completely take hold. Six or seven months was the minimum before he could chance it. This was what, late December? He would be on crutches for at least six weeks; after that, he could start some work on a stationary bike, lift weights, start running again in late May—but no cutting or sprints.

"So," Dr. Sparks said, after outlining all this. "No promises. But if you work hard, you have a real chance."

This was no more than we expected, but even so, it was a hard reality for Matt to swallow; for the first time he confronted the possibility that his soccer days were over. He had gone a long way with the game, had wonderful memories and nothing to regret, and yet missing his senior season, the year that in normal circumstances he would probably remember longest, would be devastating. Haverford had improved tremendously in his three years there—they were poised to have their best season in decades—and Matt at center back was the rock the team was built on. This was at risk now. Having played soccer for more than fifteen years, put all his passion and drive into it, he needed closure on the whole experience. Not the kind of closure that comes in a windowless exam room when a sympathetic doctor levels with you, but the kind of closure that comes on Senior Day, when you walk onto the field before your last game, handing flowers to your mom and dad.

This was not the first time we thought Matt's soccer career was over. Those of you who've read *Soccer Dad* know that, when I started the book concurrently with the beginning of his senior year in high school, I did not think he would be playing in college. This turned out to be a wild underestimation, and, four years having gone by, now it takes some explaining.

Underestimation was our game plan right from the start—a backlash against those parents who decide, when their kids are six, that they will be, they *must* be, college athletes. We'd gone the opposite route, enjoying Matt's soccer, encouraging his love for the game, but not running him through all the hoops that are out there if you're inclined to run your son or daughter through hoops.

What changed things was Matt's continued improvement as a player and his continued physical growth as a man. He was never *the* star on the teams he played on, but the third or fourth best, which took the pressure off him, let him develop at his own speed. His game had always been about intelligence, anticipation, reading the flow, talents he had been born with; he combined this with focus, courage, and hustle—plus his love for the sport, which never flamed out, but only increased year after year.

Many young players hit a wall beyond which they never advance. Matt never hit this plateau—he would finish his soccer-playing career without ever hitting it—but improved measurably, quietly, each season. At the same time, never having experienced the growth spurt that rockets many kids to temporary stardom, he was steadily getting taller . . . and taller . . . and taller. As a sophomore in high school, he was playing at 5'9"; as a junior, 5'11"; as a senior, 6'1". Four years later, a senior in college, he was 6'3", and often the tallest, strongest player on the pitch.

In short, he developed under the radar—and then suddenly people started noticing. He was starting center back on the best defensive team in New Hampshire history, winner of three state championships in a row. He was a first-team All-State selection as voted by the coaches; he was included in the best eleven players in the state team selected by the state's largest newspaper; he was going to captain the New Hampshire team in the summer Lions Cup All-Star game against Vermont. Suddenly he had clippings. Clippings! It was late now in the recruiting process, almost November, but when we sent them out, coaches began calling the house.

Haverford, looking back after Matt's four years there, turned out to be so perfect for him that it's difficult to remember why we held off visiting it for so long, or why, other than for safety's sake, we considered any other college. We knew it was one of the top schools in the country, known for its quiet excellence and Quaker traditions of brave intellectualism and seriousness of moral purpose. The campus, on Philadelphia's Main Line, was said to be just as bucolic and lovely as any New England school's, yet was only a twenty-minute train ride from downtown Philadelphia. When we read more, we were pleased to learn they didn't have two things we didn't want—neither a football team nor fraternities. They had core requirements—I didn't trust colleges where students could just do their own thing—and, unlike ninety-nine percent of American colleges, they had an honor code the students took seriously.

We liked the sound of this so much we spent little time investigating the soccer. We learned that Haverford had the oldest soccer program in the county; they had formed a club in 1902, then played in the first intercollegiate game ever, against Harvard on April 1, 1905, winning 1-0. After years of producing All-Americans—and after becoming the first college team to reach 700 victories—they had fallen upon hard times, winning only three games in the season (2007) that had just ended. They were members of the Centennial Conference, which included such D-III powerhouses as Johns Hopkins and Swarthmore, but in the eighteen years they had been in the conference, they had never once qualified for end-of-the-season playoffs.

So, a weak team—but that didn't matter to Matt; if anything, he saw this as his chance to come in and immediately make an impact. He called coach Joe Amorim and told him we were flying down for a visit. Joe said fine, he'd be glad to see us, and so on a perfect early December day, Matt and I drove to Manchester's airport and took the flight down. We did it in a day—down in the morning, back in the afternoon—and it was eight hours that changed Matt's life forever.

Guidance counselors tell you that when you find the right college you'll know. Matt hadn't really felt that yet, in the dozen we had visited. Now, as we walked across the campus from the train station (past the duck pond, across the cricket pitch), I could sense this was it, just from the way he stared, the little comments he made out of the side of his mouth. Haverford's campus gives off an atmosphere of serious endeavor and great calm, and I think he responded to that balance immediately. What impressed his father were the buildings. Up in New England, colleges are just as beautiful, but they're granite or marble, casting an austere feeling that can be intimidating. The light, grayish-yellow limestone of Haverford exudes the same venerability, but a much warmer sense of welcome. Matt, growing up in New Hampshire, had seen enough granite to last him a lifetime—he was ready to graduate into another kind of stone.

Campus tours, meeting with the soccer team captains, meeting the coach. We made the rounds, caught a cab to the airport, flew back to Manchester, drove two hours back to Lyme, got home after midnight—and Matt never stopped talking about Haverford the entire time. The deadline for early decision had already passed; then, too, as a financial aid applicant, it would be smarter to go the regular admissions route, and see what aid offers he got from which colleges. So, he would have to cool his jets for a while, but not before sending off a note to Coach Amorim letting him know that Haverford was his first choice—vital info for a coach trying to decide which "prospectives" to put his admissions chips on.

The letter arrived April 9th while Matt was in school. I'm the one who saw it first—and yes, it was fat, obviously stuffed with pamphlets and forms. When he came home and opened it, his smile was unlike any other I'd ever seen on him. It wasn't his little boy at Christmas smile, or his little kid scoring his first soccer goal smile, nor his smile of general everyday routine happiness. It was the smile that flashes across a young person's face when, at long last, one of the puzzle pieces of that overwhelmingly exciting, existentially tormenting, utterly mysterious something called your future materializes at last.

"What does it say?" I said, when he finally put the letter down—easily the dumbest question I ever asked.

D-III is by far the largest division in the NCAA, with over 440 member colleges and 163,000 participating athletes. These are not the big guys like Notre Dame or Michigan, but smaller programs with more modest ambitions—though, like most generalizations about D-III, this has to be immediately qualified, since some member schools have 20,000 students, a few play D-I in one sport, D-III in others, and some are very ambitious indeed.

For players, the difference in commitment between D-I and D-III is huge. One athlete we know, who started out at Bates then transferred to UConn, put it this way. "D-III was a serious hobby; D-I is a serious job."

D-III soccer is even harder to generalize about. As in D-I, schools that have the easiest admissions requirements and are weak academically usually have stronger teams than the ones that are super selective and academically challenging, but there are exceptions to this each year. During his time at Haverford, Matt played against a forty-two-year-old, 230-pound striker . . . that's on one hand . . . and, on the other, against a striker skilled enough to be drafted by Major League Soccer. He played on dusty fields that were so rough and choppy a grade school team would have walked off in protest, and on artificial turf fields set inside stadiums of professional quality. He played in Mississippi, California, Massachusetts, Maryland, Virginia, Pennsylvania, New Jersey, and Sweden—and yet most games were an hour away by bus, so the team could get home early and start work on their studies. He even played against a team (Cal Tech) that included girls.

As mentioned, Haverford soccer had tremendous success in the early years, placing players on All-American teams, but since joining the Centennial Conference it had never once qualified for the conference playoffs, which means never rising above sixth place; it had been eight long years since the team had managed to win one more game than it lost. Now, losing had become habitual. Prospective recruits, no matter how impressed they were with Haverford as a whole, were turned off by the prospect of playing for losers, and for the last couple of seasons, anyone—*anyone*—who showed up for pre-season with a pair of cleats made the team.

Was this because Haverford's academic standards were so rigorous that good players couldn't get in? Partly—athletes were never cut much slack by admissions, but had to have the grades and test scores everyone else needed. Facilities? Walton Field is historic, bucolic, well-manicured, but you have to wonder if recruits, used to playing on turf under lights, would be as charmed by it as their parents. Few foreign players? Haverford, otherwise so generous, does not give aid to foreign students, so the Zimbabwean strikers and Brazilian midfielders go elsewhere. Lack of support? One of the biggest surprises for us during Matt's first season was the dearth of any parental involvement in the team; we came from a high school where the tradition was just the opposite. Haverford parents didn't sit with each other at games and hardly even knew who the other parents were, even after their sons had played together for four seasons.

If soccer success breeds soccer success, then soccer failure breeds soccer failure. Whatever the reasons, Haverford men's soccer was stuck in a losing cycle that was going to be damn near impossible to turn around. Would Matt's fellow freshmen be the ones to bring

Haverford back to what it once was? "You guys are going to win the conference your senior year," Coach Amorim predicted, but their balloon was quickly popped by a cynical senior saying, "Yeah, that's what he tells every class when they come in."

Matthew spent the summer before college getting in shape. The coach sent a chart outlining daily workouts, as well as suggestions regarding diet. Matt did his best to puzzle these out; some drills were extraordinarily complicated, and many "lifts" he had never heard of. "Do ten repetitions in sets of five with a three-minute rest of double-squat liptosuction curling tripods," it would say, or some such gibberish. Matt asked his weightlifting buddies to interpret, then, when he got really baffled, called Haverford's excellent strength and conditioning coach, Cory Walts, for some tips.

In late July, playing for New Hampshire in the Lions Cup All-Star game against Vermont, he collided with a Vermonter and ended up with what the Brits call a "dead leg," which set his training back. But he was patient with it, and by the time we drove him down to Philadelphia for pre-season, he was in the best shape of his life. The first morning of practice everyone had to run two miles, and Matt had the second-best time of all those on the team. Good for him—but had the older players bothered to train at all?

That night they scrimmaged after dinner, and he now discovered not only that he belonged there as a player, but that he was probably one of the better ones. The coach had praised him. He had saved a goal-bound shot off the line. His fellow freshmen were friendly and enthusiastic.

And now might be the time to introduce these freshmen, since they play such an important role in the story that follows. To save ink, I'll not use two adjectives in my thumbnail sketches, though both apply to every one of them—"smart" and "nice." You have to be smart to go to Haverford, and, if you play soccer there, you seem to have to be nice, too, though how they measure this on applications I have no idea.

Steve Griffith was a quick, aggressive midfielder with a great work ethic, as befits a Green Mountain boy from Vermont. David Restrepo had played striker at his Texas prep school, but Amorim put him at right back near Matt—and while he went at this gamely, you could tell he'd rather be up front where he could score. Alejandro Rettig y Martinez, from New Mexico, was the only freshman as tall as Matt, and looked even stronger, with serious soccer legs. He hadn't played much as a kid and had started late in high school, so his technical skills were a little behind his physical ones, but he clearly had tons of potential.

Tyler Freeman is from Boston—easily the fastest among the recruits, he was a wide middie who was going to see lots of playing time right from the start. Jake Seeley grew up in Champaign-Urbana, Illinois—a digger on the field, someone who never backed off from a challenge or gave up on a ball. Jamie Field and Scott Cohen would play on the team for two seasons, then move on—and yet they both stayed involved with Haverford soccer, and, after the great upset victory I'll eventually be writing about, led the charge onto the field to embrace their great friends.

The freshmen weren't able to make much of a difference that first year. Haverford would end the season 3-10-3. There were no Centennial Conference wins—none, zero, zilch. What made it worse was that many of the losses were close, by one goal, so it seemed they weren't losing from lack of talent, but because they were destined to lose, and there was nothing they could do to change their fate.

Celeste and I saw one of the non-conference wins. Coach Amorim had scheduled two games in Los Angeles during the college's October break; we decided to fly out to Yosemite, enjoy a vacation, then go down and watch them. They tied Occidental with us in the stands; the next afternoon they played Cal Tech, way around on the other side of Pasadena. We decided to walk to the campus. There weren't many students in evidence, since it was their October break, too, and the ones we did see—future Nobel Prize winners—had no idea where the soccer field was.

"We have a soccer team?" one of them said.

Yes—and Cal Tech is famous in American sports for the length of their losing streaks. In soccer, it must have been twenty or thirty games since they'd last earned a win—but these young men and women were winning big-time elsewhere, so what happened on the pitch was merely an ironic footnote.

There were only three of us watching the game, there on a beautiful field widening out from some of the more strikingly modernistic buildings on campus—Celeste, me, and a loud, obnoxious Cal Tech soccer mom type, who started yelling even before the game began.

Cal Tech played like intellectually-inclined, modestly athletic young men who were huge fans of Manchester United or Real Madrid; they tried emulating their heroes with wildly speculative crosses, optimistically long-range shots, and wild flying tackles that were always too theoretical to do much harm. They played, I decided, like they were measuring their passes with slide rules, computing logarithms, doing geometry proofs.

Haverford also played poorly—this was a classic case of a bad team dumbing down the better one—but we still managed to score four goals. The Cal Tech coach sent in his reserves. Girls! We hadn't noticed them on the bench, had no idea any D-III team included females. (Since Cal Tech doesn't field a women's team, any girls who want to play soccer play on the men's.) Matt and his teammates hadn't played a coed game since fourth grade—and as it turned out, the Cal Tech women played better than the Cal Tech men, probably because our boys, gentlemanly to a fault, allowed them too much space.

After the trip, the rest of the season was anti-climatic, at least until the last game of the season away against Swarthmore, their traditional rival. We didn't drive down for it . . . I'll wait until later before describing what a Swat game is like . . . but we heard from some friends who went that Matt played well, as he always did in big games when his adrenaline was pumping. Still, the Fords lost 1-0—another agonizing defeat to finish off a discouraging season.

That was the autumn that Barack Obama became president. Our local congressman conducted an on-line lottery for inauguration tickets, and we won two. Matt went down with a friend, was part of the huge mass of humanity lined up along the Mall—but when he called us later in the afternoon, it wasn't the inauguration he wanted to talk about, but something he had just learned when he got back to Philadelphia.

"Joe Amorim announced his retirement," he said. "It's pretty sudden I guess. They're going to get a search committee going to find his replacement. Sounds like they've already started."

Surprising news, pregnant news, with all kinds of implications. The end of a soccer era at Haverford—but would the new one be any different?

Kevin Weiler, Joe's able assistant, took over as interim coach, taking care of recruiting and running spring practice while the search committee searched. They had many qualified applicants, and, after phone interviews, brought five finalists to campus to meet the team. The one who impressed Matt most was Bill Brady, head coach of D-III Greensboro in North Carolina. Friendly, handsome, outgoing, exuding confidence, still a young man despite his long resume, he impressed everyone mightily and was offered the job.

A lifetime job, if he did well. In the last eighty years, Haverford had only had four soccer coaches; Brady would be the fifth.

It wasn't until pre-season that players and coach got to know each other, but then it was pretty much love at first sight—the players were excited to be part of the new beginning, the new attitude. And the freshmen looked promising. One was a slender midfielder from Boston, Matt Gorski, who was the creative playmaker the team was desperate for. Dan Garfing was also a middie, the strong aggressive kind who would keep other teams from shoving us off the ball as they had always done in the past.

A third recruit—and we couldn't have been happier about this—was Trevor Barlowe, Matt's teammate from Hanover High. When last seen in *Soccer Dad*, he was part of the record-setting defensive back four, the Border Patrol; Trevor was the redheaded right back who didn't let a player get past him all year. He was the classic case of a superior student who wanted to play soccer without sacrificing anything academically, and so Haverford was a perfect fit. "People already love him," Matt said, two days into pre-season, so it was clear the feeling was mutual.

For all the hope and improvement, progress turned out to be very slow. The team doubled its victory total from last year, but that meant they only won six. Shaky goalkeeping meant almost any shot could go in all season. The offense struggled. Alejandro Rettig y Martinez, after showing so much promise as a freshman, broke his toe and missed most of the season.

The highlight was beating Ursinus at home, the *first conference victory in three years!* The seniors on the team wept in happiness at the final whistle, never mind that every other conference game was a loss. Coach Brady was bringing lots of talented recruits to campus, determined to turn things around, but patience was still the key. At the team dinner in November, the two Matts were voted co-captains for next season—Matt Gorski, Matt Wetherell. It's unusual for underclassmen to be given this kind of responsibility—young Matt was going to be a sophomore; old Matt was going to be a junior—but they were the players who led on the field all season, and thus the natural choices. Matt Wetherell, selected as the team's Most Valuable Player, got a nice plaque to add to the ones already in his bedroom.

Celeste and I were grizzled veterans of countless soccer road trips, but in high school these had all been in New Hampshire, a ninety-minute drive at the most. Driving to Philadelphia was an entirely different ball game—industrial-strength driving through the concrete heart of megalopolis, flanked by eighteen-wheelers all the way. And with tolls, gas, hotel rooms and meals, it was far from cheap. When we did manage a trip, we had lots of fun—but following the team from New Hampshire was pure torture. We'd seen practically all of Matt's games in high school, and not being able to know what was going on, not being able to root for him in person, was a difficult adjustment, since if anything we felt even more invested in the outcome. Luckily—or unluckily—there was another way to follow his games, one that requires some explaining.

D-III games are not broadcast on ESPN—or even PBS. What small colleges have begun to do is utilize the internet to "broadcast" the home games live, occasionally via web-cam video, but more often with something called "live statistics."

Say Haverford is playing Franklin & Marshall in Lancaster, PA on Saturday afternoon. Say some Haverford parents living far away want to follow the game in real time, not wait for a recap when the game is long over. We turn on the computer, type in *Franklin and Marshall men's soccer,* and wait until the site comes up, clicking on the line that says *Play by play.*

If things are working correctly—and often they are not—the names of the starting lineups appear. You look at your watch: 2:15 o'clock. Surely the game has begun by now—but nothing further appears on the screen. Five minutes go by . . . still nothing . . . but then a line appears toward the top of the screen: *5:43 F&M corner.* A few more minutes go by, then another entry scrolls over the first entry: *8:59 HVCMSO shot.*

And so on and so on, for ninety excruciating minutes, more if the game goes into overtime. Quite often it seems that the student volunteer handling the software has turned his attention to his girl-friend or gone back to the dorm to study. There are lots of pregnant pauses in "watching" a game on live stats, and your brain can fill them with all kinds of negative imaginings. No entries for ten minutes? Is someone hurt? Has my son broken his leg? No entries for twenty minutes? Thunderstorms? A fight on the field?

Since the software only allows entry of statistics (corners, shots, fouls, free kicks, substitutions, goals, cards), and permits no interpretation or color, it can be a horribly misleading way to follow a soccer game. At halftime, those of us "watching" often grow sick of it, try e-mailing other parents to see if anyone has better information (they don't, of course) or try calling someone we know is at the game in person with their cell phone. And yet, for all its faults, live stats are totally compelling, and we began spending Wednesday evenings and Saturday afternoons glued to our computer screen, trying to influence the entries in the boys' favor, but—these were the bad years—inevitably being crushed.

A sardonic sense of humor and great reserves of sympathy—that's what you needed rooting for Haverford men's soccer during Matt's first two years. We went down for the last game of the season, home against Swarthmore. Swat is always the biggest game of the year, and on a perfect soccer afternoon—a light mist in the air, leaves blowing down from the oak leaves, the air burnished in that autumnal, prestigious-small-liberal-arts-college way—there must have been 1,000 fans at Walton Field, so it felt like Army-Navy was about to be played, or Harvard-Yale.

We had heard that the rivalry was intense, but we had no idea it was *this* intense. Thirty minutes before the game, there was already plenty of abuse being exchanged by the Ford fans on our left and the Swat fans on our right. Much of this was the witty kind of banter college students are very good at, but there was a nastier undertone, too, and I think this was because the Swat team, even during warm-ups, was borderline despicable.

They'd had a great season and were nationally ranked, and this seemed to have gone to their heads. They swaggered through their drills, making no secret of their contempt for our boys warming up on the other end of the field. Their best player was the worst offender; it's hard to strut when you're dribbling a soccer ball, but he knew how.

It was Senior Day, where the team's seniors are honored with their parents before the game starts. Matt—who gets very emotional in these situations—threw his arms around his great partner at center back, Brian Pepe-Mooney, who was starting despite a bad hamstring. All the seniors started, and with their energy leading the way we were at Swat early, surprising them with our aggressiveness, as the Ford fans, led by the college's president, screamed encouragement (at us) and abuse (at them).

A good start—and then disaster.

Matt and Brian were playing a high line near midfield with the play in the Swarthmore end. The arrogant Swat striker lazed his way upfield behind them, well offside. A Swat defender kicked the ball to him; surprised, he trapped it, turned, broke in alone on goal, and scored. Offside, by a country mile—and yet the linesman's flag stayed down, so the goal counted, putting Swat up 1-0.

Pandemonium on the field, on our bench, on the Ford side of the stands. President Emerson's hands flew about like he was trying to find something to throw, and that was mild compared to most fan's reactions. Offside! Ten yards offside! Easily the worst refereeing decision or non-decision I'd seen in fifty years of watching soccer—but only for five minutes, when it became the second-worst. Again, the Swat striker lazed behind our defense as we moved the ball upfield; again, a Swat player intercepted the ball and passed it to him, fifteen yards offside this time—and yet once again the linesman missed it, and once again the striker scored.

Any team with a shred of honor or decency (I told parents Ron Restrepo and David Cohen watching horrified next to me) would have immediately kicked the ball twice into their own net to make up for it. But not Swat.

The Fords fought back, but ended up losing 4-2, sunk by the linesman's ineptitude. The Swat players swaggered through the first half, then got chippy and mean during the second, and one particularly repellant worm of a midfielder was sent off with a long-overdue red card.

Haverford's revenge on Swat came a couple of weeks later when the Centennial Conference Academic Honor Roll selections were announced. Haverford men's soccer led the way, with almost half the team being honored, which was far more than any other team in the conference, despite the fact that A's at Haverford weren't inflated but real. And if you looked at the team as scholar-athletes and gave equal weight to the scholar part, Haverford was clearly one of the best teams in the country. They are better at soccer than any school that is academically more challenging (ie, Cal Tech), and are better academically than any college that is better athletically (ie, Messiah), so doesn't that make them top?

The 2010 season, Matt's junior year, was different from the very start. Coach Brady had recruited heavily, and the admissions office had supported him, so there were eleven freshmen fighting for spots in pre-season, including those who would play key roles in Haverford's resurrection.

Adam Morollo was a defender from Boston—tall and linebacker solid, utterly unflappable at center back where he partnered Matt W. David Robinson was the Clark Kent type—mild-mannered looking, but aggressive and crafty once he put on the uniform. Colin Lubelczyk from Maine was a digger in the old-school style, with his buzz cut and hustle. Matt Johnson—the third Matt—was quietly solid, a natural at full back. Over on the other side of defense was Jamie Reingruber, probably the most natural athlete on the team. Nick Kahn, a smiling, friendly young man from Georgia, looked to be the reliable goalie the team was desperate for.

Coach Brady had scheduled tough games against high-caliber programs, reasoning that even if the boys lost they would learn plenty and elevate their game. This meant a doubleheader the first weekend down in Tidewater, Virginia, with a game against Christopher Newport, one of the top D-III teams in the country.

They started the game like they would blow us off the field. (Celeste and I were watching up in New Hampshire on a reasonably good video feed; the announcer kept calling us "Hay-ver-ford.") Still, we bravely held them—Haverford, even in the darkest days, never lacked spirit—and you could see the boys' confidence grow as the half wore on. Christopher Newport scored two goals to our one, but it proved to the boys that things were different now, and they could play with anyone.

The previous year, players had cried in happiness when they beat Ursinus; this year, not only did they beat Ursinus, but McDaniel, Franklin & Marshall, and Washington, giving us four conference wins. Haveford was a team on the rise, though penetrating the top layer would be tough, since the five teams above us were all nationally ranked.

A couple of games stand out. Franklin & Marshall had lost a tough game the week before playing us. One of our players had a pal on the F&M team—call him Lionel. Lionel did not like his coach, and so passed on a piece of information that motivated our boys greatly. "Thank God we have Haverford next week," the F&M coach told his team—and that became our rallying cry as we beat them soundly at home. "Thank God we had you this week!" President Emerson shouted from the stands.

A very sweet win—followed by an even sweeter tie. Haverford had lost every game against Johns Hopkins since 1995, but we tied them this time, 0-0, surviving two tense overtimes. This was followed by two games in Boston, a hard-fought loss to Wheaton, the team Coach Brady had starred for in college, then a win over Lasell, who played like a gang of muggers, hate criminals, and kindergarteners all combined.

Matt Wetherell, as he did sometimes, seemed to make winning that game his personal mission, playing just as much offense as defense, desperate to right the moral order, restore dignity and justice to the game he loved . . . and then David Restrepo, ever reliable in the clutch, buried a shot in to the lower left corner of the Lasell goal, putting an end to everyone's misery.

Another big change for Haverford that season happened off the field, but proved to be another key part of the renaissance.

Celeste and I, when Matt started playing as a freshman, were surprised and dismayed by the lack of parental support for the team.

Parents didn't even know who the other parents were, let alone make friends with them or root together. Things were different on Matt's high school team, and we knew that other Haverford parents, coming from the same kind of background, missed this aspect of soccer as much as we missed it. And so some of us began talking about making Haverford parents a much more organized, visible, and supportive presence, not only for the boys' sake, but for our own.

During pre-season I made out a master list of parents' names and contact information so we could communicate with everyone. I am not an organizer, and am definitely not a cheerleader, but making the list led to my becoming both, backed up by Celeste who *is* a cheerleader. With Matthew being co-captain, we had a good line of communication with the coach, and a source of reliable information. I missed going to all of Matt's games, missed that terribly, and this was an alternative way to be involved; someone had to do it, and it seemed simplest if that was me.

We decided right from the start that we would have no formal name and absolutely no hierarchy. If someone wanted to organize a function, even freshman parents, they were welcome to go right ahead. Organizing food "events" was our main focus (and the main focus of these was providing snacks and drinks for the team for their bus rides home after away games), but we also led the cheerleading, updated people on scores if we learned them first, exchanged information on how best to access live stats and/or video, answered freshman parents' questions, and, in general, acted as the virtual meeting place where team parents could connect.

All this—but nothing more. Early on it became apparent that some parents thought of us as their go-betweens with the coach. We were e-mailed questions about playing time and other sensitive issues—and immediately pressed *Delete*. We were pom-pom wavers, social directors, food commissars, but not soccer mediators and not soccer shrinks.

Soccer moms and dads in college are not the same as they are in high school. They're usually more knowledgeable about soccer—these are parents who have been spending every weekend for fifteen years watching their sons play. They seem less competitive, too. Here at Haverford, all the boys were at the college of their choice and were playing soccer there, so the most obvious prizes had already been gained. Parents seemed more relaxed. Our kids, for a few years, shared the same destiny, and this gave us something to bond over ourselves. We started making friends with the other parents; our soccer social life, which had taken such a hit during Matt's first two college seasons, flourished in his third.

That season's Swarthmore game was played before a big crowd under the lights at their place on Halloween—fittingly, since so many Swat students act like clowns. (OMG! My prejudice is really getting out of hand.) The Ford parents held a most excellent pre-game tailgate in the parking lot, during which I did a brisk business selling red and white supporters' scarves out of my box to raise money for the team's summer trip to Sweden.

Haverford had provided buses for any students who wanted to come, and so the stands were evenly divided between, on the left, Garnet fans dressed like Where's Waldo, Harry Potter, or Darth Vader, and, on the right, Black Squirrel fans dressed like Where's Waldo, Harry Potter, or Darth Vader. This was a crucial game for us; Swat had already secured the first seed in the Centennial Conference playoffs, but we needed the win to qualify for the fifth and last seed.

We played them even eighty-eight minutes of the way, but the key difference was Swarthmore's arrogant striker, the one who at this time next year (and this was all but unprecedented in D-III) would be playing in the MLS. Our fans, having cut red cards out of construction paper, flourished them at Swat after every tackle, but it didn't do much good, and the loss put us out of the playoffs for another year. Our Harry Potters, Darth Vaders, and Wild Things threw their red cards into the trash and trudged back to the bus. Our parents went down to the field to console their sons. I reached into my wallet, took out $400 in scarf money, and handed it over to the coach. We had brownies for the boys, cold pizza, wings, and chocolate milk.

An 8-6-2 season—the first winning season for the team in a decade. Haverford soccer had made BIG strides; it was competitive again, respectable again and then some, and yet they hadn't made the playoffs, so it wasn't quite the breakthrough everyone was hoping for. But that was okay. Surely next year, with the freshmen more experienced and the seniors leading the way, playoffs were all but certain. 2011 promised to be the Year of the Black Squirrel.

Matt's rehab from knee surgery was slow, painful, and torturous, but steady. The worst part was walking the tightrope between optimism and realism when we talked about his future. Yes, he could probably play in the autumn if he worked hard on his training; no, we couldn't count on that, lots of athletes didn't come back that fast. Probably play, maybe not play . . . probably, maybe not . . . and teetering between alternative futures can be a hard balancing act to pull off.

We needed to convince ourselves, not just him—convince ourselves not only to be hopeful, but not too hopeful. What bothered me most was not being able to anticipate his senior season like I would have if he wasn't injured. The team was going to be outstanding, Matt's senior season as co-captain would be the capstone of his long and happy soccer experience—but maybe not. I'd feel optimistic—I'd start running through the schedule gauging their chances—and then, a second later, I'd feel a pressure around my neck, reality's choke collar would tighten, and I'd go through moods when I wished with all my heart that his junior year had been his senior year, and he had finished his soccer days with his knee intact.

No one ever had a better soccer experience than Matt, no soccer parents ever enjoyed it all more, and yet, if it ended with him spending his senior season watching his team from the bench, the whole experience would forever come attached with life's wretched asterisk—*what might have been.*

I've written before about the bonds a father and son forge through their love for a sport, talked about my fears that if soccer went, those bonds would go, too.

But I learned through Matt's injury that my fears were misplaced. Our bonds were proving a lot more solid and dependable than his anterior cruciate ligament. They might stretch a little, might even get bruised, but severing? Not a chance. If he couldn't play soccer anymore, we would both be disappointed, but facing this possibility drew us together, made us share even more.

I've talked before about Matt's physical growth. Now, witnessing his intellectual growth, I experienced the same kind of shock, as each time I talked to him he seemed to have taken another big step toward being critically self-supporting and intellectually self-assured. Readers of *Soccer Dad* will know that I am cynical about what college can offer, but Haverford, what it brought my son, overcame all my doubts.

He was majoring in political science while fulfilling pre-med requirements. Thanks to some excellent professors, and his own realization that a nation's health might involve something more than just good doctors, he was becoming more and more interested in government policy and the way major decisions are or are not reached. We talked about this often, as he explained to me about his readings or sent papers for me to share. Not quite as much fun as talking about Manchester United or the Fords' latest game—but then it *was* just as much fun, and I realized we were talking even more about "serious" things than we were about soccer. The graft in his knee grew stronger his junior spring, and thanks to Haverford, what it was bringing him, the bond between us strengthened as well.

Working hard (at a children's hospital in Philadelphia), training hard, looking forward to the team's pre-season trip to Sweden and the coming season. That was Matt's summer—until Fourth of July weekend, when it all fell apart.

I was the one who answered the phone. The house was full of guests, and I had just started the barbecue; later, we were all going down to the pond to watch fireworks. This is easy to say in retrospect, but when I glanced at the caller ID and saw it was Matt, I felt a strong sense of foreboding. It didn't feel quite right, his calling just then. "Dad?" I heard him say, but his voice seemed to be coming from the bottom of a very deep well.

"Coach Brady resigned."

"What?" I managed. When you're thunderstruck, that's what you say.

"He's quit. He's gone. He's not our coach anymore."

"But he's taking you to Sweden."

"Not anymore he's not. He's taken a job at the prep school right across the street."

"Pre-season starts the moment you get back. The season begins in six weeks."

"Without him," Matt said—but it was hard to understand him through the tears.

X Prep, the private school across the street from the campus, is one of the most expensive and lavish private schools in the country—a place for the wealthiest 1% of the wealthiest 1% to send their sons. They had hired Bill Brady to be their soccer coach and to run something called their "Leadership Institute."

The reaction on the Haverford side built slowly over the holiday weekend, but on Monday, my e-mail was full of responses from team parents. Everyone felt, in varying degrees, surprise, shock, anger, bewilderment, betrayal, and, eventually, grudging sympathy. The coach had recruited their sons, led the team into respectability, gone out of his way to be their friend and mentor, become someone we all admired—and now, over Fourth of July weekend, this was gone.

With players and parents desperate to know what would happen next, Athletic Director Wendy Smith (who was as surprised as the players) stepped up big time. She assured everyone that the Sweden trip was still on, never mind that fundraising was still alarmingly short of target, then hired as interim coach the third assistant at Amherst, someone who'd grown up in Pennsylvania and knew the area well. His name (and it's a great coach name, suggesting a brave sheriff riding into Dodge City to restore law and order) was Shane Rineer.

His greatest virtue or greatest handicap—time would tell which—was his age. He was only a few years older than the young men he was now in charge of, and had never been a head coach before.

The parents were somewhat mollified, now that the situation had been dealt with so quickly. Our surprise and shock now gave way to absolute determination to support the team even more than last year—e-mail after e-mail reiterated this—so, in a similar process to what the players were experiencing, our disappointment was being transmuted into resolve.

The seniors felt this especially. Counting ever-faithful Kevin Weiler, who had served as interim head coach one spring, this would be their fourth coach in four years. "Fuck it," you could sense the players thinking. "We'll win it this year for ourselves."

This resolve, this forging of purpose, began with the trip to Sweden.

The team flew from Philadelphia to Frankfort, then transferred for the flight to Gothenburg. Matt's knee had made a lot of progress, but Dr. Sparks recommended two more weeks of taking it slow, so, while Matt worked out with the team while in Sweden, he didn't take part in any of the games. This freed him up to keep a blog of the trip; late at night, when everyone else was sleeping, he would be typing away at his laptop, letting everyone at home know how things were going.

"Update from Gothenburg; Thursday, Aug. 11:

After some much needed sleep, our team left the hotel to play our first match of the tour, against the U-19 prospects from IFK Gothenburg, one of Sweden's most successful teams. Prior to the game, Matt Gorski and I presented their captains with a Haverford soccer scarf, while in return received an IFK Gothenburg banner we plan to hang in our locker room as a tour memento. . . .

At halftime, Coach Rineer encouraged us to view the second half as a clean slate, and build on the positive momentum of the first half. Although Gothenburg added another goal against the run of play, David Robinson answered emphatically with by far the goal of the match. Having picked up the ball in midfield twenty-five yards from goal, "DRob" took one touch to prepare the ball before blasting an upstoppable rocket into the top corner of the goal."

(WD speaking. This was *not* the last time DRob would do this. Stay tuned—and be patient.)

"At the final whistle, the teams shook hands and exchanged greetings—a nice end to the first international soccer game for the majority of the team.

After showering and grabbing lunch at restaurants near the hotel (kebabs for some, fried fish platters for others), the team met for a guided boat tour of Gothenburg . . . The day ended with a pasta dinner at the hotel, before many headed out to further explore the streets of Gothenburg at night."

(WD. This, for some of the lads, meant going to a disco. Matt, e-mailing off the record directly to me: "Never have I seen so many beautiful girls all at once.")

"Next on the itinerary was a trip to Lisberg, Scandinavia's largest amusement park, packed with roller coasters, concession stands and excitement.

The best story of the day happened right at the end. The setting: the Flume Ride, a 610-meter water slide in log boats with two major downhill drops. The characters: Coach Rineer, Jamie, Ford, Adam and Matt J. The plot: In a boat designed for three passengers, five big men squeeze in. Midway through the ride, sagging with weight, the boat comes to a complete stop. The players free the boat by pushing off from the sides of the railing. Drop #1—free-fall into a giant splash, soaking them all. Drop #2—even greater fall causing a giant splash, soaking not just them but everyone waiting on line. Receive standing ovation from onlookers for the biggest splash of the day."

Next they moved on to Malmo, where they watched the famous Malmo FF take on AC Milan at the Swedebank stadium. There were more games against young future pros, a sauna followed by a plunge in the icy Baltic, a day-trip to Copenhagen, a round of "soccer golf"— and meal after great meal, described by Matt in loving detail. As well as the fun and games, you can sense these young men bonding, getting to know their new coach, forging the kind of determined resolve that forms, not just out of shared hardships, but shared fun.

While the boys pack their souvenirs and get on the plane for the long ride home, it might be a good time to abandon the soccer dad stuff for a moment and morph into Joe Sportswriter, the better to appraise the boys' chances in the coming season.

The defense was excellent, with arguably the best back four in the Centennial Conference—strong and solid, with the kind of mutually supportive understanding that you see in a good string quartet. Behind them, goalie was still a question mark. Midfield featured Matt Gorski, the Maypole around which everything spun—his distribution was top-notch, his vision outstanding. Size and strength would be supplied by Dan Garfing, "Garfdog," who was ready to take on a starting role after two years as a sub. The wings had Colin Lubelczyk and Tyler Freeman, who shared a never-say-die work ethic and speed afoot. David Robinson had shown flashes of brilliance his freshman year. Steve Griffith would bring hustle and experience off the bench.

The challenge for midfield was to chip in with more goals, something they hadn't done last year.

Strikers? This was the team's greatest challenge. David Restrepo was certain to get his five or six goals, some of them game-winners. Alejandro Rettig y Martinez would get his share of goals, too—hopefully, more than his share. When he was on his game, he was unstoppable—big, strong, determined. Would he be on his game this season? He started off injured, and there was no obvious replacement.

Other factors? The freshman class was small, only three recruits, but one of them, Nikko Giannasca, looked like being a starter once he got used to the college game. Leadership was strong—Matt W. and Matt G., in their second year as co-captains, had settled comfortably into their roles. ("We'll go as far as the two Matts take us," Coach Rineer predicted.) Coaching? This was the wild card, and it was hard to say, pre-season, whether the switch from smooth, charismatic Coach Brady to rough-and-ready, what-you-see-is-what-you-get Coach Rineer would bring the team together or pull the team apart. Intangibles are, well, intangible, but it seemed to neutral observers like a team with great heart.

As usual, the Centennial Conference was going to be very tough. Swarthmore was defending champ, a nationally ranked team, and while they would get no awards for sportsmanship (spitting at the ref when the game ended was their idea of good sportsmanship), they would be favorites yet again. Johns Hopkins, a D-I school masquerading as D-III, would challenge them at the top. Muhlenberg, Dickinson, Franklin & Marshall, Gettysburg—they were always strong, too. Six teams fighting for five playoff spots, and it was hard to see how Haverford, even if they played well, could wedge their way into that final quintet.

The first game of the season was away against a strong Neumann team. Matt, having taken that huge psychological first step—forgotten about his knee and just 'effin *played*—started and lasted 104 minutes as the game went into overtime, before David Restrepo buried one for a 2-1 win.

The next game was away against Messiah, a Christian college just south of Harrisburg. Matt begged us to come—Messiah were defending national champions. Switch soccer to basketball, change D-III to D-I, picture Kentucky or North Carolina, and you have some idea of the status Messiah has in small-college soccer. "Pursuing athletic excellence and developing Christian character" is the slogan on their website, and in case anyone misses the point, they reiterate ungrammatically further below. "Our student athlete's purposes goes beyond what other's purposes may be; their purpose is to glorify God."

Obviously their purpose(s) trumped Haverford's purpose(s)—did we even have a purpose(s)?—but it might be fun to watch rival purposes duke it out. It's a long drive from New Hampshire, so Celeste and I drove down to Connecticut through the swath cut by Hurricane Irene the week before, checked into a motel, turned the news on—and damn if it wasn't about to happen all over again. Hurricane Lee, after drenching Louisiana, was forecast to stall over central Pennsylvania, dropping thirteen inches of rain.

Would the Messiah game even be played? When we woke up in the morning it was already raining, though we were still hundreds of miles from the storm's center. We turned the Weather Channel on; they had gone from the anchorwoman with big boobs to the guy who looked like a professor, so it was clear the situation was grim.

We drove toward New York tentatively, not sure what to do. Approaching the Hudson, we had to make our decision—keep on toward Pennsylvania hoping the game would be played, or turn around and head home. Finally, just before the toll booth, the cell phone rang.

"We're playing," Matt said. "The game's been switched to Gettysburg since they have an artificial turf field. Starts at seven."

"See you there," I said. I snapped the phone shut, pointed out the windshield.

"South."

Celeste squinted through the wipers, nodded—and six hours later, after driving through the fiercest rain either one of us had ever experienced, we pulled into a Gettysburg motel and fell exhausted across the bed.

(And yes—novelist that I am, the irony of being in Gettysburg under a hurricane named Lee did not escape me.)

It was nearly dark out when we woke from our naps; we drove through the deserted downtown looking for a pizza place to put in our order for the team's bus ride home. The Gettysburg College soccer field is tucked in below McPherson Ridge with its monuments. The fighting on the first day of the battle had been fierce here. General

Abner Doubleday's men were flanked by Ewell's Confederates charging directly over what would eventually become the college soccer field, site of tonight's smaller, less significant battle. Boys had run faster, more desperately across this patch of earth than any scholar-athletes would run tonight, and there can be no more solemn place in the world to play a game of soccer.

And not many college games have been played under worse conditions. Pouring doesn't begin to describe it—this was sheet after sheet of rain, volleys of rain, cannonades. The Haverford parents—the "Gettysburg 7" we called ourselves—managed to find each other at the edge of the field, and all but collapsed into each other's arms as survivors will.

"Go Fords!" we yelled, or tried yelling—the storm stuffed the syllables down our throats.

The game had been hastily switched here and someone had forgotten to arrange for ballboys, so Celeste volunteered to run the near sideline. She pulled the hood of her parka over her head, put that determined look on her face, grabbed a ball, and started running to catch up with the play, the true soccer mom in action.

Bad weather is said to favor the underdog—we seemed to cope better with the sheer miserableness of it all. We started on the front foot, while Messiah—obviously a highly skilled team—played like they were wearing galoshes. The half ended goal-less, but a boxing referee would have awarded the first round to Haverford.

I went in the woods to pee (urinating outdoors at Gettysburg is a historical experience), and, in seeking a sheltered spot, ended up within hearing distance of where the Messiah coach harangued his troops. He sounded concerned, even worried, and this heartened me greatly—it was like listening to General Lee ordering General Pickett to take Cemetery Ridge at all costs.

Haverford's big first-half effort tired us out. Instead of controlling events, events began to control us—and when this happens, you can bet the other team will score.

They did, on a cross that sailed over our defenders to a striker alone in the box. That I thought he was marginally offside didn't matter much; that our defenders thought he was offside mattered greatly. Our fab four, who had played so heroically until then, raised their hands like old ladies simultaneously calling "Bingo!" or the smartest kids in class. But it isn't so smart, anticipating a call that way. The linesman's flag stayed down, and Messiah was up 1-0. Their over-the-top celebration testified to just how worried we had made them.

So. A narrow loss to the national champs. The boys had held their own with UConn or Duke. They ended the game as wet as it's possible for soccer players to be, but proud, and ready to come back for more. (They would be playing here against Gettysburg in October in what would surely be one of the most important games of the season.) We parents waited for them at the athletic center, loaded their arms with food, and sent them off into the storm in their bus. Celeste and I had forgotten our stadium seats, went back to fetch them, and walked along the darkened field, thinking deep thoughts, not only about the great effort from our boys, but about that greater, more desperate effort from boys who were now only ghosts.

The Jimmy Mills tournament that weekend, the first two home games of the season, was played in perfect summer sunshine. Compared to playing under Hurricane Lee, this was like kicking a ball around the beach at Copacabana—fun, laugh, R&R, with plenty of parents and girlfriends in the stands to cheer them on. Morollo, Wetherell (a ball bouncing in off his knee brace, which, in celebration, he bent over and kissed), Restrepo, and Freeman scored in Saturday's victory over Goucher, and Alejandro, Colin, and Matt Gorski had goals in beating Gwynedd-Mercy on Sunday.

Sunday's game fell on the tenth anniversary of 9/11, and watching the boys lower their heads in the minute of silence before the game started brought back memories of Matt's U-11 team standing in a circle with solemn, half-embarrassed, half-frightened postures, five days after the towers came down.

The game had begun and I was sitting in the shade just below the Walton Field press box, when I heard a small voice to my right yell, "Good going, Matt!" I looked around. At the far end of the stands was an Asian-American boy of about ten, along with his slightly older brother and their Haverford-cap wearing dad. They stared toward the field with real intensity—they were literally sitting on the edge of their seats. "Go, Matt!" the boy yelled again, and then his brother felt emboldened to add his own cheer: "Good, Matt!"

We had three Matts on the field—which one were they rooting for? The ball came wide into our end and my Matt cut over to the sidelines to intercept—then, with a trick he had perfected in high school, managed to keep the ball in with his left foot, his weaker foot, hooking it upfield without it going out of bounds.

"I love it when he does that," the younger boy said.

I felt an overwhelmingly pleasant sense of déjà vu; their rooting for Matt brought me back to the days when he was ten himself, sitting tight against me at Dartmouth soccer games, picking out his favorite players, rooting for them, sitting with the same absorbed posture I saw in these boys.

At halftime, I went over and sat down next to them.

"I heard you guys rooting for Matt Wetherell," I said.

They looked a bit worried at that, like they might have done something wrong.

"Are you friends of his?"

They shook their heads. "We just like watching him play," their father explained.

"Wow. Well, I'm his dad. That's really nice to hear. Maybe I can have him sign an autograph for you?"

That was going too far with it—the boys looked embarrassed and very shy—so I changed the subject, asked them if they played soccer, then went back to my roost in the shade. But it was a moment to remember all right—probably my favorite soccer dad memory of all time.

Conference play started next weekend with Johns Hopkins at home. Last year, the 0-0 tie had been the highlight of the season, and this game seemed headed the same way, with neither side having scored and only two minutes left on the clock. Then, just before going to overtime, one of their strikers stumbled over his own feet in the penalty area. The referee—stationed so far upfield he was in a different time zone—blew his whistle for a penalty. The striker buried the PK—and a minute later we had lost.

On Wednesday came a non-conference game against Eastern University, where Coach Rineer had gone; we dominated, but they scored a goal and we didn't. Franklin & Marshall came on Saturday—and again, it was a 1-0 loss. Three games in a row, 270 minutes of soccer, and we had not scored. This happens in soccer—frustratingly long stretches where a team simply can't find the net. Strikers break in alone on goal and stumble; a midfielder with a simple tap-in whiffs; a shot that beats the goalie hits the bar and caroms out; a defender heads in a corner only to be whistled offside. It's hard enough to score in normal soccer circumstances, but suddenly you begin to feel jinxed;

the goal seems to shrink, the time you have to shoot shortens, goalies look bigger—and so the pressure mounts, which makes scoring even harder.

Next up was a Wednesday night away game against a weak Washington College team in Maryland. (At Haverford, classes are so demanding that it's hard to play guilt-free on Wednesday nights.) The game was not only on video, but featured a play-by-play announcer, so watching on the computer was like watching television circa 1949—players had a tendency to disappear into the murkiness on the far side of the field. Washington scored first on a shot our goalie should have handled, but then David Restrepo, running the channel, took a great first touch and buried his shot for our first goal in over 300 minutes.

I was sure our boys would come out flying in the second half, but they seemed lethargic and out-of-sorts—I felt like shaking the computer screen to wake them up—so it wasn't a complete surprise when Washington, shooting long-range, scored a second. We tried feebly to respond, but couldn't. The boys had lost to the weakest team in the conference, and, at 0-3, had all but eliminated themselves from the post-season playoffs.

The low point of the season? At least until the next game, when morale sank even lower.

The team has an academic advisor, a professor who's available to help with anything related to their studies. He's a fine man—but maybe he should be choosier about where he buys his meat. On Friday night before the vital Muhlenberg game, he had the team over to his house for chili. Very generous of him, and it was great for the boys to relax. Unfortunately, the chili had more of a kick than it was meant to have, and half the team spent the night on the can or throwing up. Groggy, nauseous, and feeling more than a little self-pity, the team boarded the bus to the game in the morning—and then, halfway to Allentown, the bus broke down.

The game was rescheduled for later in the day while the boys waited by the highway for a new bus. Muhlenberg scored in the first few minutes, while the boys, after no warm-up time, were still groggy. We played them even after that, but once again some lowdown cheating Haverford hater had erected an invisible shield across the goal. Our fourth conference defeat in a row dropped us to the bottom of the standings, and it was impossible to put any kind of gloss on this or find any bright spots.

And then, of course, the bus, the replacement bus, broke down on the way home.

Matt called us while they waited for help. Usually after a defeat he couldn't talk about it at all, but this time he sounded relaxed, as in resigned. Yes, for all intents and purposes their season was over now—no team that started 0-4 ever made conference playoffs—but he was thinking while he was out there on the field how lucky he was to be playing college soccer, under the lights in front of a good crowd in a big game. He'd had a great soccer career, and if it was going to end on a low note, well, so be it. They still had an outside chance to at least have a winning record, and there was always the possibility of a consolation win over Swarthmore at the very end.

Matt's week of hell didn't end there. On Monday around dinner time our phone rang with the call I'd been dreading all season. Matt's knee had popped during practice and immediately swollen up. The trainer thought it might be scar tissue breaking up—Matt would need an MRI to check things out. Clearly, he wouldn't play against Widener on Wednesday and probably not against Dickinson on Saturday—and after that, who knew? That Muhlenberg might turn out to be his last game ever was a real possibility; maybe he even had a premonition of this, which is why his post-game phone call had seemed so elegiac.

We tied Widener 0-0. We had now scored one goal in 470 minutes of soccer.

It was Celeste's idea to drive down for the Dickinson game. I'd never said no to a soccer trip before, but when I thought about the hours in the car, the cost of a hotel, all the tolls we'd pay, the meals, I just couldn't do it, not to watch the boys lose again, not to watch Matt sit on the bench. Was that defeatist of me? Damn straight it was, but there you are.

"He needs us now more than ever," Celeste said.

I didn't cheer up until we sat in the stands at Walton Field. Matt's place in center defense was taken by Trevor Barlowe and nothing could have pleased us more. We'd been watching Trev play soccer almost as long as we'd been watching Mattie, and, of course, I'd written about his prominent role in Hanover's state championships. And he played wonderfully well against Dickinson, as did all the boys—this did *not* look like a losing team.

Still, Dickinson scored first, only ten minutes in. HERE WE GO AGAIN—you could see the words scroll themselves across the green Walton Field grass. But somewhere in the soccer heavens, the delicately balanced scale that keeps track of a season's fortunes must have hit bottom now, and stared tilting its creaky way back up toward the good luck side of the equation.

Alejandro went up for a cross along with two defenders, and while he didn't actually manage to head it, somehow the ball was redirected off his face or back past the goalie into the net. Wild celebrations, both on the field and in the stands. Haverford had actually scored!

Fourteen minutes into the second half, Alejandro . . . Alejandro our gifted, sometimes underachieving striker; Alejandro, who always came to practice suffering various aches and pains; Alejandro our potential superstar . . . stole the ball from a Dickinson defender, rolled around his shoulder, and then, from the top of the box, rifled in a shot that was the sweetest, most professional goal I'd ever seen a Ford score.

Dickinson tied it up, but out of a scramble in the box, freshman Nikko Giannasca took charge and poked one in—3-2 Haverford. And that's the way it stayed for the last seventeen minutes—our first conference win of the season, and the first victory over Dickinson the seniors had ever had.

It was a somewhat subdued celebration when the whistle blew. Beating Dickinson was a nice footnote to their poor season, but mathematically not much had changed. The boys needed four more conference wins in a row to even have a chance of making the playoffs, and even a tie would doom them. Still, it was a perfect autumn afternoon, parents had brought all kinds of goodies, and everyone enjoyed our post-game picnic to the max.

I went over to Alejandro to congratulate him on his goals, particularly the classy second.

"Thanks, Mr. Wetherell," he said, appropriately modest. Then he asked me a favor. "Uh, it was all kind of a blur to me. Can you tell me how I did it?"

It kept raining Haverford goals on Wednesday when the boys beat Penn State-Abington 3-0. That put them in a bullish mood going into the must-win game at Gettysburg on Saturday afternoon. Haverford hadn't won there since 1979—not for thirty-two years!

The game was going to be on live video, but Celeste and I had a wedding in Boston to drive to. Agony—but then the phone rang, just as we were stuck in traffic on I-95.

"We won!" Matt said—behind him, even before the words got out, I could hear the excited chatter on the bus. "David scored. A beautiful pass from Steve Griffith."

"Unbelievable!" I yelled, genuinely elated (the wedding was going to be a lot more fun now). Then the soccer dad part of me kicked in. "Did you play?"

"My knee's still sore, but coach says I'll start against McDaniel."

Ah, the McDaniel game.

There was no live video this time, only live statistics. The stats flashed across the screen in their torturously slow way, and the only thing that made it tolerable was the sudden appearance of a line reading *HVMSO goal 17" Alejandro Rettig y Martinez.*

At halftime, I snapped. The waiting to see whether a stream of electrons would make me happy or break my heart; my hatred of computers in general; our boys' inability to put a game away early and let their fans relax. I'd been patient with this all season, and then between one second and the next I couldn't stand it.

"I'm going fishing," I told Celeste. "I'll bring that cell phone thing, you can call me with updates."

"You won't get reception."

"Better yet."

It was one of those late October afternoons we get up here after the leaves have fallen and the leaf peepers gone home. Still beyond still, quiet beyond quiet—the brown of the remaining leaves seemed to leach out through the water, so what my canoe floated on was a burnished sheet of bronze.

I was drifting in the middle of the pond, my fly rod across my lap, when, miraculously, the phone rang.

"McDaniel just scored," Celeste said. "It's tied 1-1."

"Shit!" I said, loud enough to send a ripple across the pond. "How much time left?"

"Twenty minutes."

Twenty minutes went by. The phone rang again.

"It's going to overtime."

I tried visualizing the boys in Maryland, whether they were trudging back to the bench feeling defeated or whether they were digging in deep, tapping their reserves of resolve. It seemed like an hour before the phone rang again.

"Alejandro just took a shot. Their goalie saved it."

"You called me for that? Just call when something definite happens. Jeezus, this is torture."

As I said, the pond was very still, and any sound echoed its way toward shore. I saw now that I wasn't alone. A bait fisherman had come down to the boat launch and set up shop on a little stool. He certainly heard me, and I could picture him thinking, "What an ass, to bring his phone out fishing on an afternoon like this."

The phone rang, and this time, with extra urgency, it wobbled back and forth.

"Well?" I said, with a heavy heart.

"It says Haverford scored. It says Matt Wetherell header."

"It says what?"

"Haverford goal. Ninety-five minutes. Matt Wetherell HAVMSO headed goal."

Her voice was calm, that was the good news—or was it good? How could she stay so calm if what she was telling me was true?

"You're kidding, right? Are you still in front of the computer screen? Read it to me again, very slow."

"HAVMSO . . . that's Haverford men's soccer, right? . . . HAVMSO goal ninety-five minutes. Matt Wetherell headed goal. End of period."

"Then we won! A golden goal! Matt scored a golden goal!"

"Do you think so?"

It was ludicrous, how uncertain we were, how we refused to believe in Santa.

"I'm coming home," I said. "I'll believe it when I see it for myself."

Never has a canoe been paddled so fast. I pulled it up the boat launch, shrugged apologetically toward the bait fisherman, drove home at reckless speeds, and rushed downstairs to Matt's bedroom where we kept the computer. And sure enough, there it was, the final line on the live stats: *HAVMSO goal 95 minutes Matt Wetherell. End of period.*"

I started to let myself believe with that—and then the phone rang, and it was Matthew, and only then did I trust myself enough to yell.

"We won, Dad!"

"FUCKING UNBELIEVABLE!"

It took me a while to understand how they had done it; it really wasn't Christmas break, when Matt took me outside and demonstrated in front of his snow-dusted goal that I began to connect the dots. Five minutes into overtime, Haverford had been awarded a free kick just inside the half. Matt ran up from defense to stake out a position in front of the McDaniel goal, and decided that whatever happened he would stick around for a while in case something promising turned up.

Dan Garfing's free kick was beautifully lofted, luring the McDaniel goalie out but not allowing him to catch it—he had to punch the ball, straight to David Robinson's right foot. He struck the ball hard, but it looked to be sailing wide—and then the McDaniel defender in front of the ball, instead of letting it sail on past for a goal kick, stuck out his leg.

The ball must have said "Thank you," it came off his knee so politely—straight to Matthew, loitering in front of the goal. Without any time to think about it (i.e., worry about it), not needing even to jump, he snapped his head down and redirected the ball past two lunging defenders into the back of the net.

A golden goal. Haverford wins 2-1. The dream lives on.

Matt couldn't breathe, he was so excited, so dizzy with disbelief. Every kid, when they practice soccer, basketball, baseball, this is what they picture—winning the big game at the very last second. And now, after thinking his season was over, his career finished, he had done it!

A herd of wild Fords stampeded toward him across the grass. He had enough time to worry about his knee getting hurt again, enough perspective to realize that this was the best moment soccer had brought him (so far), and enough leadership skills that, as his teammates finally peeled off him, he remembered to lead them over to shake the distraught McDaniel players' hands.

This was the team's third conference win in a row, but they were still flying under the radar, and it would be another week before the Centennial Conference website began referring to them as "the hottest team in the conference." Two games left, and both had to be wins—away against Ursinus, then home against Swarthmore. We outshot Ursinus 23-1 in the first half, yet none of the shots went in; was the famous Haverford goal drought returning? No, thank God. Alejandro, Mr. October, settled things in the sixty-third minute. Five wins in a row, four conference wins in a row; we really *were* the hottest team in the Centennial, and how many centuries had it been since that phrase could describe us?

The build-up to the Swat game, tense as it was (whoever won would move on to conference playoffs; whoever lost was out), came with an overlay of emotion that made the occasion even bigger. It was going to be Senior Day—the last home game of the season, with a ceremony before the game honoring seniors and their parents. The Wetherells, walking past Founders Hall on the way to watch the final practice Friday afternoon, noticed posters taped to every dorm entrance. COME WATCH THE SENIORS CRUSH SWAT the captions implored, with pictures of the seniors looking suitably grim and determined.

Before practice, Coach Rineer read the boys inspirational goodluck messages from alumni. One was from a man who played soccer for Haverford in the 1940s, on a team consisting of 4Fs and returning GIs; he described how much beating Swat had meant to them. Another alum explained that he was in charge of an adult, just-forfun soccer league in D.C., and he still hated Swarthmore so much he wouldn't let anyone who'd gone there be in the league. One grad said it most starkly: win, lose or draw, they would remember their last Swat game longer than any other college memory.

Matt had gone one step further to pump the boys up. He taped to the locker room wall a comment off a Swarthmore website, their coach saying that while Haverford had improved, they weren't yet capable of winning a big game.

The boys looked relaxed and confident at practice—we parents watching all agreed on that. The weather forecast was a bit iffy— well, a *lot* iffy. Snow was forecast for Saturday, but it never snowed in Philadelphia in October, so we decided it was nothing to worry about.

Matt's sister Erin flew down from Boston, and we took him out to dinner. He was quiet, even testy, as he was before big games. He apologized several times for this, but we understood, and took him back to the dorm early so he could spend the rest of the evening with the team.

When I woke up in the morning in our hotel, I hesitated a long time before opening the shades; when you've lived in northern New England as long as I have, you develop a sixth sense about what's waiting for you when you first look out. And sure enough, it was snowing, with glutinous white flakes that were piling up fast. We'd had our once-in-a-thousand-year event with Hurricane Irene in August. We'd had our once-in-a-century storm under Hurricane Lee in September. Now we were in the first stages of what would turn out to be the worst October snowstorm in Philadelphia history— and Philadelphia weather history goes back to the days of Benjamin Franklin.

I felt sure the game would be postponed, dreaded the actual phone call announcing this—and that phone call came around 9:00 a.m. Conditions were impossible, Matt said—the game would now be played on Sunday. Families who had come down for the game would have to rearrange their travel plans; some wouldn't be able to do this and so would miss it. Even worse, the boys would have to tamp down their adrenaline, then get psyched up all over again for Sunday. In the meantime, parents and players alike would have to slog through a miserably disappointing afternoon.

I didn't have to peek out the curtains Sunday morning—a brilliant sun sent its beams right across our beds. There was no question in my mind but that it would burn the snow off Walton Field by mid-morning. We grabbed some coffee and checked out, then headed right to campus, though it was still early. Ron and Candace, David Restrepo's parents, had come up with a great idea a few weeks earlier—a Sunday brunch for the seniors and their parents. This was meant to celebrate the end of the season, the end of their four years, but with the game moved to Sunday, there didn't seem to be any reason not to go ahead with our plans, making in a pre-game brunch instead.

We were driving down Lancaster Avenue, about two minutes away from the Ardmore Café, when our cell phone rang.

"The game's been postponed again," Matt said. "It's Monday night on Swan Field under the lights."

The official explanation was that there was still too much snow on Walton for the game to be played. Moving to Swan Field's artificial turf was the obvious solution, keeping it a home game, but it meant redrawing the lines for soccer (it was marked for field hockey and lacrosse), and this would take time—hence the move to Monday night.

We found a parking lot, trudged through the frozen slush to the café. The other senior parents were already there starting on their coffees. We couldn't understand why they smiled and laughed so brightly, and they couldn't understand why we looked so glum—and then I realized they hadn't heard about the postponement. It was left to Celeste to break the news. Never have I seen expressions change so fast.

People reacted like I had—anger, disappointment, confusion. Some of them immediately began figuring out how they could change flights, rearrange appointments at work, manage to stay for another two nights. Some knew they couldn't.

I was still trying to figure out our own plans when Matt came in with Steve and Jake. The players hadn't shaved since the Dickinson game, and by now they all looked like desperadoes. If I looked grim, then Matt looked even grimmer; he edged his way between tables, came right up to me, and asked the question I'd been dreading.

"Can you stay?"

Daughter Erin had to be back at work Monday morning, and with the air system messed up by the storm, flying her back was not an option. I was worried about what the snow had done to our house—areas close to us were said to have received twenty-one inches. Our furnace was broken, and a man was coming to fix it. We had spent a lot of money coming to see Matt play, and two more nights in a hotel would be difficult. Our hopes had been crushed twice now in two days, and, frankly, we felt defeated, ready to throw in the towel.

I brought my eyes up to his. If it had just been the twenty-one-year-old, 6'3" center back of the Haverford men's soccer team I was talking to, I think I could have said it quite simply, without emotion—but that's not who I was looking at. Who I was looking at (never mind the beard) was my son age nine who needed me very badly—and for once I couldn't help.

"No."

What I was telling him was, in effect, that his parents were going to miss what either would be, if they lost, the last soccer game he ever played, or, if they won, one of the greatest moments of his life. So it wasn't just no to a game.

"We'll come down if you make playoffs," I promised lamely. I don't think he heard.

Other parents were going through the same emotion—like us, they couldn't stay. We talked it out, realized that the worst part was missing out on Senior Day. Parents and players had been looking forward to this for four years—the chance for the seniors to be honored before the last home game, have the announcer read off their accomplishments, have their parents come out with them and accept flowers, have the crowd (and there would be a large, raucous one, it being the Swarthmore game) stand and applaud. Now all this was gone.

Or was it? Deb Cohen came up with the idea. Our boys were going to have a light practice on Swan Field and maybe it would be possible to have the Seniors Day ceremony before practice, say in the gym?

Matt went outside where the reception was better and called Coach Rineer.

"It's all arranged," he said when he came back.

We all drove over to the athletic center. The room was one of those large function rooms every college has. The freshmen, sophomores, and juniors, wearing their practice uniforms and socks, formed a double row out from the mirrors on the wall, while the seniors waited with their arms around each other's shoulders directly behind them. Everyone looked solemn—borderline teary-eyed, and not embarrassed about that at all. Coach Rineer stood at the head of the line ready to hand flowers to the seniors as their names were called, and then we parents would walk out to meet our sons, accept the flowers from them, have our pictures taken, then wait together along the window for the next senior to be announced.

Matt Gorski read out the brief biographies Matt W. had written—but before doing so, he had a few words to say about how much he had enjoyed playing with the seniors, how great an inspiration they had been. All the things you might expect him to say, and said very well, but then he added something that really caught my attention.

"You know, tomorrow's game is not the last game the seniors are going to play," he said, looking us straight in the eye. "We have a lot more games to play before this season is over."

Sounds like the clichés any co-captain has to mouth to inspire his team—but that's not what they sounded like to me. "This guy really means it," I said to myself. "And if he means it, and that reflects what all the boys are feeling, then for sure they're going to beat Swat."

Not a dry eye in the house once the ceremony was over. And then, the final name announced, the last bouquet handed over, the boys all came together for a picture—and I'll have more to say about that later.

Monday night was Halloween. We spent it not answering trick-or-treaters, but downstairs in Matt's bedroom following the game on live stats. Those of you who've read *Soccer Dad* know about my superstitions; my newest involved tossing a miniature soccer ball from hand to hand throughout the course of the game. If I dropped it—if it touched the carpet—we were doomed.

Superstition aside?

"We need to score first," I told Celeste. "And we need to score twice."

Karen Garfing promised to call from Swan Field any time there was anything important to report. She tested the system now, with a phone call just before the game began.

"Hear it?" she said. "This place is going nuts!"

It's hard to picture a game with more at stake. Win and Haverford would make it to the Centennial Conference playoffs for the first time ever, and have the exquisite satisfaction of knocking out arch-rivals Swarthmore--the defending champions, the nationally-ranked program. The Fords, as they took the field, were playing to achieve a fairy tale; the Garnet were playing to avoid a nightmare.

I'm sure in future years I'll be convinced I was at the game in person, so many vivid stories did I hear about what it was like. This was the first time any soccer had ever been played on Swan Field, the first time Haverford had played a home game under the lights. Then, too, it was Halloween—it was always Halloween when Haverford played Swarthmore, exuberant spirits were abroad in the night.

We came out playing on the front foot. Adam and Matt. W. rushed up to the box as Matt G. readied a corner kick. It sailed to Dan Garfing, who passed to Wetherell lingering just outside the penalty area. Matt had already spotted an unmarked DRob near the far post and he crossed it to him with a soft chip. Robinson got off a header, the ball dropped to Alejandro right in front, and our star was simply too strong for the defenders to stop. First blood (and with that kind of intensity, I do mean blood) to Haverford!

One of the unhappiest quirks of the season had been the Fords' habit of surrendering goals immediately after scoring themselves. This time they dug in and concentrated—the half ended without Swat scoring. The second half was a repeat of the first, at least initially—Haverford playing as if their lives depended on it; Swarthmore increasingly desperate.

Coach Rineer had played a lone striker up front all season, alternating Alejandro and David, but now he made a bold substitution and put Ford Borhmann in the game—Borhmann, who was big and strong but had never scored a collegiate goal. . . . until now. He collected the ball inside the penalty area, swiveled left, and in a move he had worked hard on in practice, volleyed the ball past the leaping Swat goalie into the net.

Matt W., celebrating, ran over and kicked off a chunk of snow from the drifts piled along the field; he raised his fist in triumph toward the Swat fans, who responded by showering him in abuse. Just to show he had a softer side, he kissed Ford on the cheek. Surely his would be the winning goal?

Or would it?

Again, that fatal habit, letting the other team respond too quickly. Ninety seconds later, Swat scored themselves. Fourteen minutes left in the game, a one-goal lead. Could we do it? Surrendering a goal seemed to galvanize our defense, and they smothered the Garnet rushes before they became dangerous. The crowd had already begun counting off the dying seconds . . . "Five! . . . Four! . . . Three! . . ." when a cross came into the box and a Swat player rose for an unmarked header. Wide! Goalie Nick Kahn, outstanding throughout, booted the goal kick safely out of bounds and the celebrations began.

And what celebrations! The students lining the fence along the sideline had already vaulted it before the ball even flew out of bounds, and now they were mobbing the Haverford players, everyone dancing, yelling and laughing in a huge swarming pile. Even parents were caught up in this—*especially* the parents. Mike Reingruber and Ron Restrepo, two dignified middle-aged men, had spent the last few seconds of the game debating whether it would be seemly for them to jump the fence and join the mob. *What the hell,* they decided, and ran out with the rest of the fans, slapping their sons on the back and all but crying from happiness.

Up in New Hampshire, Celeste and I *were* crying. And then the best part, a part that took a while to come, but then was all the sweeter for our waiting. Matt on his cell phone, people shouting and laughing behind him, and, out of the joyous static, these words managing to emerge.

"This is the happiest moment of my life."

In the morning, Athletic Director Wendy Smith sent out this e-mail.

"To Co-Captains Matt Gorski and Matt Wetherell,

I just wanted to say congratulations again and to let you know how happy I am for you and proud. Last night was very special—a memory you will carry with you for the rest of your lives, and replay many times at reunions and other gatherings. You and your teammates have worked incredibly hard to get where you are right now. After meeting with you this summer, I told people that this team would have a great season—they were taking the coaching change in stride and remaining focused—terrific leadership and team chemistry. I have been part of Haverford men's soccer for close to thirty years, and last night was one of the best moments I can ever remember. Be very proud of yourselves—it's been a long time since Haverford men's soccer has had such a significant win—many years of alumni laying the foundation and maintaining strong ties to the program. You did it for yourselves and I know they could not be happier for you.

　　Best of luck in the playoffs,

　　Wendy"

What struck the players hardest, when they reported to practice next day, was the novelty, the strangeness, of playing soccer in November. Always before, their season had ended Halloween weekend—there were never any playoff games to prepare for. Now, it was as if they had entered a different time zone, a different latitude, with a different quality of light. This was all uncharted territory, beginning with that weak November sun setting already behind the Walton stands while they were just warming up. Being in conference playoffs had always seemed like something out of Harry Potter—alluring, mysterious, enticing, but nothing that was real enough that they could ever dwell there themselves. *What's it like?* they must have wondered each October, so tormentingly close did it seem, so frustratingly far. And now, thanks to their miracle victory (five miracle victories), they were taking a bus on Wednesday to Hogwarts, there to play Quiddich against Franklin & Marshall.

To describe the events of the week would require a sequel to this soccer sequel. There's no room for that here—and so I'll have to shrink a hundred pages of experience and emotion into a few brutally brief pages.

Celeste and I were there in the stands in Lancaster as promised, having left New Hampshire at 4:30 that morning. Much later, after what happened happened, I sent a breathless e-mail to those parents who couldn't be there.

"Beating Swat was a fluke, eh?

Among the memories . . .

Arriving early, seeing the boys, in civies, walking slowly around the field, getting to know it, getting themselves in the zone.

Bright moon overhead. Freight trains steaming along behind the field. Crazy Haverford fans—not many of us, but boy did we yell.

The wild first half. Our boys playing really well, but F&M staying pesky. Penalty against us in the box, ouch, then a nice play by them for their second goal. For us? Reingruber rising high to meet a corner, then Giannasca's perfectly placed shot.

Second half very different. THIS WAS THE BEST PLAY I EVER SAW FROM H'FORD. Beautiful beautiful soccer. The effort, the intelligence, the understanding. Alejandro's beautifully taken winner, breaking in on the goalie one-on-one, with just enough time for him to realize he *was* one-on-one, which realization can often freak a striker out—but not this time. 3-2 Fords!

A victory sprint over to their adoring fans. Chocolate milk, string cheese, and brownies for the victors—then pizza from Rosa Rosa, Lancaster's finest. Their not wanting to leave right away, wanting to linger over what they've done, hardly believing.

What impresses most about these boys is the fact they have no prima donnas on this team, no egomaniacs—they are really a modest bunch! Committed to team play, a band of brothers.

Hopkins will never know what hit them!

Avanti Fords!"

Celeste and I couldn't follow them to Baltimore for the semifinals—the drab realities of owning a house and working intruded once again. Matt seemed okay with that—we'd seen him play one last time, in a big win. When we said goodbye there by the F&M field, there was none of the heartbreak that had come with our missing the Swat game.

"It's funny," Matt said once it was all over. "All that week I had the feeling that if even one small detail had been changed, it all would have come crashing down. If you and Mom had been watching Monday, somehow we wouldn't have won. If we hadn't gotten those cool new warmups to wear just before Swat, we wouldn't have won. If you hadn't come to Lancaster, we wouldn't have won. If I had something different to eat for lunch before F&M, we would have lost. Does that sound crazy?"

"It's call predestination," I said. "I felt just the same way."

Fate involved facing Johns Hopkins next, the playoff's number one seed (we were fifth seed). On paper, it was the worst draw possible. Haverford hadn't beaten Hopkins since 1995 (our seniors were in kindergarten), and Hop had powered through to every Centennial Conference final for the last six years. On the plus side, losing to them on that phantom penalty during the regular season would supply us motivational fuel—not that we needed it, at least not the seniors. They remembered being sarcastically taunted by the Hopkins' women's team (watching from the stands) as they trudged off the rain-soaked field after a pasting their sophomore season. A lot had changed since in the world of Haverford soccer. A *lot*—and most of it just that week. Now it was up to the boys to prove it.

We watched from New Hampshire on a live video feed. And say this for Hopkins, it was the best video we'd ever seen, TV quality, with a play-by-play announcer to boot.

(There was a downside to this. Late in the first half, Matt went down injured. "Looks like it's number 6 who's down," the announcer said, then "We have a policy of not focusing on players when they're injured." The picture on the screen immediately switched to the Hopkins logo, a beaming blue jay. After an agonizing minute, the bird disappeared, and we were back to watching the game again. Matt was back up, though he looked groggy; it wasn't until later that we learned he'd taken a ball straight in the groin.)

The first half was even—both teams seemed wary of each other, but if anything Hopkins seemed warier of us than we were of them. Two minutes into the second half, Alejandro took charge of a scramble in front of the Hopkins' goal. 1-0, Haverford takes the lead!

The goal seemed energizing—but for Hopkins, not for us. They scored, after some pretty teamwork. With twenty minutes left, our best hope seemed to be to hold on until the end of regulation, then regroup for overtime. There was some nondescript play inside midfield, about thirty-five yards from the Hopkins goal and slightly to the right. The ball, instead of just being kicked around like the boys were engaged in a bitter shin fight, dropped to one of our players who stood somewhat apart from the mob, like a bystander who was too smart or aloof to get involved.

David Robinson, DRob, was among our most talented players, but he'd had a difficult season, at least when it came to scoring goals. How many had he scored to this point? Zero. There may have been fans watching who remembered reading on the blog about his preseason thunder-strike back in Sweden, but I confess I was not one of them. When he gave the ball a little tap to position it, swiveled, and shot long range, I was as surprised as anyone—except maybe the Hopkins' goalie, who was clearly startled . . . or why else was he leaping so desperately to his right like that?

If you had drawn a line from DRob's right foot to the top left corner of the goal you would have traced exactly the flight of that ball. His first goal of the season—from thirty yards out! Our players swarmed over him in celebration. The game wasn't over yet, but it was as good as over; you could see the Hopkins' players shoulders literally sag.

Another triumphant Haverford celebration on the field, players, parents and fans all smiling and laughing in wondrous disbelief, and then—and Celeste and I were getting addicted to this now—Matt's post-game phone call to us in New Hampshire, his happy, excited voice cutting through the miles.

Some of you reading this, with sons or daughters playing in high school, will be wondering whether playing college sports, D-III soccer, is a good idea or a bad one. My best advice is to let your son or daughter decide for themselves—but now that I've gotten that platitude out of my system, I have a few things to say from a parent's perspective.

And I'll say this first, though you probably already know it. Sports can be very cruel. Not cruel like war or poverty can be cruel—it never remotely reaches that level—but crueler than ordinary, run-of-the-mill life, at least for young people who are armored against so much just from vitality and sheer exuberance.

Where pain comes from in sports is asking more of it than can be delivered. A young eighteen year old, having devoted his life to soccer right through high school, finds out that he's not good enough to play in college, not smart enough to get admitted, or not rich enough to attend. A freshman, having made the team, sits on the bench all season and is not invited to spring practice. A starter, playing wonderfully well, breaks his leg and wakes up next morning as an ex-player, someone whose soccer is in the past. Referees blow big calls and deprive you of a deserved victory; beloved coaches quit without warning; you deserve all-conference recognition, but it goes to a lesser player with a more influential coach. Bad enough—but then, after a tough loss, your girlfriend announces she's breaking up with you; your father calls to say he's lost his job; your mother is entering the hospital to begin chemotherapy. Life doesn't grant you a four-year bye in heartbreak just because you happen to be playing college sports.

Matt had the happiest, luckiest, most joyous soccer career anyone ever had—and yet even so it was full of upsets, disappointments, defeat, and injury. If you had talked to his father after the Washington game, he would have wished with all his heart that the season was already over, that his son's soccer career was over, that it was something in his past. His fainthearted father, who had no way of anticipating what would happen over the next four weeks.

"This is the happiest moment of my life," Matt said, as Haverford danced in victory and Swarthmore lay sobbing on the turf. But it was another phone call that impressed his dad more, when he called after the Muhlenberg loss. Food poisoning, bus breakdown, his knee troubling him again, yet another game where the team couldn't score—and here Matt was calling his father to say that all he had been conscious of was how lucky he was to be out there playing. In soccer terms . . . in *any* terms . . . this was the moment he grew up.

Again, as with so much else in sports, a parent's enjoyment comes from not pushing too hard—for accepting that less often means more. A lot of men deliberately set out to live vicariously through their son's or daughter's sports careers. You have to take my word for this, but living vicariously through my son's soccer was never one of my failings, though God knows I have plenty. But it's just because I didn't think in those terms that, in the end, I managed to live vicariously through my son's soccer. Yes, that meant taking on some of the pain and some of the heartbreak, but it meant I shared some of the triumph and victory as well. Sweet stuff for a man my age, when the lines on the happy-sad graph tend to flatten out. I would miss soccer terribly.

Sunday morning here in New Hampshire, Centennial Conference finals morning, and I've already turned on the computer and checked the Baltimore weather. Warm and sunny, perfect soccer weather, and surely the boys are already on their way there in the bus. Still some time left then, and I've decided to take a moment and look at the pictures sent us after our improvised Senior Day celebration in the athletic center's function room.

One is of the three of us just after Matt handed the flowers to Celeste. Behind us, you can see chairs stacked on tables, dance mirrors along the wall, the green pointy fronds of a potted palm. I have my sunglasses on, and a red and white Haverford scarf is looped around my neck, which complements quite nicely my red hair; my hands are held quite high, and the left one seems like it's just returned from Matt's shoulder or is about to go there. I've turned my head to face him. My expression is ridiculously easy to read—pride is written across my face in capital letters, Helvectica, eighteen point bold.

Celeste looks *way* up at him from the other side—his arms are around us both, hugging us closer. She has her Haverford scarf on, too, and the ends bunch against the flowers of her bouquet. If my expression is *PRIDE,* hers is *LOVE.* Really, we could be actors modeling this, only for us it's totally sincere.

In the middle, wearing a white Haverford jersey with a red number 6, stands Matthew—unshaven since the last time we played Dickinson. He fills out that shirt pretty well—I knew he'd shot up right after high school, but when had that strength and breadth kicked in? His expression is also easy to read, even though his eyes are modestly downcast, perhaps to keep from crying. It's regret that his soccer is almost over, sadness that we can't stay for the Swat game, but there's acceptance and satisfaction there as well. Call it *BITTERSWEET,* and you can picture what I mean.

Wetherell, alphabetically, was the last senior to be announced. Once we had our family picture snapped, he joined the other seniors so they could have their photo taken as a group with their arms around each other's shoulders. That's the second photo beside me as I write. Six of them stand there, their red and white uniforms standing out boldly against the black curtain that forms the backdrop.

On the right, Steven Griffith with a determined grin on his face—unmistakably a Vermonter, though I can't really say how I'm reading that, other than from the quiet resolution in his face. Beside him, raising the altitude, comes Alejandro, number 15—if he looks like a bearded tower of strength, it's because he *is* a bearded tower of strength. David Restrepo stands next to him, with a boyish smile impossible to resist—always the Texan, he's got a red turtleneck on under his jersey, so that notorious Philadelphia cold won't bully him once they start practice. Matt comes next and he's beaming; they're *all* beaming, you notice now—Swat doesn't have a chance in hell.

Tyler's certainly thinking that—his smile is so confident it's like they've already won. Jake Seeley, number 11, stands furthest to the left, the only one of the six who's beardless, which makes him look very much like his own man; if he's going to influence the outcome of the game, it's going to be from intelligence and hustle, not three-week's growth.

A similar photo op ends *Soccer Dad*, where the high school seniors have just won their state championship and stand with arms around each other's shoulders staring off toward their futures. The Haverford seniors have a different look on their faces. There isn't quite as much happiness (the triumphs of the week are still ahead of them at this point), but there is more confidence, more certainty, more—for lack of a better word—manhood. They've already achieved a significant part of their future—they have all played four years of college soccer—and it's very much a picture of young men looking back in satisfaction at what by hard work and good fortune they've managed to accomplish. And maybe a bit of surprise is in their look, too—surprise that life works that way . . . that something you love passionately can already be slipping into the past.

The conference finals, the game against Dickinson, were tense all the way. We started brightly, and it wasn't long before our aggressiveness paid off. Colin Lubelczyk, flying down the wing, played a classic through ball to David Robinson running the channel, and DRob slotted home a stretchy/slidy finish. It wasn't until the second half that our dike started leaking—Dickinson attackers were pouring through the cracks—and we were reduced to desperately plugging holes, rather than boring holes ourselves. Even so, it looked like we would make it, steal away with a win, but at seventy-six minutes Dickinson tied it up.

The game went into overtime, but then after 110 minutes, the score was still tied, which mean the game, the Centennial Conference championship, would be decided by penalty kicks, which means, in effect, by luck.

Luck that went Dickinson's way. The surfboard of fate the boys had been riding had finally hit the beach, with a rather inelegant, unsatisfactory bump that spilled them over—but what a hell of a trip it had been, the ride of a lifetime on a wave out of dreams. They had pulled off the best Haverford season in twenty years, a breakout season, bringing Haverford back to soccer excellence after so many years in the wilderness.

Matt called from Baltimore before getting on the bus for the ride back to campus. He wasn't crushed or even particularly disappointed, knowing what they had accomplished. I followed up by writing a consolatory e-mail that would be waiting for him back at the dorm. I said the usual things a parent says in these situations, but then, when I came to the ending, I wrote a sentence that made my hands shake because of the tense of the passive verb—a tense I had never used in fifteen years of watching him play, not until now.

"Remember this, Matthew Wetherell. You were one hell of a great soccer player."

And it's Matt who deserves the last word here. Just before the season started, as the boys flew to Sweden, the coach, as coaches do, asked each player to write down their goals for the season. Matt wrote his and balanced his way up the plane's aisle to hand them over to Coach Rineer.

"TEAM GOALS:

—Make the Centennial Conference playoffs. Our team plays well when we have a chip on our shoulder and knowing that no previous Haverford team has ever made the playoffs should be more than enough motivation.

—Beat Swarthmore. We all hate Swat with a passion, but none of us have been part of a team that has beaten them . . . and this must change.

—Use the memory of last season. Use the memory of being one point away from playoffs to remember how important every Centennial game is, not let any slip away like last year at Gettysburg.

—Even though I'm a senior, and this is somewhat selfish, I really want my entire class to have a great senior season. We were 3-10-3 my freshman season, 6-11 my sophomore season, and 8-6-2 my junior season. I think improving on this record and qualifying for the playoffs will fill our class with lifelong pride knowing that we helped turn around Haverford men's soccer into a dominant force for years to come. This isn't going to be easy, but one of my goals is to have all the seniors help lead, perform well in games, and set a strong example through the year.

INDIVIDUAL GOALS:

—My immediate goal is to return to full contact soccer. Having played exactly once since last season, the day I tore my ACL, I need to manage my expectations upon return and remain upbeat. Get to

100 percent ASAP. I've been dreaming of my first start after return-ing and I can't wait to be back on the field with my teammates.

—I have been a captain of this team since the end of my sophomore season and have never cared more about my teammates and having a great year. I want to use what I've learned in the past and continue to improve as a captain, and be an effective and respected leader on and off the field. Continue to develop and establish friendships that will last a lifetime.

—Ultimately, I want to end this season with no regrets and achieve some closure with the game of soccer. I've played and loved soccer almost non-stop for as long as I can remember, and trained incred-ibly hard to recover from my injury. I know that this is the season I'm going to remember longest, and I am committed to making sure it is my absolute best."

Goals—but also wishes. And, like in a fairy tale, every one of them came true.

ACKNOWLEDGEMENTS

Readers finishing *Soccer Dad* always had two questions. What happened next for Matt? What happened next for Rob Grabill, Hanover High's vibrant and charismatic coach?

Soccer Dad ends with Rob in a rare moment of uncertainty where his future wasn't quite clear. I'm glad to report he rebounded in inspiring style. His Hanover High soccer team went on to win three more state championships after 2007's for six in a row, making the team one of the most successful high school soccer programs in the country. Rob himself was just as successful. He ran sports camps in Vermont for a couple of summers, then moved to a boys' school closer to home in New Hampshire, where he helps direct their summer programs. He had time now to pursue a longstanding ambition: working toward a master's degree in divinity at the Bangor Theological Seminary in Maine, making the long commute during the week. As if this wasn't enough to keep him busy, he's become Director of Religious

Education at the Church of Christ at Dartmouth College. He took an active, supportive interest in Matt's college soccer career, as he does with all his graduates; when Matt came out of knee surgery, the first one who called him was Rob—not just to wish him well, but with his secret plan to beat Swarthmore.

Many readers also ask about what became of Matt's teammates after high school. Many of them played soccer in college—a very high number, considering the fact that a lot of college coaches, when they see where a prospective is from, are liable to start off the conversation saying, "I never recruit players from New Hampshire or Vermont."

Eric Barthold played striker for Colby College in Maine, and, fighting back from many injuries, became their leading scorer his senior season. Angus Kennedy played four years on an excellent Williams team. Trevor Barlowe, as described, was part of Haverford's dream season, then stepped into a starting role in 2012. Ben Harwick, Hanover's goalie, played at Skidmore. Oliver Horton played for Knox. Eric Jayne, the diminutive goal-scoring freshman, filled out to the point he was recruited by D-I Dartmouth and plays there now. Dam Remillard, another of the younger players in 2007, plays for Bates up in Maine. Yosef Osheyack played for the Rochester Institute of Technology. Counting Matthew, that makes nine players from the team who went on to play in college, an extraordinarily high number.

In a short recap like this, not all of the players on the 2011 Haverford's men soccer team had the chance to strut their stuff on the page—but the ones who didn't all played a huge role in making the season so memorable: Andriy Mshanetskyy, Charlie Crawford, Julien Calas, Mike Gould, Robin Brooke, Gebby Keny, Geoffrey Henderson, Charlie Michele, Charlie Espinosa. As Matt said, "This was the closest team I ever played on," and even someone watching from the stands like me could tell how deeply this team bonded, first in defeat, then in victory.

The parents bonded, too. Again, some managed to find their way into my story, some did not. But heartfelt thanks to Rick Singer, Peter Gorski, Jan and Joe Seeley, Amy Stephens, Charlie Barlowe, Steve Lubelczyk, Mike and Missy Reingruber, Laura Coyne, Charlie Freeman, Olivier Calas, Terry and Gary Griffith, Peggy Bressler, Brady and Martha Bohrmann, the Goulds, Peter and Laura Henderson, Gail Weiss and Sam Brooke, Leslie Reed, Bill Espinosa, Alice O'Connor, Claire Bloom, the Gianassca family, the Kahns, Barbara and Tony Morollo, May Reed, the Michele family. And, of course, Ron Restrepo and Candace Baggett, two of the Gettysburg 7.

Matt could not done have done so well with his ACL recovery without the support of a great crew. Thanks to Dr. Michael Sparks at Dartmouth-Hitchcock; Dave Barlow at BE Fit Physical Therapy in Hanover; Steve Vincente at DHMC; Roxanne Smith for rehab on campus; Curt Mauger, Tifani Melendez; Heather Hellem. Cory

Walts is a strength and conditioning coach to die for; there's no one finer in his trade. Trainer Melissa Cruice went above and beyond to help Matt out throughout his career.

Thanks to the great Haverford soccer staff, past and present. Matt Brown, David Owens, Bonnie McAllister, Carole Gormley, Jim Kenyon, Gregg Petcoff. Dave Sauerhoff did an outstanding job coaching the goalies from pre-season right through finals. And, as mentioned, Kevin Weiler was a faithful mentor and friend to the seniors throughout their four years.

Matt's friends on the women's soccer team, Anna Rayne and Erin Verrier, were highly successful athletes themselves and part of a class that made playoffs every year, with the highest winning percentage in the history of the program. Their parents Nancy and Todd Rayne, Barb and David Verrier, were hugely supportive of Matt.

The Fords have a very loyal group of alumni who cheered the team on. Thanks to Joe Howard, Andrew Poolman, David Poolman, Jonathan Propper, Max Stossel, Jim Wiltsee, Panos Panidis, Brian Pepe-Mooney, Jeff Rickert, Chris Dioguardi, Adam Care, Taylor Sundby and, especially, Dan Braz.

The Haverford College Squirrel Squad led the cheerleading efforts in the stands. Thanks to founders Mike Troup and Ethan Glor, as well as Joe Banno and Jixi Teng, for energizing the student body. Keep it up!

It takes a village to support a successful soccer team, and a pretty populous one at that. The students, professors, coaches, friends, and family listed here deserve a cheering section of their own.

Jenine Abbassi, Tamara Agins, Sarah Andrade, Tom Apicella, Molly Braun, Jake Chaplin, Liz Coward, Liz Cohen-Sheer, Emily Cunningham (thanks Emily!) Gemma Donofrio, Annelise Herskowitz, Emily Dutrow, Matt Forster, Edward Gracia, Debbie Gilbert, Michele Taylor, Cheryl Mathes, the Applegate family, Ian Goldberg, Roxanne Jaffe, Audrey Johnston, Rebecca Joseph, Logan Meltzer, Joel Michel, Juliana Morgan-Trostle, Calvin Okoth-Obbo, Sam Permutt, Julia Pringle, Katie Raymond, Lindsay Ryan, Lily Warnke, Zack Woerner, Will Garrett and Kaitlyn Shank.

Also Bruce Agins, Bridgette Black, Cate Brown, Megan Cain, Zachary Dayno, Cooper Dodds, Meg Donahue, Natalia Fadul, Georgia Griffith, Clark Johns, Julianna Lord, Bryanne Leeming, Ethan Mann, Tucker Little, Andry McLaughlin, Dylan Riessen, Danny Rice, Sam Rosen, Bill, Sofia and Conrad Brady (good luck with your soccer career, C-man!), Tommy and Susanna Clark, the Cosci family, Lydia Dagenais, Christopher Haines, Joe Amorim (big thanks!), Sue Higgins, Tamara Davis, Kaye Edwards, Laura and Noel Cunningham, Casey Londergan, Christina and Bob Lane, Jess Lord, Gregg and William Tousignant, Donna Mancini, Chris Maxey, Jason McGraw, Bobbi Morgan, Bruce Partridge, Steve and Becky Powell, Judy Owen, Zachary Oberfield, C. Everett Koop, Gary Waleik,

Raisa Williams, George Nofer, Carol Walkley, the Fields of Portland, Oregon, Terrence Williams, Jane, Steve and Ron Arena, and that great Bi-Co couple, David and Deb Cohen.

And let's not forget all the Haverford soccer greats who came before, including Christy Morris who scored the winning goal against Harvard in 1905 and kept coming to cheer at home games deep into the 1960s . . . and the legendary Jimmy Mills, coach from 1949–1970, commuting to the campus every afternoon from his job working a loom at a Philadephia carpet mill, and now a member of the U.S. Soccer Hall of Fame.

And just enough time to add a sequel to a soccer sequel. The 2012 Haverford soccer team continued the program's brave renaissance, shutting out Dickinson and Swarthmore in the playoffs to win their first Centennial Conference championship ever, and advance to the NCAA tourney.